All Things Natural

Commentaries by Ficino on Plato's Writings
a four-volume series

Gardens of Philosophy
Evermore Shall Be So
When Philosophers Rule
All Things Natural

All Things Natural

FICINO ON PLATO'S *TIMAEUS*

ARTHUR FARNDELL

Notes and Additional Material by
PETER BLUMSOM

SHEPHEARD-WALWYN (PUBLISHERS) LTD

© Arthur Farndell 2010

All rights reserved. No part of this book may be
reproduced in any form without the written permission
of the publisher, Shepheard-Walwyn (Publishers) Ltd

First published in 2010 by
Shepheard-Walwyn (Publishers) Ltd
107 Parkway House, Sheen Lane,
London SW14 8LS

British Library Cataloguing in Publication Data
A catalogue record of this book
is available from the British Library

ISBN: 978-0-85683-258-1

Typeset by Alacrity,
Sandford, Somerset
Printed and bound through
s|s|media limited, Wallington, Surrey

CONTENTS

Acknowledgements   ix
Translator's Note on the Latin Texts   xi

Marsilio Ficino's Compendium on the *Timaeus*   1

1. The subject matter of the book   3
2. The arrangement of the book and its parts   4
3. Introduction to the dialogue   4
4. An allegory of history; contents of the prologue   5
5. The fall of Phaethon; floods; fires; a description of Minerva   7
6. The finest directions concerning prayers and entreaties   8
7. The world has three causes higher than itself, depends on the incorporeal cause, and is ever in flux   10
8. The Good Itself, rather than subsequent causes, is the cause of all things, and it has no direct relationship with anything   13
9. The dependence of matter on the Good Itself; the action of the mind and soul upon matter; and the intelligible world   15
10. The Sun, light, radiance, brilliance, heat, procreation; likewise unity, goodness, intellect, soul, nature, the body of the world, the image of the higher worlds   16
11. Individual orders are taken back to individual heads, and the universal order is taken back to the universal head, by which all things are composed through action and power   18

CONTENTS

12 Matter was not in disarray prior to the world in time, but was arranged according to some principle of order or origin — 20

13 Two views concerning the origin of the world — 21

14 A threefold inference drawn from Plato's view of the world, and what is undisputed about his view — 22

15 By the grace of the Good the world has been brought into being in the likeness of the divine principle and the divine word — 24

16 Why the world is one, why it is spherical, and why its movement is spherical — 25

17 Why the world is divided into five or six regions; how the number seven is right for it; circular number; and how the world is arranged in the likeness of the intelligible world — 26

18 Why there are distinct parts within the world and why there is opposition among them; also concerning the four elements — 27

19 Numbers linear, plane, and solid; why a single intermediary is sufficient between planes but is not sufficient between solids; how mathematical ratios are related to physical ratios — 29

20 The first consideration: why the number four in relation to the elements befits the world — 32

21 The second consideration: proving the same — 33

22 The third consideration: confirming the same — 34

23 The fourth consideration of the same; and the powers and ratios of the elements — 35

24 The whole world is composed of four elements; how these elements are under a particular principle in the heavens and under a different principle beneath the Moon — 37

25 Circular motion is the property of every sphere in constant movement; and light is the principal property of fire — 40

CONTENTS

26	A confirmation of what was said earlier; concerning fire, ether, the composition of the heavens, and the daemons in the heavens and beneath the heavens	42
27	On the spirit of the world, that is, on intellect, soul, intelligence, and nature	44
28	On the composition of the soul, and why the soul needs five elements for its constitution	47
29	Why the soul is compared to a compound and to musical harmony	51
30	The propositions and proportions related to Pythagorean and Platonic music	54
31	In musical harmonies one is produced from the many; how harmony is defined	58
32	Which harmonies arise from which proportions	61
33	On the harmonious composition of the soul	66
34	The main points about the harmonic numbers which lead to the composition of the soul	71
34*	From the intervals of the spheres Plato seeks the intervals of the ratios between the parts of the soul	74
35	How the intervals of the double and triple numbers are filled	75
36	The division of the soul; motion; and time	77
37	The arrangement of the living world through its limbs; the opposite movements of revolutions; and the intersectors of axes and orbits	80
38	Right and left in the cosmos; the movements of the firmament, of the planets, and of the fixed stars; the arrangement of the soul	83
39	The great harmony, within the cosmic being, between the soul and the heavens and between the heavens and the elements, in relation to the higher worlds and the orders of divinities	85
40	Those things which come into being directly from God, and those things which come into being through intermediaries; the words of God in relation to the gods; and the providence of the gods	87

CONTENTS

41	Man's relationship to soul and body	89
42	How the world is composed of mind and necessity	91
43	Natural phenomena are based on the principles of mathematics; concerning the elements and compounds	93
44	More on man: how much regard he gives to the soul, and how much to the body	96
45	On the outward and inward breath, according to Plato and Galen	99
46	On the good health and poor health of the body and the soul	101

The Chapter Divisions of the *Timaeus* with brief commentaries as given by Marsilio Ficino   105

Notes to the Compendium   169
Soul Numbers   198
Glossary   200
Bibliography   204
Index   205

ACKNOWLEDGEMENTS

SINCE THE TIME work on this series began, there have been wars and rumours of wars, accompanied by vast changes on the national and international stage.

In the midst of reflections on changes of any kind, it is good to acknowledge what is constant. As far as this series is concerned, the constants, in terms of human contributors other than myself as the translator, are my wife Phyllis, John Meltzer, Nathan David, Anthony Werner, and Jean Desebrock.

Work on this particular volume has been enormously helped by a group of composers and musicians who graced our home three times a year for almost a decade to consider Chapters 28 to 35 of Ficino's *Compendium*. Leading regulars in this group were Peter Blumsom (who kindly wrote the notes and additional material to this volume), Bruce Ramell, and David Goymour, and valued contributions were also made by David Fletcher, the late Geoffrey Mulford, Noel Skinner, and David Ward.

For the supply of source material I am deeply indebted to Adrian Bertoluzzi and Christophe Poncet.

The constant of constants is the source of all, the Truth itself, acknowledged as supreme by Plato and Ficino. To this Truth, which shines in the hearts of all, this final volume and the whole series are dedicated.

Arthur Farndell

TRANSLATOR'S NOTE ON THE LATIN TEXTS

THE FLORENCE text of 1496 is the principal authority for the translation of the *Compendium*, but use has also been made of the Venice edition of 1491 and the Basle version of 1576.

Minor differences, too numerous to list in this volume, appear in these three versions: for instance, the last word of Chapter 8 of the *Compendium* is given as 'confirmavimus' in Florence and Venice, but as 'confirmabimus' in Basle.

The major variations in these three publications, however, are given below, with references from the English of this present translation:

Compendium, Chapter 7: Six consecutive paragraphs almost at the end of the chapter ('When we say – if we follow Plato ... according to the poets.') occur in Florence only.

Compendium, Chapter 11: The final paragraph ('He says that ... would come forth from it.') is in Florence and Basle but not in Venice.

Compendium, Chapter 19: In the sixth paragraph, the words beginning 'since in this way twelve borrows two sides' and ending 'from the further cube, namely, eight' are in Florence but not in Venice or Basle.

Compendium, Chapter 23: Basle gives a table of the elements and their qualities which does not appear in Florence or Venice.

Compendium, Chapter 26: This chapter is not in Venice. In Basle it is numbered XXVII.

Compendium, Chapter 27: In Basle this is numbered XXVI. Thus Basle reverses Chapters 26 and 27 of Florence. In the second paragraph, the second sentence and the single word 'moreover' of the third sentence appear only in Florence. Likewise, the penultimate paragraph of this chapter appears only in Florence.

Compendium, Chapter 29: The final paragraph occurs in Florence and Basle, but not in Venice.

Compendium, Chapter 32: Paragraph 23 ('But when we said that Saturn …') and paragraph 24 ('We should, however, assign …') appear only in Florence.

Compendium, Chapter 33: Paragraph 3: The words beginning with 'Stillness, and Motion', which conclude the first sentence, and ending with 'the Same, and the Different' in the third sentence, occur in Florence and Venice, but not in Basle.

Compendium, Chapter 34: The penultimate paragraph is given in Florence, but not in Venice or Basle.

Compendium, Chapter 34★: The second paragraph occurs in Florence only. Note also that the English translation follows the Florence text in attributing the number 34 to two consecutive chapters, this being the second of those two chapters. The result is that, from here until the end of the *Compendium*, the chapter numbers will lag one behind those of Venice and Basle.

Compendium, Chapter 35: Both Venice and Basle include a triangular figure with numbers. In Basle the topmost number shown is 6, whereas Venice shows the numeral 1 above the 6. This figure does not appear in Florence.

Compendium, Chapter 36: Venice has only the first six paragraphs of this chapter.

Compendium, Chapter 37: Venice lacks this chapter.

Compendium, Chapter 38: Venice lacks this chapter. It is erroneously numbered XXXVII in the Basle text.

Compendium, Chapter 39: This chapter is not in Venice.

Compendium, Chapter 40: In the title, only Florence has 'the words of God in relation to the gods; and the providence of the gods'. Venice has only the first six paragraphs of this chapter.

Compendium, Chapter 41: Paragraph 6: Only Florence has 'We have also spoken about sight in our commentaries on Plotinus.'

Compendium, Chapter 42: Basle erroneously gives the number XL to this chapter.

Compendium, Chapter 43: Basle assigns the number XLI to this chapter. The eighth paragraph ('Euclid demonstrates …') occurs only in Florence. In the tenth paragraph, the words 'and so twice sixty

TRANSLATOR'S NOTE ON THE LATIN TEXTS

scalenes are produced. In this shape there are twelve solid angles, each produced from five planes' and the words 'having eight solid angles, each of which is made of three right-angled planes' likewise occur only in the Florence text.

Compendium, Chapter 44: Basle gives the number XLII to this chapter.

Compendium, Chapter 45: This chapter appears only in Florence.

Compendium, Chapter 46: Venice and Basle have this as the final part of the chapter entitled 'More on man: how much regard he gives to the soul, and how much to the body' [Chapter 44 in Florence]. The chapter title is therefore only in Florence. In the third paragraph, the words 'that no one who has clearly perceived, at the outset, the misery which depravity brings in its train will voluntarily direct all his desires towards this end. You should also understand him to mean' occur only in Florence. In the penultimate paragraph, between 'just as the poets do' and 'So take these', Venice and Basle have 'Atque Timaeus Locrus in Lib. de Mundo fabulosa haec esse fatetur' ['And Timaeus of Locri, in his book *On the World*, says that these things are fictitious (or mythical)'].

For the translation of 'The Chapter Divisions of the *Timaeus*', the Florence text has remained the principal guide, but the Basle of 1576 has also been consulted. In this part of the work there are numerous minor discrepancies between the two texts, but no major divergences.

Marsilio Ficino's Compendium
on the *Timaeus*

Chapter 1
The subject matter of the book

JUST AS Plato devotes his energies, in the *Parmenides*, to encompassing all matters divine, in the same way he embraces, in the *Timaeus*, all things natural; and in both dialogues he is principally a Pythagorean, his discourse being uttered through the mouths of Pythagoreans. In the *Parmenides* he emulates two Pythagoreans from Elea, Parmenides and Zeno, who wrote on divine matters. In the *Timaeus* he follows a Pythagorean from Locri named Timaeus, who wrote a book on the nature of the universe.

All this he does in such a way, however, that he includes in these writings the mysteries as well as eloquence. But since the divine world is the cause and model of the natural world, while the natural world is the effect and image of the divine world, it is for these reasons, too, that Plato, while speaking of the divine world in the *Parmenides*, occasionally moves down to the natural world, and when dealing in the *Timaeus* with the natural world he quite often soars up to the divine world. And it is not without some justification that he links divinity with nature, for nature is the instrument of divinity. And so Plato treats divinely of the natural world, as does Aristotle, and he treats of the divine world naturally.

He also interweaves mathematical items as the means between the divine world and the natural world. Through numbers the study of mathematics indicates the divine world, and through measurements it indicates the natural world.

The subject matter of this book may therefore be said to be the very nature of the universe, that is, a seminal and quickening power pervading the whole of the cosmos, being subject to the world-soul but exercising control over matter, and begetting all things in the sequence with which the soul itself conceives, while looking up to the divine mind and seeking the Good.

Chapter 2
The arrangement of the book and its parts

IT WILL BE SHOWN that the universe and its nature are not self-existent but depend on a higher, divine cause. It will also be shown that nature is arranged in many levels: celestial, elemental, simple, compound, rational, and irrational. All creation beneath the Moon will be seen to be related to a rational being, which is its end and its lord. Many more things will be said of this being, in relation to both the soul and the body; and more will also be said about those things which are compounded by nature beneath this rational being. Indeed, to put it briefly, the threefold world will be considered: the divine, the celestial, and the human.

It will further be shown that for all the things that are compounded in this world, and for the world itself, there are two chief internal elements: matter and form. But there are three external principles: the efficient cause of the world, the model cause of the world, and the final cause of the world. The efficient cause is divine power, intelligence, and will; the model cause comprises the Ideas conceived by divine intelligence; and the final cause is the Good.

Chapter 3
Introduction to the dialogue

LET US PROCEED, in any case, to the contents of the dialogue. Plato devotes five successive days to discussions. On the first day Socrates is at the Piraeus, discussing the State in the company of Polemarchus, Glaucon, Adeimantus, and Thrasymachus the Sophist. On the second day, in the city, he goes over the same topic again with Timaeus, Critias, Hermocrates, and a fourth person, an anonymous foreigner, who is perhaps a companion of Timaeus. On the third day they make an end of this topic. As if starting afresh, Timaeus immediately talks about nature, in the company of Socrates, Critias, and Hermocrates; for the fourth person, who anonymously attended the second discussion, is absent from the third, since it is not right for all to share in matters that are somewhat secret. On the fourth day Critias speaks out. The fifth day has not yet dawned.

After the arrangement and concluding speech about the divine Republic in the world of men, Plato moves in the *Timaeus* to the celestial Republic, which is the model for the earthly one and is composed by God Himself. Then he proceeds to the antiquity of the world and of the human race, and to the wondrous deeds that were energetically accomplished by the ancients.

Chapter 4
An allegory of history; contents of the prologue

NEAR THE BEGINNING of this dialogue Plato relates an account of the war that was once fought between the Athenians and the men of Atlantis. It is clear that Crantor, the principal expounder of Plato at the time, takes the account to be devoid of any allegory. Some, on the other hand, take it as pure allegory, but they are refuted by Platonists of the highest standing, who declare that it is an historical account because Plato has uttered it. The tale that follows is indeed amazing, but totally true. They also consider that an allegorical meaning should be given to Plato's account, for he never exerts himself without good reason.

They therefore think that the war between the Athenians and the Atlanteans presents an image of all the confrontations in the universe. For, according to Heraclitus, war or opposition is the father of all things. Amelius gives the example of the opposition between the firmament and the planets, especially since it is said in *Critias* that the island of Atlantis was divided into seven circles. Origen, for his part, cites the opposition of the higher daemons towards the lower daemons and their victory over them, for the higher daemons had more power, whereas the lower daemons were greater in number.

Numenius refers to the pre-eminent souls which follow Pallas and which are hostile towards other souls who pursue the procreative process under Neptune.

Porphyry alludes to the battle between the daemons which entice towards procreation and the souls which strive for the realms above. He distinguishes three types of daemons: those that are divine; those that conform to a particular disposition, and whose ranks are filled with the specific souls that have obtained the daemoniacal lot; and those that are evil and harmful to souls. He therefore says that these lowest daemons assail the souls in their unending ascent and descent; and this is especially true of the daemons of the West, for he says that that region is considered by the Egyptians to be suitable for the harmful daemons.

Similarly Iamblichus, Syrianus, and Proclus add the never-ending opposition which holds sway everywhere between the One and the Many, Limit and Limitlessness, the Same and the Different, and between Stillness and Motion. All things are composed of these elements from the beginning. Again, being is either of itself or not of itself. Essence is either incorporeal or corporeal; and the incorporeal either moves down towards the corporeal or does not; while the corporeal is either permanent, being celestial, or it is transient, being elemental. Finally, in the heavens movements are opposed to each other, as are diverse powers; but beneath the heavens it is the qualities that repel each other.

In brief, all these differences are indicated by that war of old; and in all cases the Athenians represent what is higher and more excellent, while the men of the West stand for their opposites. Such an allegory is to no small extent applicable to the discussion by Timaeus and is confirmed by what we say in our commentary to *Critias*.

Chapter 5
The fall of Phaethon;
floods; fires; a description of Minerva

HERE I ASK YOU once more to remember that nine thousand years are calculated by Eudoxus as a thousand months; and that Phaethon, offspring of the Sun, consumed the Earth with thunderbolts, which, according to some, means that a huge comet, solar by nature and eventually disintegrating, provoked unbearable periods of heat and perhaps the fires which Moses says were sent by divine intervention.

But when the floods are spoken of, remember that fire is the most effective of all the elements; water is more effective than earth and less amenable than air. Again, fire has the power to divide and penetrate, while water always has the power to strike with great force. Thus it is through these two elements that major calamities occur.

There is still the final cause to consider: from the destruction wrought by these two elements there ensues a greater good, a regeneration of creation which is more fertile than that produced by the pestilence of the air and the fissuring of the earth. This is why providence employs these two in particular to accomplish the most widespread destruction. Just as the celestial orbits obey providence, so God has ordained that there will be destruction and regeneration at those periods of time when all the planets properly coincide with the fiery or watery signs and when the fixed stars lead to the same position.

You will also remember that Neptune signifies natural providence, while Pallas indicates the providence of the intellect, and that Pallas herself is described by the followers of Plato as the goddess who, with her wisdom and power, adorns all that is heavenly and builds up all that comes into being beneath the heavens. Among the constellations, it is Aries over which she wields special authority; and she presides over the celestial equator, where they believe the motive power of the universe to be particularly active.

You will commit to memory the golden saying which, according to what Proclus read in the annals of the Egyptians, was inscribed in the temples of Minerva: 'I am whatever is, whatever will be, and whatever has been. No one has lifted my veil. The fruit that I have brought forth is the living Sun.'

Chapter 6
The finest directions concerning prayers and entreaties

BUT WHEN Plato speaks of God, who is worthy of adoration and supplication, you should hear Porphyry expressing his approval of prayers offered to God, for he says:

'Since God provides for us, and since our affairs can change, we certainly worship Him to good purpose by the use we make of all that is ours, provided that we are good; for in this way, being made like unto God, we are united more closely with Him. The whole power of worship lies in this union. For there is no doubt that we are the children of God, but we are cut off from Him, as if in a dungeon in the land of exile. We should beseech Him that we may be freed and thus return to our Father. Otherwise we shall be like those who have been deprived of parental protection.

'Indeed, since we are parts of the universe, we undoubtedly depend on the universe, for turning towards the whole bestows salvation on the parts. If you therefore follow virtue, you should worship Him, who holds all virtue within Himself. For the whole of the Good Itself will be for you the motivating force of that which makes the Good available to you. If you choose the physical good, there is in the universe a power that holds all physical things within itself. Thus all the parts need to be maintained in good health. But we have found that, in all nations, the men who are outstanding for their wisdom have devoted their energies mainly to prayers to the divine. This is particularly true of the Hindu Brahmanas, the Persian Magi, and the Greek theologians (although the Chaldeans worshipped something different). Giving the name of God to the power of those above, they offered their worship in this one name.'

That is what Porphyry says.

After Porphyry, let us listen to his disciple, the divine Iamblichus, whose words are fully confirmed by Proclus:

'All things are of God, so that nothing, however small, is ever away from God. For in all places divine unity prevails. Through this unity all things come to rest, and, in a never-ending circle of close relationship, they turn towards God Himself, from whom and in whom they miraculously have their being. If it were not so, they would at once rush headlong into nothingness.

'All things proceed from the divine unity, and as they proceed they retain a particular unity which has been impressed upon them as an image of divine unity. Through this particular unity they are called back to the divine unity, and, being called back, they find their completion.

'This unity seizes souls in accordance with their prayers, through which our union with God is deeply fulfilled. For if nature, which emanates from God, has introduced certain qualities which resonate with what is higher, so that through these qualities they turn in some measure to what is higher, as all that is solar turns towards the Sun, while all that is lunar turns towards the Moon, how much more deeply has the Father of souls impressed upon them powers which will seize them for Himself.

'Now these powers seem to be located particularly within a divine unity which is higher than the intellect: in fact, within the very act of the intellect as it turns back. The prayerful worship which arises from this brings our re-instatement in God to complete fulfilment, for by a natural affinity it draws into us the divine beneficence and unites the worshippers with the object of their worship. It joins the prayers of the devotees to the intelligence of the higher beings, and it moves the will of those who embrace all good things within themselves to impart good things to us in accordance with our desires. It is the agent of divine conviction, and all that we have it establishes in the steadfastness of the higher realms.

'But there are five principal prerequisites for the fulfilment of prayer. The first is some concept of the object of worship and of the reason for worship. The second is the approximation of our life to the divine life, starting with purity, integrity, holiness, discipline, and order; seeking God's blessing; and submitting our souls to His bounty. The third prerequisite is some contact through which we can for much of the time attain the divine essence and sink into it through the most exalted condition of our soul. The fourth pre-condition is entry into the forecourt of divine light. The fifth is a union which enables the unity of the soul to penetrate deeply into the divine unity and remain connected, thus making the action of the soul and of God one and the same, so that we are no longer under our own law but are under God's law, being overwhelmed and enveloped by divine glory.

'However, the supreme purpose of this worship, which should be undertaken unceasingly, is to conjoin this turning of the soul with that unchanging state, to restore indissolubly to the divine unity whatever has come forth from it, and to flood our light with the supernal light. Thus true worship alone restores souls to their home country. Holiness alone is the fullness of virtue. Only the good man, as Plato writes in the *Laws*, prays to God in a fitting and auspicious way. Only intercourse with those above confers blessings on men. Those who lead disgraceful lives are completely estranged from this; such sacrilegious people should be kept away from prayers and devotions.

'But those who are pure come to offer their entreaties in a fitting manner, bringing with them three special companions: faith, truth, and love. Encompassed by these three, let them conceive an unshakeable hope in whatever is good; and being thus taken beyond all else and beyond themselves, let them dive deeply into the divine light. For a man vainly seeks after God if he does not apply himself in solitude to that which is solitary, in stillness to that which is still, and in simplicity to that which is utterly simple. Just as we cannot be united to being through non-being, so we cannot be united to unity through multiplicity, to stillness through movement, or to simplicity through complexity, but rather do we fall back into their opposites.'

That is what Iamblichus and Proclus say.

The great Theodorus adds that anyone who carefully examines the nature of things will find that, in addition to souls and minds, everything apart from the First is engaged in worship and prayer.

Chapter 7
The world has three causes higher than itself, depends on the incorporeal cause, and is ever in flux

LATER, NOW THAT prayers have been offered, Timaeus, deeming that the world has been created, and therefore created by something outside itself, examines its threefold cause: the efficient cause, which is the divine mind; the model cause, or the series of Ideas conceived by the divine mind; and the final cause, which is the Good.

COMPENDIUM CHAPTER 7

That the world is made by something other than itself he shows by the fact that, although it is fully complete in its physical nature, it is not totally complete in its absolute nature, since it admits of irregularities and deformities through the nature of matter, and through the nature of measurement it suffers defects in its excellence and is open to division. If it is a victim of further division on account of its composite nature, it is liable to disintegrate. On account of the mutual repulsion of its parts it devises evil. On account of its motion it reveals its deficiency and suffers further deprivation. In brief, its constitution, being compounded of diverse elements, has no single higher power to hold it together, a power that has perfect being since it is from itself. The world, not having perfect being, is thus known not to be of itself.

Yet every kind of composite thing is taken back to something which is not composite within the kind: dimensions to a point, which has no dimensions; numbers to unity, which is not composed of numbers; elements to that which is not compounded of elements. In this way the entire order of all beings is taken back to that being which does not consist of beings. This will be a substance unmixed with contingent attributes, a substance without quantity or quality, a substance whole and indivisible.

That which is single, utterly simple, and alone does not have less than those things which, apart from substance, are subject to contingencies, for those attributes which are contingent within all that follows must be a substance within the supreme and, indeed, the finest substance. But the more you add to what is excellent, the further do you force things away from excellence itself, for from the admixture there arises a quality that is new and inferior.

This world, therefore, being composite in all respects, depends, as does any world that is higher but still composite, on a higher simplicity which stands above even eternity and from which are derived the fullness of eternity within divine minds, the eternity that is mixed with time within rational creatures, the temporal everlastingness within the spheres of the world, and a portion of time within those things which arise from the motion and power of the spheres.

Thus whatever is considered to be above the soul always is and never becomes. But the soul itself is and ever becomes. The world never is, but ever becomes. Whatever is born in the world never is, but becomes for a time. Indeed, we say that to become is to be enacted by time, and since the world is driven by ceaseless movement and unending time it is judged to be ever becoming. But because it is becoming, it is not yet, and so it is said never to be, just as the reflection of a mountain in a rushing stream is ever becoming and being re-formed, ever led into becoming and never staying at rest in being.

But the followers of Plato think that the difference between the soul and the world is that the heavens are continually becoming, both in action and in essence, whereas the soul becomes through action, but through its essence it is from God and does not become from God; and since essence is indivisible it has a generative power of its own by which it projects into itself its own life and movement, while the heavens are fully dependent on something other than themselves.

In brief, just as from the same rock, which lies between the still pool and the rushing stream, the reflection in the pool constantly is, as it appears, and in the rushing stream constantly becomes and after vanishing is constantly re-created, in the same way they both depend on God, but in different ways. For from God the soul ever is, while the world ever becomes.

When we say – if we follow Plato – that the world is always becoming, we must understand that the heavens, too, are in some way becoming, through motion that is, as it were, both spatial and natural. For since the entire mechanism is beneath soul which is set in motion through action, it itself must naturally be subject to motion.

Consistent with this kind of susceptibility to motion are matter without form, dimension that is naturally divisible, polarity of qualities, and motion that is extremely swift; so that, just as the intelligible world always is and never becomes, so the whole of the perceptible world, as Timaeus says, is always becoming but never really is.

This is why, in the *Republic*, Plato calls all perceptible things images and shadows. This is what is implied by that divine statement, 'All is vanity'; and again, 'The world passeth away'. Concerning this kind of passing away we have spoken at greater length in the *Theology*.

We shall therefore say, in company with Plato, that nothing flows externally into or out of the world as a whole, but that outflow and inflow always occur within the world, and this causes the world to always become. The elemental region does not in any way change into the celestial region, or vice versa. The elements gradually penetrate each other and, intermingling in this way, they allow outflow and inflow within their respective regions, whereas the celestial spheres, like eight worlds, do not intermingle, for each sphere is held intact by its own extremely powerful soul. But from the stars something flows everlastingly through their heavens and flows back again; and this reciprocal flow is assisted by the circular movement of the heavens.

Thus in the eighth sphere, through those stars known as the fixed stars, and in the subsequent spheres, through the planets and the other dwellers in the heavens which are hidden from our eyes, mutual interchange takes place. The stars, however, appear ever the same, for the outflow and inflow are always brought into balance by the governing soul: their shape remains unchanged and their light remains much the same, but their matter is replenished. In addition, beneath the Moon, there are aeons in which the inflow is equally balanced in all places with the outflow for very long periods of time, but not for ever.

In this way, if we accept that the Sun of Thales, Democritus, and Heraclitus is new every day and that everything is in perpetual flux, there will be no discord at all between the ancient writers and Plato, and it will not escape our notice what banquets and nectar and ambrosia of the gods they require, according to the poets.

But let us now make a new start.

Chapter 8

The Good Itself, rather than subsequent causes, is the cause of all things, and it has no direct relationship with anything

ALL THE FOLLOWERS of Plato concur in declaring that this universe receives everything from the supreme God, including action, power, and essence; for this is what they find in all his books and what they hear confirmed in his letters. Indeed, in all his writings he most mysteriously withdraws the tertiary effects into the tertiary cause, the secondary effects into the secondary cause, and all effects into the one cause of all. He does not say that the primary effects are to be withdrawn into the primary cause, lest by calling them the primary effects he might mislead us into thinking that they alone depend on God or that God combines with the other causes in every genus and with the effects in some kind of lordship. And so he shows that all things come forth together from Him and that He is completely free of all contact with whatever comes forth.

On account of its absolute simplicity he calls it the One Itself; and on account of its unbounded beneficence, through which, and as the beginning, it creates all things by bringing them forth and, as the end, perfects all things by bringing them back, he calls it the Good Itself. But he thinks that whatever comes into being depends more on it than on the other causes, since in every activity it operates earlier, for longer, and more powerfully than the other causes; and whatever the other causes are, it is under its operation that they are so; and whatever they do, they do under its authority.

But in order to show that each and every thing emanates from it rather than from the other causes, Plato says three times that it is the beginning of all. For he says that all things surround the King of all, that all things exist for His sake, and that He is the cause of all, in order that we might understand that all things arise primarily from Him and that God is the maker of all, the model of all, and the end of all. In the same way Plato clearly shows, in the sixth book of the *Republic*, in the *Parmenides*, and in the *Sophist*, that the One Itself, the Good Itself, is higher than every essence and every intellect and is the cause of both essence and intellect.

But it is clear that the One and the Good are the same; for if they were different there would of necessity be two supreme principles. The principle, or beginning, must of course be utterly simple and utterly good; and nothing is simpler than unity or better than goodness. Unity is not better than goodness, and goodness is not simpler than unity. Thus both are one, the supreme God. That this is wholly above essence and mind we have clearly shown in the *Theology* and elsewhere.

Chapter 9
The dependence of matter on the Good Itself; the action of the mind and soul upon matter; and the intelligible world

FROM THIS UNQUALIFIED One, the Good that soars above every essence, Plato, in his *Parmenides* and *Sophist*, derives all the levels of beings; next, the levels of those things that truly are, the separate forms; then the levels of those that truly are not, the forms inherent in matter; and finally, the lowest level of matter, which is so far from the truth that it is next to that which is imagined to no longer have true being. This unqualified matter, which in the *Parmenides* is derived from the Good Itself and found at the last level of creation, Plato accepts in the *Timaeus* as already begotten by the maker of the world and as subordinate to the effect of cosmic operation.

But can it be said that God, the creator of the world, is also the producer of matter? The followers of Ammonius and Origen will reply that He is; that the *Parmenides* deals with how matter receives being from God; and that in the *Timaeus* the way in which matter receives well-being from God is carefully thought out, although it must receive some measure of being before it can receive well-being. A different reply will be given by the main body of Plato's followers, who will say that the one who makes matter and the one who shapes it soon afterwards are not the same God; that matter is, in fact, from the highest Good, but is shaped by the intellect and then moved by the soul; that all these things are indeed from the First, but being is from the First only, is shaped by the First through the intellect, and is moved and, being moved, is quickly given shape by the First through both the intellect and the soul.

In a similar way, let us imagine a potter who prepares the clay with his own hand and, once it is prepared, shapes it on the wheel, and as he shapes it he defines and fashions it with a wooden spatula. No one would say, without some qualification, that the vessel was made by the spatula and the wheel rather than by the potter, although it does come into being from the potter by means of the wheel and spatula.

They deem that this universe likewise comes forth from the Good Itself by means of a divine intellect and the soul of the universe; that from the One Itself the world is made primarily one, and from the

Good Itself it is made primarily good. But since this visible world, on account of its manifold division into parts, the opposing natures of its qualities, the diversity of its effects, and the imperfections of its material forms is not primarily one or primarily good, they deem that prior to this world another world emanates from unity itself and from divine goodness, a world which resembles the visible world as closely as nature will allow, a world which is not visible but intelligible and intellectual, containing the models for all those things which come into being in this visible world. They call this other world the divine intellect, not the Good Itself, but the noblest child of the Good. If we understand this to be of one substance with the First, we shall unite Plato more closely with Christian theology, but the other interpreters of Plato will voice their protests.

Chapter 10
The Sun, light, radiance, brilliance, heat, procreation; likewise unity, goodness, intellect, soul, nature, the body of the world, the image of the higher worlds

THEREFORE LET the truth, Christian and Mosaic, persist. But in the meantime, as most expositors agree, it was possibly the view of Plato or of Pythagoras that the intelligible world is intermediate between the visible world and the Good Itself, an image of the Good and the model for the physical world; it depends on the Good, just as the radiance outside the Sun depends on the light within the Sun; and it very soon brings forth from itself the soul of the world, just as radiance pours forth brilliance from itself; and through the soul it continually begets all things, just as brilliance begets bodily forms through heat.

These six levels are arranged in a hierarchy. The first is the very substance of the Sun; the second is that light which is substantial and innermost; the third is the radiance emanating from it; the fourth is the brilliance which pours forth from the radiance; the fifth is the heat kindled by the brilliance; and the sixth is the procreation produced by the blazing heat.

The six other levels are distinguished in a similar way. The first is unity, and the second is goodness, but these two are not truly distinct – although reason can distinguish them to some extent – for they have the same divine nature; and because unity soars high above everything, yet at the same time fills everything, it is called goodness. This unconditioned power to fill all things Plato, in the sixth book of the *Republic*, calls the Idea of the Good, but in his letters he calls it the Idea of good things; and so he calls it the Idea of the Good Itself and of those good things that come forth from the Good. At the third level, corresponding to the radiance which emanates from the light, is a divine mind, which, if I may express it thus, conceives within itself manifold Ideas from the warmth of the single and supernal light and of the Idea of the One, just as within the radiance many rays originate from a single ray of light. Not only are the Ideas of created things comprised within this mind, but to this mind are related, as to their leader, many hosts of minds springing forth from that same divine light from which that mind itself also comes forth.

All of this is called the higher world, but all that concerns the subsequent minds is called the intellectual world, while whatever concerns the leader is called the intelligible world.

But that mind which is the leader of minds is called partly intellect and partly intelligible: intellect insofar as it applies itself to distinguishing the principles of created things, and intelligible insofar as such principles are held within its Ideas.

Finally, the Idea of the Good presides not only over the intellect but also over the intelligible.

After this world-archetype there follows, at the fourth level, the soul of the physical world. This is the rational world, coming forth from the intellectual world, as brilliance comes forth from radiance. And just as the brilliance is now combined with movement, so the soul, with a quick movement, reaches and pervades the principles of the unmoving Ideas. This is followed by the fifth level, the nature of things, the seed-world, proceeding from the rational world of the soul as heat proceeds from brilliance. At the sixth level is found this physical world, arising unconditionally from the seed-world, just as the procreation of things arises from warmth.

And if you wish to draw a more suitable comparison with all the items that have been omitted, you will consider firstly the natural power and goodness found in an architect of surpassing wisdom; secondly, the contemplative intellect related to geometry and containing the general principles of measuring; thirdly, what is called practical reason, which, through these very principles, is already deliberating upon craftsmanship; fourthly, the imagination, which forms the shapes and patterns conducive to work; fifthly, the disposition; and sixthly, the ability to move. But in such comparisons you will see that the effects are caused much more by what precedes than by what follows.

Chapter 11
Individual orders are taken back to individual heads, and the universal order is taken back to the universal head, by which all things are composed through action and power

WE SHOULD NOT be unaware that specific kinds of things need to be taken back to their respective heads, while the universal genus needs to be taken back to the universal head. For all the physical things of the world are related to a single body; all natures are related to a single nature; all souls, to a single soul; all minds, to a single mind; good things – and therefore all things, since all are good – to the Good.

In this way, all things without exception yearn for the Good, which is their end, through a natural tendency, since they have all come forth from the Good itself, which is also their beginning, through a common movement. And all things yearn so strongly for the Good that base matter yearns with a longing that is far from base, for in begetting all things it tends continually towards the very likeness of the Good, so that it is clear that it depends on the Good: on the Good, I say, rather than on the mind, for the action of the mind, being initiated through ideal forms, ends in forms, whereas the all-embracing action of the Good moves down below forms and into matter, making matter eager and able to receive good things.

But to what I am now calling matter Plato, in the *Philebus*, gives the more extensive name of Limitlessness, for he says that the Good itself brought forth Limitlessness and Limit next to each other and immediately mixed them together; from this intermingling, that is, from a formative power and an approaching form, it constituted all things. For Limitlessness is the name he gives to a formative power, as if it were not yet limited or complete; and limit is the name he gives to the form which is presented to it , because it sets a limit on an unlimited power and brings it to completion within a pre-selected species.

They hold that it is therefore from these two that the intelligible world was first formed by God, and that the perceptible world was then formed by the intelligible world from the same two, or very similar, elements. Thus the result was that that intellect, the immediate maker of the visible world, took from the Good Itself matter that was to some extent imbued with life but was close to deteriorating, formless and void, into the vast mass beneath it and on the point of wavering in disordered fashion if it were able to move of itself. But through the order of Ideas, which had been received from the Good, the intellect gave it form and restored it to order before it could stray away from order, particularly because it first imbued it with the rational soul, which presides over movement of the most ordered kind.

He says that not only would matter be formless of itself but the soul, too, would be formless, if God did not impart form to them both. But what physical type is to matter, reason and intelligence are to the soul; and if the soul lacks reason and intelligence, it will move matter in a random way. To express this, however, he viewed matter as formless and the soul as irrational, and he saw that movement without order would come forth from it.

Chapter 12
Matter was not in disarray prior to the world in time, but was arranged according to some principle of order or origin

FROM ALL OF THIS we are able to gather that matter was not coeval with the maker of the world. It was not prior to the world by any length of time, either in origin or in order. It was not tossed about indiscriminately prior to order, but it would have tended to stray far away from order if it had not been immediately set in order from above.

Anyone who might reproach Plato for speaking in this way and for imagining that, prior to the world, matter was being randomly tossed about should listen to Moses, who says that before the formation of the world the earth was void and without form, and darkness was upon the face of the deep.

For present purposes I omit the poetical word 'chaos', but it is good to hear the evidence given by Philo, the Jewish writer, who expounds Moses' *Book of Genesis* in similar terms. Anyone who wishes to inquire into the reason for the creation of this universe will not go wrong, in my opinion, if he considers what Philo has handed on from those of ancient times: the Good is the creator, parent, and author of the universe, and by the grace of its goodness it withheld nothing from substance, which of its own nature had nothing good and yet was able to become all things. For of its own nature substance was unordered, formless, lifeless, full of diversity, inconsistent, inharmonious, and inconstant, yet susceptible of changing into the opposite qualities and of accepting the principle of all that is excellent: form, liveliness, uniformity, consistency, harmony – in short, the better Idea of all things. Again, in the second volume of the same work, Philo says that when the creator had begun to shape unordered substance, which was by nature in disarray, into order from disorder, and to transfer it from disarray into discrete forms, he then established earth and water in the central place. That is what Philo says.

In the same way, if you consider the six levels of creation which were adduced earlier, you may observe how close Plato is to Moses, who says that the world was created in six days, and how similar is

Pythagoras, who proves that the number six applies to creation and to marriage, which is why he calls it *gamos*, for its parts, placed side by side, produce it and make the offspring similar to the parent.

Chapter 13
Two views concerning the origin of the world

TO THOSE WHO may doubt whether Plato really considered the world to be everlasting, my own answer is that commentators such as Severus, Atticus, Plutarch, and many others, as Proclus recounts, did not view it as everlasting, whereas commentators such as Crantor, Plotinus, Porphyry, Iamblichus, Proclus, and many others considered it to have been for ever, indeed, to have flowed for ever from God. For they say that God ever is, whilst the world ever becomes and ever flows.

If you consider the world to have no beginning in time, you will say that it is not begotten. On the other hand, if you deem its outflowing from God to be continuous, you will say that it is constantly being born and that, if it depends on God and has always depended on Him, it is no less dependent on Him than if its dependence began at some point in time and may end at some point in time, just as light is no less dependent on the Sun for its origin and does not serve the Sun less by always taking its origin from the Sun than if it flowed forth from the Sun at some point in time and still flows forth.

Chapter 14
A threefold inference drawn from Plato's view of the world, and what is undisputed about his view

WE NOW SET ABOUT considering other Platonic matters, either through inference or through knowledge.

As far as inference is concerned, Plato himself speaks, and his followers reason, in such a way that it is legitimate to put his view of the origin of the world under three headings.

For he may have thought that from nothing matter was simultaneously created and formed by God at some point in time, although in this work, which is composed of matter, it is thought that a second order of creation is produced by matter itself before being formed, that matter exists before it is given form and prior to the work that is formed from matter and that the matter from which the work had to be accomplished is constantly sought.

Again, Plato may have considered that God did not create and arrange new matter at some point in time but from eternity, although it was made in crude form before it was refined, since by nature it lacks order, which it awaits from something other than itself. And since each and every thing is considered in accordance with what it is before being considered in accordance with what it receives, it can be contemplated without reference to order, being of itself devoid of order.

Again, as I have said, Plato may have thought that matter was ever and uninterruptedly from God, yet not continually ordered by God, but only for periods of time, so that God's nature is to impart order constantly, while the nature of matter is to be ordered variably; it receives the temporal balance of its arrangement just as a clock does from its maker, and when specific periods of time have elapsed in conformity with its nature, it loses its order by degrees and ultimately loses all of it, thus returning to chaos; but God, not accepting total confusion, restores it at once to its former disposition with a single fiat of will, and it becomes totally re-shaped matter, while God is not the least whit changed.

So far human inference has prevailed among the followers of Plato. But in accordance with the knowledge available to us, we declare that our Plato states that the world does not exist from itself but from a cause: not from a chance cause but from a definite cause; not from a merely natural cause but from an intellectual cause; not from an intellect determined by the ways of nature but rather from an intellect that operates voluntarily; not from a will that is compelled by some natural impulse but from a will that is free. For nothing enjoys more freedom than that which is of itself and acts of itself in every respect, without the contingency of any will, since there is no contingency when will and necessity are one and the same. Again, there is no violence when, conversely, necessity and will are one and the same.

But in order to show this in his account of the making of the world, he speaks of the divine will no less frequently than he speaks of intelligence. And he adds that the will of the Good is the supreme cause and the most dependable of causes. He shows that it is free, because he often says that God, in the manner of an architect, pondered and deliberated on the construction of the work. By using these words Plato intends God to be understood not as being uncertain but as making a free choice.

In a similar way, he does not say that the making of the world proceeded only once from God, but he says that it proceeds continually and is continually preserved by God. And furthermore, the highest divinities of the world, together with the world, would of themselves be subject to dissolution if they were not ruled by the divine will.

It is sufficient, then, to have affirmed these points, and this point in particular, about the philosopher who makes these statements, for once these have been accepted you will find it easy to say that, when God makes the world from His provident free will, He has made it new but without its coming into existence for the first time. And if you hear that He has brought it forth new, not at some time but from eternity, you will be able at the same time to attribute its dignity to God, on whose will – a will that is indeed free – the world, of necessity, depends no less if it is always necessarily dependent than if it came forth at some point in time.

But since Plato frequently says that we should make a solemn profession of things divine as far as is approved by the divine precepts, we should give our assent to the sacred Scriptures rather than to our own conjectures.

Chapter 15
By the grace of the Good the world has been brought into being in the likeness of the divine principle and the divine word

HE THEREFORE MADE the world through His own will, His own goodness, which naturally and of its own volition overflows through its limitless fertility, rejoicing in itself first and then finding delight in its own image, but doing so in such a way that it establishes the end of this delight, not in this image, but in the model and the beginning. Since He therefore made the world through goodness, He made it for the sake of the Good, for He did not bring it forth merely that it might be, live, and perceive, but that it might be well, live well, and perceive and attain to the Good. This is fully in harmony with what Moses says: God saw that this and that were good and that all things were very good.

And because beauty is the glory of goodness, Plato adds that the transient world was brought forth by almighty God in the fullness of beauty as an image of the eternal model. And he frequently says that God has ordained there to be as many forms within the creation as there are living, intelligible, and reproducible types within the archetype, that is, within the primordial world; and that He has made it like unto Himself, with the result that those who understand the Ideas of the creation are not standing with their heads in the clouds, as certain slanderers say, but are established within the mind of the Architect of the world.

Yet when he says that Ideas are within life itself, he seems to be presaging this statement from the Gospels: 'In him was life'. And when he says, and frequently repeats, that the world has been established by divine providence, he is confirming religion in its entirety. Indeed, when Theophrastus had observed that this was something astonishing to find in a philosopher, he said that Plato, alone of philosophers, or at least much more than all the others, attributed the causes of creation to divine providence. But, my Theophrastus, whatever your intention in speaking of Plato may be, you will no doubt admit that he alone, or at least much more than all the others, is himself providential and divine.

Chapter 16
Why the world is one,
why it is spherical, and
why its movement is spherical

PLATO SHOWS NEXT that the divine model for the world, which the Evangelist, with a more divine understanding, calls the divine word, is one, for it embraces all things, leaving nothing outside itself, and is thus necessarily one. However, we have spoken of this at greater length in the *Theology*.

But since this world reflects, as faithfully as possible, the world and the divine intellect, so that anyone who descries forms within this matter, as if discerning a divine countenance in a mirror, will undoubtedly portray this world as the single work of the single Architect within the unity which makes and preserves all things. The one world is therefore of the one God. Indeed, if a human architect were able to master matter, he would, after creating many buildings, each of which is single in itself, encompass them all with a single common factor. But God is able to do this in all respects, for He is the Master of matter.

And it is not right to dream up numerous worlds, like balls, some apart from others; for in this way the divine work would be diffused and there would be empty spaces separating the worlds. If, instead, you consider spheres within spheres, as many as the worlds which you are imagining to be scattered throughout the void, you are more likely to think that each sphere is a world within a world, that the universe is a single work, ordered within itself, and that nothing will be found that is either empty or devoid of order and union.

But let the form of the world be spherical, for in this way it is fully uniform, spacious, cohesive, and energetic; and this is the only way in which one mass can be placed inside another without any void or can move without any collision. This is not the case if squares are placed within squares or within circles, but only if globes are placed within globes. In brief, there is a special cause of this world-sphere: the nature of the divine world is circular, being turned back to itself through the act of understanding and loving, while the principle of spherical motion is both the shape itself, which receives the movement, and the innermost revolution of the world-soul, which moves through the intellectual types.

Chapter 17
Why the world is divided into five or six regions; how the number seven is right for it; circular number; and how the world is arranged in the likeness of the intelligible world

THIS IS WHY numbers are justifiably applied to the arrangement of the world. The first roots among these are of the circular numbers: the number five from the odd numbers, and the number six from the even numbers. Now we say that the number twenty-five is multiplied from five in the manner of a circle, since from the same there is a return to the same, while five times five is reckoned as twenty-five. Again, by means of a similar circle, we have the number one hundred and twenty-five, for this is the product of five and twenty-five. There is the same ratio of the circular number six in relation to thirty-six and to two hundred and sixteen, for six times six gives thirty-six, and six times thirty-six gives two hundred and sixteen.

Although they call some of these numbers square and others rectangular, according to their origin, they also call them circular on account of their outcome and end. And so, by means of the numbers five and six, which are the first roots of the circular numbers, we divide the spherical body of the world, firstly into five parts: celestial fire, ethereal fire, and the sub-lunar air, water, and earth. This division is ratified in the *Epinomis*. The second division, by means of the number six, is when we subdivide the celestial fire into the 'fixed' and the 'wandering'. This division is quite often employed by Plato.

But we shall find it more convenient to derive the arrangement of the perceptible world from the arrangement of its model in the following way, as Plato does: God devises, within the intelligible world that is close to Him, one power that is able to receive form and another power that is able to impart form. The first of these powers, as I have said, is what the followers of Pythagoras and Plato call Limitlessness, and the second is what they call Limit. He also devises the intermingling of these two powers and understands that a third form at once arises from this mixture. But He is aware that this form is threefold, for it has something of Limitlessness, something of Limit, and something of its own.

The result is that after the number two, the number of Limitlessness and of Limit, the number three immediately arises, as the third form is added to these two. The number five also arises, as a form of this kind is arranged in a threefold manner. Finally, the number six is born when the favour of that world is extended to bring forth the things that are lower. And the number seven is born when that world is referred, like an image, to its father. At this seventh step, as on the seventh day, there is rest.

But if you return each to its own, you will observe that this physical world receives fire as its form from the very Limit of the supernal world, earth as its material from the Limitlessness, but from the intermediate form of the supernal world it receives moisture, the reconciler of fire and earth, holding together the earth, which is by nature liable to dispersion, and nourishing the fire, which is of itself dissoluble. It possesses three things within itself, being fiery on the one hand and earthy on the other hand, with something of its own which is pure and airy and which is midway between these two, since it turns towards fire through that which is highest and towards earth through that which is lowest.

After this number five of the world there is the number six, if you have thought out the general form of all things. Then the number seven comes into being, if you have restored this actual form of the world to its model, in which it may indeed rest on the seventh day.

Chapter 18
Why there are distinct parts within the world and why there is opposition among them; also concerning the four elements

WITHIN THE WORLD we see not only a differentiation of forms but also a state of opposition; for the world comes forth from the First, and as it comes forth it declines. Indeed, the outward movement causes differentiation, and the decline causes the opposition. The fact is that the origin of the division is the fecundity of the cause, overflowing on all sides and spreading far and wide; but as the division moves forward through many steps, it eventually reaches the state of opposition, especially since the material of the world is unable, on account of its own weakness, to reconcile the forms in the way that the higher world reconciles them within itself. Thus it came about that God spread forth matter and measured it out in order to collect, at various resting-points, forms which are likely to be mutually opposed.

In short, since we say that those things are mutually opposed which are furthest apart within the same genus, and that those things are different which are separated from each other by genera, the fact that there are opposites within the world shows that each genus contains a vast number of species; and the fact that there are differences shows that the universe contains a huge number of genera. But since all species are ultimately taken back to genera, and all genera to the universe and its common form, it is concluded that, just as the higher world is both uniform and omniform, so this world is both omniform and uniform.

However, the opposing qualities and forms of the elements and the heavens are conducive to the daily begetting of new forms through the variation of movement. For either there was a single element, so that absolutely nothing will be begotten, as Hippocrates avers, or there were many similar elements, so that nothing new will be produced, as Heraclitus demonstrates.

It is, however, incumbent upon this world, through the unceasing production of new forms, to imitate, with all its power, the eternal action of the higher omniform world. And so, as the poetry of Empedocles proclaims, let there be mutually opposed elements. And let there be an intermediary between opposites when the opposites are furthest away from each other and they can find no harmony without an intermediary. But this intermediary cannot be indivisible, for, if it were, then the opposites would not be far from each other; and so it has dimension. But the part with which it touches one of the opposites does not touch the other opposite. And it also has, of necessity, a middle part by means of which it is equally out of harmony with the two extremes.

This is why Plato also inserts at least two intermediaries between opposites, as is clearly apparent from his words. He introduces a third when he says that the intermediary has the power to protect the unity of the extremes and its own unity as well. But, for now, we do not dispute the fact that he clearly posits two intermediaries, as when he places air and water between fire and earth. That at least two intermediaries are required between opposites that are totally physical he demonstrates from numbers and measurements, which in some way precede natural bodies.

Chapter 19
Numbers linear, plane, and solid; why a single intermediary is sufficient between planes but is not sufficient between solids; how mathematical ratios are related to physical ratios

WE HAVE STATED elsewhere that, according to the followers of Pythagoras, numbers are of three types: linear, plane, and solid. They say that linear numbers, which are measured by unity alone, as if by marks on a scale, are, for example, two, three, five, and seven. Plane numbers, they say, are those which are the products of numbers acting as sides: thus the number six is made from two threes or from three twos. We call those plane numbers square and equilateral which are produced from any number multiplied by itself: thus the number four is produced from two twos, nine from three threes, and sixteen from four fours.

The non-equilaterals, however, are those which are produced from the multiplication of a smaller number by a larger number, such as six, the product of two and three. We call them oblong if they are produced by the multiplication of a very small number by a much larger number, such as the number ten, which is the product of two and five, since two times five makes ten. If in the tenth book of the *Republic* we have called this number linear in some respects, we would like it to be understood as oblong.

In addition to this, we were speaking of those that are solid, for they are produced from the multiplication of any number by itself twice, like a solid mass produced in three dimensions, such as twice two doubled, which is eight; three times thrice three, which is twenty-seven; and four times four times four, which is sixty-four.

Take the first two plane numbers, which are produced by the first linear numbers: four, which comes from two, and nine, which comes from three. You will, of course, be able to unite these two plane numbers, nine and four, with a single appropriate intermediary or mean, which is the number six. For the ratio of nine to six is the same as that of six to four, since in both instances the ratio is the *sesquialteral*, as nine contains six and one half of six, which is three. In the same way, six contains four and two more, a half of four. But that six is the appropriate mean is apparent from the fact that it is composed of them both, for one side of four is two, and one side of nine is three; and the product of two and three is six.

Similarly, if you take nine and the next square number, which is sixteen, the mean will be twelve, which is made from the sides of these two squares; for the side of nine is three, while the side of sixteen is four, and if you multiply three by four you will reach twelve, which, as their mean, connects them both by the same ratio, which is the *sesquitertial* ratio, for sixteen contains twelve and one third of twelve, while twelve contains nine and one third of nine. You will thus see what Plato says: that plane numbers can be linked by a single mean.

Next take the first of the solid numbers, I mean the first ones produced from the first linear numbers when multiplied by themselves and then multiplied again by themselves, in the way that eight is produced from two, and twenty-seven from three. You will not be able to join these with a single mean, but you will be obliged to take two means at any rate, namely, twelve and eighteen. For you will obtain twelve from twice two times three, and eighteen from three threes times two, since in this way twelve borrows two sides, that is, twice two from eight, the cube nearer to it, and one side, namely, three, from twenty-seven, the further cube; and the other mean, namely, eighteen, also borrows two sides, namely, three times three, from the nearer cube, that is, twenty-seven, and one side, namely, two, from the further cube, namely, eight. And by means of these numbers you will harmonise the two extremes with the *sesquialteral* ratio, since the number twenty-seven contains eighteen and one half of eighteen, which is nine, and eighteen exceeds twelve in the same way. Again, twelve exceeds eight by the same ratio. It is thus clear that solid numbers always require more than one mean to join them harmoniously.

But what we have expounded in the case of numbers can also be shown to apply to measurements, both plane and solid, for we can show that between planes which are mutually compatible a single mean is frequently sufficient, whereas in the case of compatible solids more than one mean needs to be employed. It would be a very lengthy process to demonstrate this, and it has already been demonstrated by Iamblichus, Proclus, and Chalcidius.

But since Plato here accepts such mathematical propositions, not for their own sakes but for the sake of natural forms, let us pass over them but consider briefly which natural mysteries in particular he is alluding to through the mathematical images. First of all, that God, as we read in the Scriptures, created all things according to number, measure, and weight is clearly touched upon by Plato, who presents numbers, measures, and solids as his witnesses. For with solids he includes weights, as he indicates when, after referring to measurements, he speaks of the forces of inclination as the causes of weights. By numbers he intends us to understand the actual species and substantial forms of natural things, which Aristotle, too, compared to numbers. By measures we are to understand particular instrumental shapes or magnitudes which are appropriate to particular species. Finally, by solids and powers he means the qualities which are fully extended together with vast masses of material and which provide the momentum for movements and actions.

But he considers that all the species within the whole creation, as well as the shapes, sizes, and qualities of the species, are composed of geometrical and musical ratios, so that the lowest species are surpassed by the intermediate species, and the intermediate by the higher, in accordance with the same ratio.

Again, by numbers he indicates the arithmetic mean, which consists of the equality of numbers; by dimensions and measures, the geometric mean, which lies in the sameness of ratio and proportion; by weights and forces, the harmonic mean, which in the equality or likeness of proportion holds by its power the place, briskness, and slowness of movements and the height and depth of notes.

Chapter 20
The first consideration: why the number four in relation to the elements befits the world

BUT MORE OF these things elsewhere. Let us now go back to the division of the cosmos into parts, so that we may be able to descry their harmonious composition. We were saying earlier that the numbers five and six harmonise with the spherical shape of the world. Now we are saying that the number four, too, matches its fullness. Indeed, four first fulfils all the difference of the numbers, embracing within itself the first even number and the first odd number. Four also fulfils the simple sequence of numbers, since with its limits it fulfils ten, perfectly completing ten with one, two, three, and four. Again, it fills the development of dimensions, achieving this with four limits: point, length, breadth, and depth. It fulfils musical harmony, for between its limits are held the *double*, the *triple*, the *quadruple*, the *sesquialteral*, the *sesquitertial*, the *diapason*, the *disdiapason*, the *diapente*, and the *diatessaron*. It fulfils nature, which extends as far as four limits by means of substance, quantity, quality, and movement. In short, it fulfils all, whether it be something within nature or something above nature, through essence, being, power, and action.

The followers of Pythagoras were therefore justified in using the number four to designate the fullness of the cosmic body and the cosmic soul and to testify on oath that the fount of ever-flowing nature is fourfold. It is undoubtedly from this fount that the four elements emanate. Hence the fourfold triplicity in the heavens. Hence the four seasons under the heavens. Hence, beneath time, there appear the four humours, the four complexions, and the four dispositions. Hence, above time, there arise the four virtues. Hence, in eternity, there are the four models of the virtues.

Chapter 21
The second consideration: proving the same

AGAIN, IF I DID NOT fear prolixity on the one hand and novelty on the other, I would list some remarkable statements by Iamblichus, Syrianus, and Proclus, who designate four levels higher than the celestial world: One, Limit, Limitlessness, Combination. In the same way, below the celestial world, which is the first intelligible mind, they place the mind and world which are partly intelligible and partly intellectual, and below this the mind and world which are wholly intellectual. But in the fourth position they place the mind and world which are filled with soul and lead the sensible world.

Again, they maintain that the supreme mind looks up to those four (One, Limit, Limitlessness, Combination) and has four elements in its own nature: unity on the one hand, and essence on the other, as well as essential unity and uniform essence and all the Ideas of created things that likewise partake, without exception, of a fourfold nature.

They also say that the intellectual and Jovial mind, the maker of the world, looks up, in the act of making the world, to the intelligible supreme mind as the model, and looks up to the Good as the end. And for this reason, that which they call Being Itself and Living Itself within the intelligible world perceives that the world is arranged into four regions by principles and Ideas of a fourfold nature.

The first of these regions extends from the first heaven, through the sphere of fire, to the beginning of the air. From here the second region extends as far as the middle part of the air. From here the third region extends to the earth, and the fourth region is the earth itself. To this type of division there correspond, respectively, the four hosts of denizens endowed with reason: the world deities, the angels, the daemons, and the individual souls.

But, setting these things on one side, let us return to the work we have taken in hand.

Chapter 22
The third consideration: confirming the same

THERE ARE FOUR elements in metaphysics: essence, being, power, and action. There are four in mathematics: point, line, plane, and depth. There are four in natural science: the seed-power of nature, natural growth, mature form, and organic nature. See how they correspond respectively: the point and seed correspond to essence; line and growth to being; plane and form to power; depth and organic nature to action. And in all cases, the extremes, like solids, are united by two means.

But, of course, that which is a point in mathematics is considered by Plato to be, in natural science, the indivisible, steadfast seed-power. That which is linear extension in mathematics he considers to be, in natural science, the growth of the budding form, if I may express it thus. The plane in one he sees as the form in the other, for just as a plane surface limits the body, so does form limit matter. Finally, that which is depth in mathematics is the organic nature in natural science: I mean a twofold nature, being both formal, that is, compounded of many forms, and similar to a solid sphere, and also material, being composed of form and matter, more like a cube.

Thus when he says that between two planes one mean is sufficient, understand that between two forms a single mean is sufficient: the formal mean. For when forms touch other forms with their extremities, they harmonise through a single formal mean, which reveals both the similarities and the differences. But when he says that solids are linked to other solids through a double mean, he is indicating that between two natural organic forms twin means of separate natures are interposed, the first of which is formal, while the second is material. For in each and every organic form the principal form is considered on the one hand and what is suited to the form and is subject to it is considered on the other hand.

Hence it comes about that two differences arise between any two organic forms. The first difference is based more on the principle of form; and the second difference is based more on the principle of that which is subject to form.

Chapter 23
The fourth consideration of the same; and the powers and ratios of the elements

THESE THINGS RECEIVE further corroboration if you go down from the groups of four that have just been described to the fourfold nature of the sphere. In the sphere the nature of the centre is certainly considered, as is the nature of the surface, the two aspects furthest from each other both in nature and in position. The space is also considered, firstly as the extent to which the power of the centre stretches and secondly as the extent to which the power of the surface reaches.

This is how the four regions of the world are calculated, as also the four elements. Of these elements, that which is placed on the surface, according to its nature, is the most extensive and therefore the finest of all in substance, the keenest of all in power, and the one best equipped for penetration, as well as the one that, in its action, is most inclined to movement. That which is positioned in the centre follows the nature of the centre and is therefore most constricted and compacted in substance, blunt in power, and in action least capable of movement. The nature of the two means is middling in these respects.

Just as, within the sphere, the surface and the centre are as far apart as is possible, so fire and earth, through their positions and natures, differ as far as is possible. For fire seeks the surface and thus never naturally seeks the centre, while earth seeks the centre and thus never goes naturally to the surface.

Air, for its part, sometimes goes down, as when it is put in the lofty realm of fire, while water rises if it is forced under the earth. But just as in fire and earth there are three aspects to consider – substance, power, and action – so there are three particular qualities: in fire there are fineness of substance, incisiveness of power, and nimbleness of action; in earth are the opposites, namely, coarseness of substance, bluntness of power, and cumbrousness of action.

Now the natures of all these are said in Plato's writings to be solid, because they possess three qualities, like three dimensions. If they had only two qualities, they would resemble planes, and it would be sufficient to have a single mean, which would agree with the extremes in one respect and differ in another. But since they have three contrasting qualities, two means are necessary to bind them together. Each of these means agrees in two qualities, and disagrees in one quality, with the extreme closer to it, and also with the other mean, and it agrees in one quality, and disagrees in two, with the extreme further from it.

Thus air follows fire, being very similar in fineness and nimbleness, but it differs on account of some bluntness in its power, and in this one respect it has some similarity with earth, while it concurs with water in two qualities: bluntness and nimbleness. Water follows air, being similar to air in these two respects; but it is similar to fire in respect of its nimbleness alone and dissimilar in the two qualities of coarseness and bluntness; and it is dissimilar to earth through its nimbleness, but like earth through its coarseness and bluntness.

Indeed, it seems that fire is comparable to earth through some analogy, that is, through some likeness of principle. For as the fineness of fire is to the coarseness of earth, so the incisiveness of fire is to the bluntness of earth, and the nimbleness of fire to the cumbrousness of earth.

It is clear that there are further comparisons – on stronger grounds and through the harmony of qualities – between fire and air, air and water, and water and earth. But it seems that the agreements between one element and its immediate neighbour are twice as many as the differences, while the differences with an element further away are twice as many as the agreements. Fire seems twice as fine as air, three times nimbler, and four times more incisive. Air seems twice as incisive as water, three times nimbler, and four times finer. Water seems twice as incisive as earth, three times finer, and four times readier for movement.

But musicians are not allowed to go beyond the fourth ratio obtaining between related items, for the ears are offended by any further development. Moreover, the perfect principles of music are held within these ratios. Within them we move through three qualities, inevitably and 'solidly', as if through three dimensions, as far as the solids, and we do this on three occasions. For through the *double* at the fourth step we reach eight, which is the first solid. Again, through the *triple* at the fourth step we reach twenty-seven, which is the second solid. Through the *quadruple* at the fourth step we reach sixty-four, which holds the third place among the solid numbers. For eight is made from the number two taken or drawn 'solidly', that is, three times; twenty-seven is from three taken three times; and sixty-four is produced from four likewise multiplied three times by itself.

Moreover, that it may be better known how much harmony, according to Plato, there is in mathematics in relation to the natural sciences, those two means for the first solids will be stated again. For between eight and twenty-seven we placed two appropriate means: twelve and eighteen. The number twelve is born from eight and twenty-seven, since the side from which eight is multiplied is two, while the side from which twenty-seven is multiplied is three, but from two and three is produced twelve, if you take two times double three, where the arising twelve takes two of its sides from eight and one side from twenty-seven. Again, from two and three arises the number eighteen, if you take three times three twice, where eighteen, the number coming to birth, takes one of its sides from the distant eight, giving 'twice', and two of its sides from the number twenty-seven, giving 'three times three'.

In the same way, the two elements between fire and earth are tempered by the extremes while at the same time bringing back two natures from the nearer and borrowing but a single nature from the further one.

Chapter 24
The whole world is composed of four elements; how these elements are under a particular principle in the heavens and under a different principle beneath the Moon

ALL THE FOLLOWERS of Pythagoras and Plato consider that the whole world has been compounded from these four elements, through geometrical and musical proportion, which are united to each other in such a way, however, that the harmony of the elements never suffers any discord in the heavens, although beneath the heavens some dissonance seems to arise at certain times and in certain places, but when it arises it is immediately and miraculously restored to a concordant form through the higher harmony.

Doubtless no one will deny that these elements are beneath the Moon, but some natural scientists will deny that they are in the heavens.

Let them, I pray, listen to the metaphysicians, who demonstrate that the elements, by means of their own Ideas, are within the very Maker of the world; that, by means of their proportions, they are within the soul of the world; and that, by means of seeds, they are within nature. Thus through their powers they are in the heavens, and through their forms they are under the heavens. For how do the natures of the elements pass below the heavens from causes which are above the heavens, and how will they give direct assent here, unless the regulating powers of the elements pour through the heavens at the same time? Indeed, just as a farmer does not rule the master-builder since he holds none of the principles of architecture, but rather does the geometer, who possesses these principles, rule him, so will the heavens never govern the powers of the elements and of all composed therefrom, unless they comprehend them all. But as they govern they embrace, and by embracing they govern.

Let them also listen to the astronomers, who indicate the natures of the elements in the constellations as well as in the planets and confirm them by their effects.

Finally, let them listen to the holy Scriptures, which frequently locate the waters in the heavens and also locate there the earth of living beings. For if these two, being unlike the things of the heavens, are placed there, all the more firmly are fire and air, which are more similar to the things of the heavens, located there by the holy Scriptures.

Some, I think, will reply that the finest powers of the elements are to be located there as causes, while in the spheres of the elements beneath the Moon their natures are according to their forms, and in compounds they are present through some participation; but they will deny that the actual natures of the elements are present in the heavens. With reference to these matters, the followers of Plato point out that particular excellences are universally based on particular natures, and therefore, if the excellences of the elements are in the heavens, their natures are there too; but just as the excellences reside there in a genus far superior to these here, so their natures reside in a genus that is more excellent, indeed, to speak more accurately, in a genus that is most excellent.

And the highly outstanding nature of fire provides the heavens with perceptible light, life-giving warmth, and the keenest of movements. The nature of earth bestows firm and unshakeable stability; it grants density to the stars, that they may be seen, and to the Moon, that it may ward off the rays of the Sun. The nature of air affords a very clear quality known as translucence. The nature of water introduces a most delicate and uniform gentleness. And the greatest benefit of all is that it imbues the very flanges of the spheres (with which they contact each other) with the excellent nature of cold and wetness which ensures that, however rapidly and strongly they come into contact with each other as a result of their great speed, there is no heat and no damage.

The Hebrews will give their strong support to these waters in the heavens. They will, I believe, also give their approval if they hear that, on account of the nature of earth in the living beings there, it comes about that the otherwise extremely tenuous materials do not get dispersed by the excessive movement.

But it should be remembered that in the substance of the heavens the excellence is so great and so capable of bringing about unity that the qualities and movements which are at odds with each other in our world show no opposition there, and there the remaining elements have been immediately restored, from the very birth of the world, to the form of the most outstanding element, that is, fire, just as in our world the four elements, through the movements of the heavens, are restored, in each and every birth, to the single form of a compound.

Again, that the elements are brought into unity there will not surprise you, if you consider that even beneath the Moon they have been compressed into a single mass, that fire partakes of earthy denseness, so that it does not get scattered immediately on account of its very subtle and nimble nature; and that earth, too, of itself inactive, acquires activity and life through its association with fire.

If the extremes are mixed, then the means are certainly mixed with each other and with the extremes. Again, if union beneath the Moon is so great, it is far greater above the Moon; but the solidity or stability of earth reigns there, without coarseness, in a vaporous form. Moreover, the equability and gentleness of water, when dissociated from its flowing movement; the nimbleness of air, as distinct from its ability to flow away; the efficacy of fire in its light and health-giving warmth: these rule the intelligence and a life that closely resembles it, without that destruction by the fire which is produced in our world by bringing together light reflected between concave surfaces and the fiery heat, penned in some rough and abrasive material, which undoubtedly shines more purely and gives warmth more wholesomely the more it is released from its earthy coarseness.

And so, together with Heraclitus and Empedocles, we shall say that the intellectual light of fire, which is within Idea, flashes as the visible light in the heavens to our eyes, but beneath the heavens, in the upper air, it flourishes as its pure harmless flame, while on earth it appears as coal, burning in coarse material. Finally, we shall say with Orpheus that there are also four elements in the lower regions: Pyriphlegethon, Acheron, Oceanus, and Cocytus.

With Plato we shall say that just as in the archetypal world all the elements are within all things, so in this reflected world all the elements are within all things; but in accordance with the nature of whatever adopts them particular ones are adopted in all cases, so that the things of the heavens are elemental within the elements, and the elements in the heavens are celestial; and the celestial region so excels the other regions that the celestial fire, in addition to the elemental fire and the three remaining elements, may rightly be called the fifth element. Thus he says that the worlds may be numbered as five, since all the genera in creation, through their own individual natures, are five in all respects.

We shall end by declaring the harmony that exists between Moses and Plato, whom Numenius calls a second Moses. For where Moses says 'In the beginning God created the heaven and the earth' Plato says 'God first created fire and earth', understanding 'fire' as 'heaven'. For first of all he considered, within the sphere of the world, its centre and its surface. All the rest he interposed for the sake of these two.

Chapter 25
Circular motion is the property of every sphere in constant movement; and light is the principal property of fire

BUT LET US NOT be troubled by those who, on the grounds that the motion of the heavens is circular, while the motion of fire is in a straight line, doubt that the heavens are fiery. For if any part of the heavens happens to be placed in the middle realm, it will at once rise up in a straight line, seeking its native home by the shortest path, and yet it remains true that the proper motion of the heavens is circular;

and if the earth is moved away from the centre, it will move downwards, although its true property is to stay motionless. In fact, every moving sphere, whether elemental or celestial, moves naturally in a circuit in accordance with its own form, so that it may take fuller advantage of its own position. But wherever there is movement in a straight line, this is not so much a natural movement as a return to nature.

If circular motion suits any body, it suits fire most of all; for since it is by nature furthest from earth, it is ever in movement, just as the earth is ever motionless. If it is always in movement, then it is in circular motion; for whatever moves in a straight line stops moving when it has traversed space, which is finite. But the orbit made by comets shows that both fire and air move in a circle. Unending inflow and outflow demonstrate that water, too, has its cycle. But motionlessness was required of earth, that it might resemble an indivisible unmoving centre and offer its benefits with the greater convenience. Yet it behoved things higher to be in movement, that they might continually bring forth their manifold blessings through the variations in their movements.

No one should say that the heavens are not hot; it should rather be said that they are not burning. Again, it should not be said that the light of the Sun heats through reflection alone, but that, through reflection alone, it reduces to ashes. For the reflected rays of the Moon give no warmth, since watery power predominates in her, while the rays of the Sun provide health-giving warmth on account of the fiery and quickening nature of the Sun. It should not be objected that the rays of the Moon give no warmth on account of the Moon's slower movement, for, even if it is posited that the Moon is slower, she is so much nearer to human beings than the Sun is that she should give, if not as much heat, at least some heat, if it is true that heat is at any rate produced from reflection.

Nor should it be claimed that heat is the property of fire, since the less it is mingled with extraneous matter the less it burns. Rather should it be said that light is the property of fire, for the greater its purity, the greater its brightness, though it is not clearer to certain eyes. Its brightness extends further than its warmth. It illuminates more quickly, indeed in a moment. It bestows heat, so that what is heated retains the heat for a time after the fire has gone; but it never bestows light, its own property, for as soon as fire departs the light goes with it.

Chapter 26
A confirmation of what was said earlier; concerning fire, ether, the composition of the heavens, and the daemons in the heavens and beneath the heavens

IN OUR WORLD, fire has no stable substance and no realm of its own, but it arises here and there from chance transformation and it requires continual feeding. And if it seeks to fly upwards away from the air, it is at once extinguished.

But somewhere, universal fire must dwell in its own province, and yet it does not have its own elemental abode – an abode which, as its elemental nature demonstrates, would be destructive – between the Moon and the air, for, if it did, such a huge fire would straightway consume all the air and all that follows after it. Fire therefore has its abode in the heavens, and there, by divine power, the fiery heat of the heavens is rendered harmless, especially as it is tempered both by the expansiveness of the region and by its life-giving sound.

And it is not right to imagine that heavens which are not at all warm can yet heat everything through their motions, as if motion, of its own nature, produced heat. Indeed, motion sometimes produces cold and puts out a fire. For since the very nature of heat, as something quite steadfast and alive, is superior to its unstable movement, it is quite probable that its first localised movement is in the nature of the heavens, which produce heat in some way even before they move.

I refer only briefly to the occasions when movement does not produce new heat but rather arouses that which is already inherent, I mean the fire infused into all things everywhere by the influences of the heavens or by the presence of the heavens. So just as air that is close to water becomes thick and misty and cold and is driven directly forward by the winds, so air that is close to the Moon becomes bright, clear and hot through the movement, light and heat of the heavens and it moves in a circle.

The heavens are indeed the true fire. But the air that is thus ignited is called aether; yet it is not so consumed by fire as is our air, which becomes violent in fuel that is dry, thin, and compact. Since Aristotle had given the name of 'fire' to that fire with which we are acquainted, he called the sublunar kind 'Pyroïdes', that is, something fiery or something in the form of fire, as if in agreement with Plato; and when, in relation to its motion, he assigns to it the everlasting and thus non-violent revolution of the heavens, he is thus clearly indicating that fire has a motion that is circular rather than straight; and in this, too, he concurs with Plato. He is also in agreement when he admits that, in that realm, fire does not burn in the same way and cannot be observed up there, because it is extremely rarefied and not very bright.

Plato believes that there is a plentiful supply of fire in the composition of the stars, so that it far surpasses there that which relates to form and life, that which pertains to objects, since they are beneath the Moon, and all that is fiery, as if it is considered to be the form and life of all else. In fact, he has it that fire dominates all else in the whole of the heavens, but in the stars it unites with a kind of celestial earth; in the other parts of the heavens, with celestial air or water; and likewise in living and celestial beings in the same realms. But neither those spheres nor those living beings can be seen by us, because their lack of solidity, their faint light, and their very nature make them impossible to detect.

Indeed, since the extremities of the world – earth and water on the one hand, and the firmament on the other – abound with their own living beings, the intermediate spheres are also completely filled with *their* living beings. The particular reason for this is that the natural order does not allow of a sudden descent from such a vast number of stars to a single living being. Thus in the spheres of the planets there are seven leading planets. Being leaders, they excel the fixed stars. For beneath a leading planet in that realm there are many beings of exactly the same kind, whatever names they may have. I now give them the general name of 'daemons'; whether they are natural or whether they are produced by man, they imitate the dominant planet in function and orbit. Likewise, there are such daemons in the air: some are natural and some are strangers from the human race. Under their respective leaders they all in some way imitate the movements in the heavens.

In brief, each sphere is, to some extent, a complete world.

Chapter 27
On the spirit of the world,
that is, on intellect, soul, intelligence, and nature

NOW WHEN HE HAS dealt with the way in which God constructed the body of the world and tempered the soul of the world, Plato moves towards a controversial subject. In the meantime he shows that he has set his gaze first on the unformed mass before considering it after it has received form, and then on the mass once it is given some form, before viewing it as imbued with life. He has done this not because formlessness was prior to form or because physical form preceded life, but because he wanted us to acknowledge that the nature which could receive form was divinely ordained for the sake of forming the body, while the forming of the body was divinely ordained for the sake of the soul as its end.

Wishing, therefore, to create a perfect work, God made a world endowed with life and intellect. It is, indeed, as the *Timaeus* says, a creature which is alive and animated and intellectual: having life, it is common to all, while its intellect is pure, and its body is animated. But some animated things possess intelligence, and others do not. And, moreover, in order that a single creature might more conveniently be produced from a combination of pure spirit and the substance of the world, God differentiated matter, as we have said, into four elements, to be the humours of this creature, because He had wanted its spirit to be differentiated into four. For four components belong to the spirit of the world.

The first is the intellect, which remains motionless within itself, the mover or ruler of the sphere, ordained by the Author of all things to rule the spheres. The second is the soul of the sphere, the mover which itself moves but moves only through itself. The third is an intelligence divinely implanted in this soul by God and the higher intellect. The fourth is nature, the seed-power, the vital power, infused universally into matter by the soul. Now the intellect and the soul are substances, while intelligence and nature are qualities. Intelligence is a quality of the soul, and nature is a quality of matter.

The images of these four are the elements; for fire is related to intellect, earth to nature, air to intelligence, and water to the soul. And just as fire has three properties, while earth has three contrasting properties, and the intermediate elements have intermediate properties, so the intellect has three properties, nature has three contrasting properties, and the intermediaries have intermediate properties. For the intellect is indivisible, uniform, and eternal; nature is, as it were, divisible, multiform, and temporary; but the soul, intermediate between these two, becomes, through its intelligence, a partaker of the intellect rather than of nature, while through its spirited power it is more in harmony with nature than with the intellect. This is why it is said to be partly indivisible and partly divisible; both uniform and multiform; eternal in part and temporary in part.

Four lives are thus enumerated, in accordance with the fourfold spirit of the world: the life of Saturn within the intellect which looks up to its heavenly Father, that is, to God, the Maker of the heavens; the life of Jupiter within the intelligence which inclines downwards to action which is already in movement; the life of Venus within the spirited power which now gives its love to matter; and the life of Dionysus within nature, a life that is, as it were, intoxicated, that is, immersed in matter.

On a similar basis, there are reckoned to be four senses in the universe. The first sense is necessarily within the soul of the world, I mean the sense that is common and single, that is, an imaginative power which accompanies its intelligence and extends to the particular forms of things, just as intelligence extends to the universal forms. I mean that it reaches them inwardly and therefore requires no mechanisms: it neither goes forth nor does it experience. The second sense is within the souls of the spheres and of the stars; it is likewise common and beyond experience, but it does go forth. The third sense is within particular souls, allocated beyond the general power by means of specific mechanisms; it extends outside itself and manifests as a result of experience but it comes to an end in the exercise of judgement. The fourth sense was attributed to plants by the followers of Pythagoras: a semblance of sense, something benumbed, having no discernment of quality but being located merely in the experience of some pleasure and pain. The first sense reveals the intellect; the second, the intelligence; the third, the spirited power; and the fourth, the natural power.

But it should be remembered that the very matter of the world does not receive a soul except by means of nature, does not receive intelligence except through the agency of the soul, and does not receive intellect except by way of intelligence. In the same way, it receives water by means of earth, air through the agency of water, and fire by way of air.

Note, moreover, that what follows from this time onwards is similar to this; for he says, 'God has placed the soul in the mean position, and He has spread it though everything, and by it He has protected the whole of the world.' This means firstly that the soul fills the entire mass of the world, governing some parts of the world with some of its powers, and other parts with other powers; and that it surpasses the world with its own supreme power, intellectual providence, which girdles the world.

That the power of the soul extends from the central position and fills the universe is expounded twice in four steps. Firstly, it extends its connecting power out in all directions from the middle part of the earth; from the centre of water it diffuses its vital force; from the air, its power of sense; and from fire, its rational force. Then, from the centre of the world-sphere it sends forth its connecting power, as we have said; from the sphere of the Moon, the centre of all that can be created and all that cannot be created, it diffuses its vital force; from the Sun, the heart of the world, it projects its power of sense; and from the middle of the zodiac of the heavens it dispatches its rational force.

The nature of the heavens is the mean between the coarse bodies of the world and the soul of the world, just as spirit is the mean within us. To begin with, then, the heavens are quickened. This is why, when you hear that life is spread throughout all things from the centre of the world, you should ponder this mystery: that is where the nature of the heavens resides, the proper receptacle of the soul. But we deal more fully with this subject in the commentaries on Plotinus and in the book *On Life*.

But since there is a double order of creation in relation to God – that whereby all things come forth from Him and that whereby all things that come forth are turned back to Him – Plato is following the order whereby things come forth, when he says, 'God placed the intellect within the soul, and the soul within the body.' But he is thinking of the return process when he says, 'God spread out the soul, which had been placed in the mean position, to fill the whole, and in the meantime brought forth something of it outside the world, so that, while it was providing for the world, it was being turned back to God.'

Chapter 28
On the composition of the soul, and why the soul needs five elements for its constitution

SINCE WE HAVE expounded more fully in the *Theology* many things relating to the souls, the minds, and the motions of the spheres, and to the composition of the soul, we have been and shall be rather brief in dealing with such matters here; for we are now hastening on to more relevant matters.

Firstly, we think that the number five accords with the composition and division of the soul, for three reasons. The first is that as five consists of the first even number and the first odd number, so the soul consists of the divisible nature and the indivisible nature. For you know that an even number is called divisible, but an odd number is called indivisible since it cannot be divided into equal parts. The second reason is that the natures by which God compounds everything are five in number. For they are Essence, the Same, the Different, Stillness, and Motion. Indeed, the soul is deemed the mean of all things, for the special reason that it consists of the five qualities of all things. The third reason is that, since the soul is the mean of the universe, it naturally assumes the number five, the mean of universal number.

For five is the perfect mean of ten, since if we duly divide ten five ways, the justly spaced mean in each division is five. If you first divide ten into nine and one, you will see that five is the mean, equally spaced between one and nine. If, secondly, you wish to divide ten into eight and two, again you will have five as the precise mean between these. If, thirdly, you make the division into seven and three, or, fourthly, into six and four, you will again obtain five as the true mean between the extremes. The mean in all these cases we call the Arithmetic. Fifthly, however, to obtain a mean of five when ten is divided into five and five is by definition superfluous.

For these reasons Plato puts forward in particular five headings in the universal structure both of the living body, as I might call it, and also of the soul. For in both cases, I mean of the body and of the soul, he deals first with the very substance and basis of the thing itself, if I might call it so. Secondly, he deals with the harmony of the parts of each. Thirdly, he deals with the type resulting from the harmony of the parts. Fourthly, with the powers of the type. Fifthly, with the actions which arise from these powers.

Indeed, the followers of Plato hold that the first three, namely, substance, harmony, and type, belong to the essence of the soul: through these proceed power and action. By harmony I mean a balanced blending of five items, namely, natures, parts, principles, forces, and actions. For the soul consists of those five natures of things through which its own parts are assigned. Again, it receives from God the principles of all the things. Hence it has many special powers through which it manifests actions.

Indeed, when he calls the soul a concord or symphony, you will remember that Plato in the *Phaedo* even denies that the soul is a harmony, that is, a harmony of bodily parts, produced from them and residing in them. But in the *Timaeus* he affirms that the soul is a harmony, that is, a harmony of its own parts, abiding within itself, and from itself moderating the body, especially when he says that from the indivisible, never-varying essence and also from that which in respect of bodies is divisible, God composed the mean form of the essence, that is, the soul. He also declares this elsewhere when he says, 'God made the world living, animated, and intellectual.'

For when he says 'living', he means the natural life spread through the bodies of the world, co-extensive with the body of the world and working through movement. But when he says 'intellectual', he is referring to the angelic intellects, which are charged with rightly ruling the spheres and which are indivisible according to place, and unchangeable according to time, in contrast to natural life and bodily form, which are divisible and changeable. And when he says 'animated', he means the very substance of the world-soul, whose essence is both indivisible and unchangeable, like the intellect. Yet it may be said to be divisible and moving to a certain degree, for it is the very source of those forces which are directed down towards the divisible and the moving.

Now power and action are partly indivisible and unmoving, insofar as they concur with the divine and act steadfastly; partly divisible, insofar as they are either composite or directed down towards the composite and divisible body; and also moving, because they operate in time.

So he calls this soul the third type of essence and the mean between the indivisible and eternal on the one hand and the divisible and temporal on the other.

Now, that his term 'intellectual world' refers to the angelic intellects is proved by the fact that through life the body of the world is prepared for the intellect, and thus, as it is related to life, so it is related to the intellect. So as it has natural life latent in the fabric of the world as well as 'living' life, that is, the soul existing in itself, in the same way it has both the intellectual quality permeating the soul and the intellectual substance dwelling within itself. For everywhere certain qualities relate to certain substances; for example, the vital quality relates to the vital substance, and the intellectual quality relates to the intellectual substance.

Now he composes the soul in five ways especially: firstly, from those five natures of things; then, from numbers; thirdly, from rhythmical harmonies; fourthly, from the rudiments of shapes; and fifthly, from the beginnings of movements. Thus the soul, possessing the principles of metaphysics and mathematics, may come to know all things: essences, numbers, harmonies, shapes, and movements.

Again, insofar as the soul is related to the divine, he says that it is composed of the natures of things which initially dwell in the divine. Insofar as it is related to the natural, he says it is blended with shapes and movements. But insofar as it holds the mean between the two, he tempers it with rhythmical harmonies and proportions.

Indeed, these five, that is, Essence, the Same, the Different, Stillness, and Motion, he calls the natures of things: for from these all things, bar the First, are made. By Essence he clearly means the formative principle of anything, and he also gives a hint that being is the proper function of Essence. The Same is so called because it concurs with anything, first with itself and then with others. Again, the Different is added, because it has some distinction, first within itself and then in relation to others. Then there is Stillness, since it maintains a certain unity for some time. Finally, Motion here means any movement out from potential to actual, either through being or through acting in any way, internally or externally.

But above these five natures are placed three more: Limit, Limitlessness, and a Combination.

Above these three is placed the One Itself.

Essence, indeed, follows the divine One Itself. Stillness and the Same follow Limit, but Motion and the Different accompany Limitlessness.

Finally, as we have placed the four elements of the world at the highest level among things celestial, at the middle level under the

Moon, and at the lowest level under the Earth, so we put the five natures by the highest principle among things divine, by the middle principle in the soul, and by the lowest beneath the soul.

For in the divine, unity is above multiplicity, Limit above Limitlessness, the Same above the Different, and Stillness above Motion. But in lower matters it is quite different: and the things which were masters there are here mastered in their turn.

In the soul more than anywhere else there emerges a uniform tempering among separate beings, so that it is not without good reason that they believe the soul to be not only the mean of all things but also tempered by the principles of music. Mathematics is like the soul, for each is deemed the mean between the divine and the natural. Musical numbers are most like the soul. For they are in motion, and on that account they rightly signify the soul, which is the beginning of motion. Indeed, the soul is described not only by numbers but also by shapes, so that it may be considered incorporeal through numbers, and through shapes it may be known to decline naturally towards bodies.

The triangle is like the soul, because as the triangle develops from one angle into two more, so the soul, flowing forth from the indivisible and divine substance, falls into the deeply divisible nature of the body, and if it is compared to the divine, it appears divided. For as those things act through one stable power, and that immediately, this works through many changing forces and actions, and after a lapse of time. But if it is compared to natural things, it is considered undivided. For, unlike the other, it does not have separate parts in separate places, but it is complete in every part of the whole; nor, unlike the former, does it follow everything in movement and in time, but it attains some things immediately and possesses them eternally.

One may compare the soul to the triangle for the further reason that the triangle is the first figure consisting of a number of straight lines. In the same way, the soul is the first of all things to be dispersed into many forces which are subordinate to the intelligence within it; and it seems to be produced in a straight line as it falls from divinity into nature. In this very descent from the highest intelligence it flows out into three lower forces, namely, discursive reason, sense perception, and the power of movement. In the same way the triangle is produced from a point and drawn down into three angles.

Now I say that the soul is by nature the first of all things to be blended in some way with many forces and to fall, if I may put it thus, in a straight line. For the angelic mind above the soul has no need of any lower forces within itself, but it is pure mind, mind that it is whole and self-sufficient. Again, it does not face towards the lower, but is turned in circular fashion to that divinity alone from which it comes. For that reason its action is compared to the circle. For it is a single uniform action, as the circle is formed from a single uniform line, and the embrace of each is marvellous. Moreover, the circle is the first and the last of the shapes. Indeed, it is the first, because it is contained by a single line; and the last, because with shapes consisting of many lines, the more sides they have the closer and closer do they seem to tend to the form of a circle as if to their end.

Likewise, the intellect is the first of all things to be created by God, and the intellectual aspect, that is, the absolute order of things, is the last of all to shine back from the mirror of nature, that mirror to which natural forms tend ever closer as if to their end. But we have written elsewhere of the intellect. Now let us return to the soul.

Chapter 29
Why the soul is compared to a compound and to musical harmony

THREE THINGS in particular about the soul are the object of our search at present. The first is why Plato likens the soul to a compound. The second is why it resembles a compound through a certain harmony. The third is why it is like musical harmony.

In the first place, although the soul is knit together indissolubly, it is made up of so much multiplicity that it has a natural tendency to turn towards those things which are wholly composite. For this reason it may be imagined as somewhat similar to composite things, with which it concurs through a natural relationship, or rather, affinity.

Then, because it is justly the mean of all things and is composed of them, and because it binds all things together harmoniously, it is therefore compared to a harmony or to something harmoniously composed; especially since the soul reconciles those things which are opposed to each other by nature, connects them when they have been reconciled, and preserves them when they have been connected. Therefore, not unjustly is the soul deemed to be a substantial harmony or an utterly harmonious and indissoluble substance.

But since those things which are perceived by the other senses are most frequently composed in a harmonious fashion, we were seeking to discover in the third place why Plato likened the soul most closely to musical harmony. The answer is that musical harmony is produced in the middle element of all and that it reaches the ears through movement which is none other than spherical; so that it is no wonder that it matches the soul, which is both the mean of all things and the beginning of circular movement. In addition, harmony, more than all the other things which are perceived, whether singing or sounding, like something animated brings the disposition of the senses and the contemplation of the soul into the minds that hear; and so, first of all, it concurs with the soul.

Moreover, those things related to sight, although they are in some way pure, yet they lack the power of movement and they are more frequently perceived through their image alone without the nature of the thing in question; so they usually move souls but slightly. And those related to smell, taste, and touch, being strongly physical, do more to titillate the sense-organs than to penetrate the depths of the soul.

Now harmony moves the body through the airy nature which has been set in motion; through the purified air it strikes the airy spirit which knits soul and body together; through its influence it affects the sense at the same time as the soul; through its meaning it acts upon the mind; finally, through the very movement of the subtle air it strongly penetrates; through its tempering power it sweetly soothes; through a similar quality it pervades with a wonderful pleasure; through its nature, animate as well as material, it simultaneously seizes and draws to itself the whole man.

And certainly if someone presented harmonies to the hearing with as much of the art and diligence of the Muses as there is natural art and care in the presentation of flavours to the taste or of soft things to the touch, we would undoubtedly recognise that Apollo seizes the soul by melody much more than Bacchus seizes the taste by wine or Venus the touch by wantonness.

Moreover, when Plato represents the Maker of the world as one who speaks both by reasoning with himself and by commanding everything else, he considers the utterance itself, like the highly musical hymn of Apollo, to be the origin both of the world-soul and of the body. He also believes that the soul which is born therefrom strikes the heavenly lyre with the same musical rhythm. But now that which is in the heavenly melody, both the low tone from the slower movement and the high tone from the swifter movement, appears beneath the heavens as the heaviness and lightness, the cold and heat, the dampness and dryness, of the elements.

The same thing in the generation of creatures is matter and form; in human nature it is gentleness and magnanimity, temperance and fortitude. And just as from a low note and from a high note, so from all the pairs in nature which we have mentioned, there is everywhere one.

Therefore, since musical consonance is as if alive, rational, and effective, and since it is very similar and pleasing to the mind, it attracts the whole man to itself, and what is even more important, since the mind is created through consonance, and all created things are maintained by it and move by means of it, our Plato has described the effective, preserving, and moving soul of all natural beings as consisting of musical numbers and ratios in particular, — I do not mean mathematical numbers, as some falsely claim, but the ideal and metaphysical ratios of numbers.

Indeed, the soul would not be able to discern the universal harmony and appreciate the absolute proportions, both in air by means of music and in the body by means of nature, unless it had their causes within itself and unless there were within it a harmony rising above the harmony produced therefrom in all else. For our soul contains all of the proportions contained in the world-soul. For this reason, both in the world-soul and in our own the ratios are not mathematical but natural; they have power, and they are to be not only judged, but also constructed and produced, in accordance with mathematical proportions.

Chapter 30
The propositions and proportions related to Pythagorean and Platonic music

THEY CALL THE SOUND fit for melodies the *phthongus*, by which anyone can easily produce both the low and the high notes in such a way that the former is not so deep and relaxed as to resemble silence, while the latter is not so high and taut as to shriek. They think that the deep sound is created by a relaxed, slow movement, and the high sound by a tauter and quicker movement. Indeed, just as the very relaxed and slow movement seems, as it were, to approach rest, so the very deep sound seems to approach silence.

Again, just as a movement which is very strong and swift seems to approach violence, so a very high sound seems to approach injury. Indeed, they give the name 'intervals of sound' to the discrete gradations in sharpness and depth, and the name 'compositions of harmonious sounds' to conjunctions of consonances arising from favourable proportions.

Furthermore, resonances of strings in musical instruments, whether in the single tetrachord, such as Hermes discovered and Orpheus confirmed, or in the two tetrachords united through seven strings, which Terpander is said to have produced, or in the double tetrachords arranged and separated through eight strings of which Lycao of Samos is said to have been the maker, or in the four tetrachords joined together and consisting of fifteen strings to the approval of all the Greeks, in all these tetrachords progressively the *diatessaron* resonates through harmony.

But now, having referred to sounds, intervals, and compositions, let us proceed to the proportions from which harmonies arise.

Equal proportion, they say, is between two precisely similar and equal portions, as between this one and that one or as between one cubit and another.

But unequal proportion, they say, is between dissimilar and unequal portions, as between one and two and as between one cubit and two cubits. The greater portion of the unequal proportion is known as the *double*, and the smaller as the *subduple*. In addition, we now need to consider the threefold proportion of inequality.

The first proportion, which they call *multiple* (such as the *double*, the *triple*, and the *quadruple*), does not divide a smaller number by means of a larger number, but gathers and multiplies the whole, as with 'twice' or 'thrice'; and just as you can multiply for ever through the method of number, so this proportion proceeds for ever.

In the second proportion, which they call the *superparticular*, the larger number contains the smaller number, divides it, and then adds the divided part to the whole; we call this the *aliquot part*, for when it is multiplied so many times the whole re-appears.

The first example of these is the *sesquialteral*, between two and three. For three, containing two, adds unity; when unity is repeated it makes two.

The second example is the *sesquitertial*, between four and three; and so the process continues for ever by means of continual division.

The third proportion is the *superpartient*, which adds to the whole a part which, being multiplied any number of times, cannot recreate the whole. An example is the proportion between five and three. For to three five adds two, which, if taken once, does not reach three, and if taken twice, exceeds three. Because this proportion divides the whole into a part which is incapable of restoring the whole, it seems unsuitable for harmony, in which every division must necessarily be restored to the whole and every multiplication to the one.

But the second proportion is considered suitable, for although it divides it does not depart from easy restoration and in it the two extremes are considered to be mutually commensurable. For the difference between two and three is unity, and unity is the common measure of both two and three. For when it is taken twice, it measures two; when taken thrice, three. But the difference between five and three is two; and two, no matter how many times it is taken, cannot possibly measure either three or five.

However, the first proportion is the one best suited to harmonies. For it does not divide, but restores by multiplying and multiplies by restoring. Unlike the *superparticular*, it seeks no measure from outside, but the smaller portion measures the larger, being twofold in the *double* and threefold in the *triple*. Nor does it fall away from wholeness or simplicity. But the *superparticular* does indeed fall away from wholeness, for it divides; but it preserves simplicity, for it divides by means of a single part.

However, the *superpartient* loses not only wholeness but also simplicity when it mixes many parts into something incapable of restoring the whole. For this reason it produces dissonance, while the earlier two produce consonance: the multiple more so, and the *double* most of all. Indeed, in the *double* we do not see one thing actually exceeding another, but we see something being exceeded by itself: for two exceeds one by one, four exceeds two by two, and so on.

Moreover, the first proportion arises between the first of the numbers, that is, between unity and two. It is the only one, I say, to arise without the operation of anything else, free and independent of all.

But the *triple*, rising as it does between one and three, has an associated *sesquialteral* which is born simultaneously between two and three. The *quadruple*, too, seems to be commingled with the *sesquitertial*. For as soon as the *quadruple* is born between four and one, the *sesquitertial* at once arises between four and three.

Again, the *double* arises from the very proportion of equality; from this, the triple and the *sesquialteral*. Again, from the *triple* are born the *quadruple* and *sesquitertial*, and it is the same with the others, as I would clearly demonstrate, were I not afraid of prolixity.

Thus all the others are brought back to the *double*, as to their beginning and their end, and they either divide it or multiply it. For the *double* is first, whole, simple, independent, and absolutely equal, so that it is no wonder that the harmony born of this is the most perfect of all; it is called the *diapason*, firstly because it pervades all, and secondly because all proportions are reducible to it.

However, before I take harmonies any further, let us note that what the Greeks call the *logos* we call ratio and proportion; what they call *analogia* we call comparison of ratio and proportionality, a name which I wish were as elegant as it is proper.

Let us also note that proportion is between two terms; and that when it is lawful, that is, when it leads to melodious sounds, it is defined as the commensurable relationship of two mutual quantities with each other, such as the *double* (between one and two), the *sesquialteral* (between two and three), and so on with similar ones.

Proportionality is defined as the mutual likeness of two ratios. Thus we say that as two is related to four, so four is related to eight, through the double ratio in both cases. The likeness that arises when there are three terms is called continuous. But it is called discrete when it is produced from more than three terms, as when we make a comparison such as: As two is to four, so eight is to sixteen. Moreover, such a comparison is threefold: arithmetic, geometric, and harmonic.

The arithmetic consists in equality of number. Thus the mean between three and seven is five, which exceeds the first term by the same number (two) as that by which it is exceeded by the second, by means of a proportion which cuts midway between the two.

Now the geometric is found in an equality of ratio in which are a multiple and a *superparticular*: thus, of course, when we compare three to nine, and nine to twenty-seven, there is a factor of three in either direction. Furthermore, as nine is to six, so is six to four, for in both cases there is the *sesquialteral* proportion.

Finally, they locate the harmonic proportion in such a relationship that, when the three terms are placed in order, the greatest term is to the least as the greater difference is to the less. For if you have three, four, and six, the difference between six and four is two, and the difference between four and three is unity; and just as there is a double ratio between six and three, so there is a double ratio between two and one.

Here the other comparison holds good also, namely, that of proportions: for the middle term exceeds and is exceeded by a similar proportion of the first and last terms, since four is exceeded by six by a third part of six, and four also exceeds three by a third part of three. The harmonic proportion operates here, because it avoids the *superpartient* proportions as separate and dissonant but admits the multiples and the *superparticular* proportions, making doubles out of the *sesquialterals* and the *sesquitertials* by means of the harmonic ratio which we have mentioned and which rejoices in the variety of harmony.

Now, as we were saying, it likes multiples and also *superparticulars*; another reason for this is that in the former there is such a strong tendency to revert to the same that when several terms belonging to the same ratio are put in a line, the middle term, being taken into itself [i.e. squared], will give the same product as the two extremes when multiplied by each other.

Take two, four, and eight: two eights make sixteen, and so do four fours. Again, take four, six, and nine: in the same way as before, four nines are thirty-six, and so are six sixes. It is a similar situation if you interpose two mean terms between the extremes: for example, if you insert four and eight between two and sixteen. For all these numbers reflect the two-fold ratio. Thus, if you multiply two by sixteen, you will have the same answer as when you multiply four by eight. The same happens in the other *superparticulars* and multiples.

But in the *superpartients* it is not the same. Take three, five, and seven. There is a *superbipartient* relationship between seven and five, and also between five and three. For in both cases two parts of the whole are added. If you multiply three by seven, you will not produce the same number as five multiplied by itself.

Thus in the first place there are the multiples: since in addition to what we were just saying, it is by means of them that all numbers look back to unity while looking at numbers.

In the second place are the *superparticulars*: for although they do not look towards unity itself, they always refer to a part which is based on a single whole.

In the third place are the *superpartients*, because they do not seem to look towards either of these. For this reason the sense of harmony is averse to this relationship which resists harmony.

For harmony chooses either to produce *univox* and *unison* from the proportion of equality or to produce *equivox* and *equison* from the rational – or multiple and *superparticular* – proportion of inequality.

But it is from the *double* that it produces that *equison* which is closest to *unison*: because in the *double* the smaller term measures the larger and by measuring equals it, and when the larger exceeds the smaller, it seems, one might say, to exceed it by none other than the smaller itself.

Chapter 31

In musical harmonies one is produced from the many; how harmony is defined

JUST AS EXPERT doctors mix certain juices together in certain proportions so that several different substances come together to form a new unity, and in addition to their elemental power miraculously acquire a heavenly power, as was seen in the concoction of Mithridates and the *theriaca* of Andromachus, so the most highly skilled musicians take the deepest notes, as if they were cold substances, and the highest notes, as if they were hot, together with the moderately deep, as being moderately moist, and the high notes, as being dry, and mix them in such proportion that from the many a single form arises which results not only in vocal power but also in heavenly power.

This indeed is evident from what Democritus and Theophrastus say and from what Pythagoras actually proved. For certain diseases both physical and mental are said to be miraculously cured by certain harmonies, so that it is no wonder that the sages of old attributed the origin of both medicine and music to the same source, namely, the god Apollo. For each is a medicine. But one cures the soul from the body, while the other cures the body from the soul.

The ancients quite rightly attributed prophecy, too, to Apollo, the source of melody. For melody alone draws the mind back from all that would draw it away, and draws it together into itself, into a kind of inner hearing, if I may so call it, by which are perceived not only the notes but also the ratios of the notes; and when the disturbances have settled down, melody tempers the mind with celestial harmony and pours forth divine oracles in heavenly fashion.

But in case someone says that a third and common note-form does not arise from the high note and the low note, it should be remembered that low notes can be mingled with high notes more effectively than juices are said to mix with other juices.

Firstly, this is because the note-substances, on account of their subtlety, their continuous motion, and their uniform quality in all parts of the airy body, merge into one more readily and more fully than juices, which are thick, ill-disposed towards movement and very diverse in quality; and if they do merge into one, then they are the more ready to assume a single new form.

Secondly, this is because the natural inner instrument of the voice, being the closest and most obedient to the power of life, spirit and reason, tempers the art of music more easily and more fully in producing that one which it gazes upon than external instruments do for doctors; and if even a lyre is touched by the fingers, the notes will obey the will of the musician more faithfully than herbs obey doctors.

And if nature, in due time, acts upon a concoction of herbs over and above the labour and care of doctors, how much greater and quicker will be its effect upon vocal material, which is extremely amenable and flexible; that nature, I say, which lives everywhere, and which is armed with celestial powers, will have an effect upon material which resembles the heavens and is, as it were, alive; to this it immediately reveals a wonderful living new form, through which, by means of a hidden power, it projects its forces onto the body and the soul.

Furthermore, just as in the body, which is naturally composed of the four elements, the four elemental qualities combine into one essence, which some call the quintessence, being subordinate to the special power issuing from heaven by secret means, so numerous voices properly commingled produce together a resonance which is the basis of a new and wonderful power.

For if from a sounding lyre something immediately resonates in another similarly tuned lyre; and if from a plucked string a similar vibration at once passes into another string equally tensioned, there can be no doubt that from numerous notes sounding in a certain proportion one note is immediately produced which is like a form common to them all and through which the many are one, and for this reason they are perceived as one by sense and they conjoin to give a single effect.

The same thing is evident in sense-pleasure, in which, since a single form arises from many, full delight arises from a single form which is likewise produced harmoniously from many. Hence it comes about that hearing unison for too long is wearisome, for in it equality is heard without any inequality. It also comes about that a dissonant sound offends, for in it the differences do not accord together in one.

For the same reason many things are clearly discerned by sense and are, as it were, tasted by it as many. I say 'tasted' because it experiences the mixture of notes just as taste experiences the mixture of flavours. Hence the words of the prophet: 'O Lord, thy words are sweeter than honey to my mouth.'

Finally, if the low sounds absorb the high ones, or if the high sounds overpower the low ones, there is no delight, and yet some sort of unity is sought everywhere. But since neither the absorbing nor the overpowering sort of unity pleases, the only unity that pleases is one that is new, effective, and tempered by a certain harmony. Hence, therefore, harmony is defined as a mixture of sounds high and low reaching the ears uniformly and sweetly.

Now this mixture is similar to that in flavours which gives satisfaction to the taste: a very sweet full flavour is likened to a very relaxed, deep note, while a very sharp flavour is compared to a very high note. But a sweet flavour mixed with a bitter flavour suggests a moderately low note, whereas when mixed with salt or sharpness it seems to represent a moderately high note. But finally, when a compound mixture fills the sense it is not perceived as manifold, but appears as uniform.

The physicians maintain that sound reaches the ears after being gradually expanded by many circles into a spherical shape, just like the circles which grow towards the shore after a stone has been thrown into a pond from on high. But we think that harmony, compounded of low notes and high notes, falls upon the ears like a single round, or rather, oval shape, in which the eighth note, as if continuing for itself the breadth of the first note through its sharper vertex, now makes a single note from itself and the first; and just as the eye sees an ovate roundness as a single shape, although it is greater in one dimension and less in another, so the hearing draws, as it were, a single note resulting from the deep note and the eighth and arising gradually and sweetly from the full deep sound as if into restrained loftiness, like the shape of an egg.

Hence we believe it comes about that nature has bestowed a shape like this upon the instrument of hearing and a similar shape upon the instrument of speaking, while art has contrived to produce a similar shape for musical instruments: the closer these are to the oval shape, the more harmonious they are.

Chapter 32
Which harmonies arise from which proportions

IT IS SAID that when Pythagoras had observed in the smithies that harmony issued from the hammer-blows by a law of weights, he gathered the numbers which held the self-harmonising difference of the weights. Then he is said to have tautened strings by tying on the various weights which he had discovered in the hammers. And, as a result, he is said to have clearly thought that from a string which was tautened more than another according to the *sesquioctaval* ratio another tone was discerned by contrast, that is, a full, complete sound, as with the ratio of nine to eight.

Nor was he said to be able to divide the tone into two equal half-tones, since nine does not divide into two equal parts; but he discovered that one half-tone is slightly more than half, while the other is slightly less than half: this he called *diesis*, while Plato called it *limma*. How much the half-tone was less than the full tone and away from the true half-tone, Plato shows in the difference between the numbers two hundred and forty-three and two hundred and fifty-six. For since an eighth of the smaller number is thirty and nearly a half, and since the larger number is thirteen more than the smaller number, it produces neither a tone nor a full half-tone.

Pythagoras next observed that what I might call the full and complete breadth of the tone consists of two sounds and an interval, and thus he arrived at the first elements of harmony.

The first of these harmonies, the *diapason*, is based on the first or double ratio, where the first string had twice as much tension as the second because of the double weight on it; when both were struck, the first resumed its rectilinearity twice as energetically and twice as quickly and sounded a far higher note than the lower one, yet one that was so friendly to the other that it appeared as a single sound, more restricted in one respect but fuller in another. By regulating and measuring the first sound when it happened to be higher, he ascertained that it is positioned at the eighth step above the note that is accounted low and that, as a rule, it consists of eight notes, seven intervals, and six tones.

Moreover, when the ratio of tension and slackness between the two strings was that of one to one and a third, he found the *diatesseron* harmony, comprising two tones, a minor half-tone, four notes, and three intervals.

In the ratio of one to one and a half he found the *diapente*, and in this he noticed three tones and a smaller half-tone, five notes, and four intervals.

Then he observed that the *diapason* consisted of the *diatesseron* and the *diapente*, for the double ratio which produces the *diapason*, where the mean occurs, is composed of the *sesquitertial* and the *sesquialteral*, of which these consist. For the first double having a mean is of two in relation to four, composed of the *sesquialteral* between three and two and of the *sesquitertial* between four and three.

But from its triple appearance he considered the *diapason diapente*, having twelve notes and eleven intervals. For the *diapason* is based on the *double*, while the *diapente* is based on the *sesquialteral*. But the unbroken *sesquialteral* of the *double* produces the triple. For six is the double of three. Consider nine, from which is born the *sesquialteral* of six, and you immediately have the triple of three.

However, it is not a *triple* if you add a *sesquitertial* to the *double*: for example, if you compare eight to six; for the *sesquioctaval* is missing, that is, the relation of nine to eight.

And since the *sesquitertial*, when added to the *double*, is *superpartient*, as in the ratio of eight to three (for here there is a double *superbipartient* relation through the *bisesquitertial*), Pythagoras forbade any continuation beyond the *double*, that is, the *diapason* through the *sesquitertial* (*diatesseron*), although Ptolemy sometimes admits this addition.

But the *sesquitertial* was agreeably added to the *triple*, for hence comes a *quadruple* proportion, and through the *quadruple* the *disdiapason* harmony, having fifteen notes and fourteen intervals; for example, if a *triple* is placed alongside nine and three, you will reach twelve, which is the *sesquitertial* of nine, and you will at once obtain the *quadruple* born of twelve in relation to three.

But for the sake of melody he forbids any progression beyond the *quadruple*, not only because violence invades the senses from the more vehement movement and from the broken sound, but also because as soon as the *quintuple* is born between five and four beyond the first *quadruple*, there immediately arises a *superbipartient* between five and three which produces dissonance.

But so that we may not go beyond the *quadruple*, he also prohibits a frequent descent below the *sesquitertial*, for the sake of avoiding heaviness. He forbids the frequent continuation of two *sesquitertials*, for two reasons: they are generally displeasing, and they do not complete a *double* or a *diapason*.

If you take nine, twelve, and sixteen, you have two *sesquitertials*, but you certainly do not have a *double*, for there is no *sesquioctaval* – that is, the ratio of eighteen to sixteen – so that the *double* is born from the ratio of eighteen to nine.

Nor does he like to continue a pair of *sesquialterals*, for when they are continued they exceed the *double* by the *sesquioctaval* ratio. This you will be able to observe if you write down the numbers four, six, and nine. For here there are two *sesquialterals*, from four to nine. Nine exceeds eight, which is the double of four, by one-eighth. From this it is clear that the power of the *sesquialteral* is greater than half the *double*.

It is also clear that the power of the *sesquitertial* is less than half by just the same amount, since the *double* is created from the two of them together. Indeed, the *sesquialteral* exceeds the *sesquitertial* by just one-eighth. For eight to six gives you a *sesquitertial*, while nine to six gives you a *sesquialteral*. But nine to eight gives a *sesquioctaval*, and you can see that the *sesquialteral* exceeds the *sesquitertial* by this one-eighth part.

However, it should be remembered that the *diatesseron* – the arrangement of four notes rising to the fourth step heard through itself – is not approved, but is happily taken from the one which, with the addition of a tone, easily becomes the *diapente*, that extremely pleasing harmony of the fifth note. Again, if it is connected to the *diapente*, it produces the *diapason* – the most perfect harmony of all.

Nor should anyone be troubled by our statement that although the *diatesseron* has four notes and the *diapente* five, yet the *diapason*, which is composed of these two together, has no more than eight notes. For when we deal with compound harmonies we arrange the strings themselves in groups of four and we proceed with the notes in such a way that the last note of the first harmony is the first note of the second harmony that follows in the compound.

Thus the situation suggests that we should go back to the seven-stringed instrument of Terpander, where the fourth string is struck twice to produce the octave. Terpander followed this grouping, I think, because the number of notes clearly distinct one from another does not rise beyond seven. But by a wonderful similarity the eighth note returns to the first, just as the double ratio through which it is created restores the smaller number which it exceeds while exceeding the same number by the same amount. The ninth turns back to the second and, like the second, is also dissonant. The tenth returns to the third and, like the third, is harmonious; the eleventh to the fourth; the twelfth to the fifth; the thirteenth to the sixth; the fourteenth to the seventh. Finally, the fifteenth returns to the eighth and with the eighth returns to the first.

The first and lowest note they call *hypate*; the next, *parahypate*; the third, *lichanos*; the fourth, *mese*; the fifth, *paramese* or *trite*; the sixth, *paranete*; and the seventh, *nete*.

Moreover, if we make a comparison with the qualities and movements of the heavens, we shall compare *hypate* with Saturn, and the following notes with the following planets respectively.

But if we compare the notes to the swiftness or tardiness of the diurnal movements, we shall compare *hypate* to the Moon, and the subsequent notes to the higher planets, and we shall discover that the low notes are mixed in the heavens with the high ones, and that the selfsame orbs utter a high note from one kind of motion and a low note from another kind.

We shall also find that great sounds come from great globes, divine sounds from divine globes, and multiple sounds proportionately from multiple revolutions. And just as an identical revolution occurs beyond the seventh note, so above the distinct orbs of the seven planets everything revolves into a single orb which miraculously embraces all seven.

But when we said that Saturn bears some resemblance to *hypate*, we do not understand Saturn to be slower than the Moon, since it is swifter in motion both after its rising and before its rising. For the space encompassed by its orbit exceeds that of the Moon's orbit to a greater degree than the time it takes to complete its orbit exceeds the time taken by the Moon to fulfil its own orbit. It is slower to none except Jupiter and Mars, Mars being the swiftest of them all.

We should, however, assign the specific causes of the slowness or swiftness of heavenly bodies to nothing except their own movers. For the nature and number of the circuits that are deep within the movers are revealed when they issue forth in those chariots of theirs. But perhaps some differences of light, which are difficult to detect, have arisen from actual differences in the intelligences.

But more on these matters elsewhere. Let us return to the harmonies and come to some fitting conclusion about them.

The ancients counted three harmonies.

The first is the *diatonic*, in which any four-stringed instrument proceeds through a lesser semitone and a tone and a tone, a harmony to which other wise men as well as Plato give their full approval, putting it before all others, as the most natural of all, since from the lesser semitone, as if from some soft substance, it proceeds naturally to the stronger substance of the tone and has a form that is simple and gentle, yet robust. The *diatonic* is also particularly suited to the four-stringed instrument, on which the *diatesseron* is produced from twin tones and a half-tone.

The second harmony is called the *chromatic*. This customarily moves through a lesser semitone and a greater semitone as well as a minor third, but the philosophers spurn it for being too soft.

The third is called the *enharmonic*: it proceeds through almost the fourth part of a tone, through another similar fourth part, and through a ditone. They disapprove of this, too, on account of the remaining difficulty of perceiving it and practising it.

Now many related subjects, which we are omitting at the moment, are dealt with more thoroughly in the eighth book of our letters.

Chapter 33
On the harmonious composition of the soul

WHEN GOD WAS about to create the soul of the world, He produced it from the indivisible essence and the divisible essence.

This first division of essence into its indivisible nature and its divisible nature is very common in the writings of Plato. For what he calls indivisible contains within itself that which is not cut into parts according to place and does not flow from earlier to later according to time. From the former fact it is called the Same, and from the latter it is called Stillness and the permanent. Likewise, what is called divisible contains within it both that which is dispersed through space and that which passes through time. From the former fact it is called the Different, and from the latter it is called Motion and the moving: I mean Motion within natural objects.

And so within this division, which declared the soul to be composed of the indivisible essence and the divisible essence, are contained the five properties of the creation: Essence, the Same, the Different, Stillness, and Motion. Yet for the sake of brevity Plato does not repeat five, but three. For he repeats Essence, the Same, and the Different, as if they were sufficient. For Stillness is concomitant with the Same, and Motion with the Different. And, conversely, the Same is concomitant with Stillness, and likewise the Different with Motion.

Now he says that God has created a single nature with such a precise admixture of Essence, the Same, and the Different that everywhere within Essence the Same and the Different are immanent; conversely, within the Same the Different and Essence are immanent; and finally, the Different is pervaded by Essence and the Same.

For Essence is enabled through the Same to harmonise with itself and with others, and through the Different to make some distinctions within itself and many more in everything else. But from Essence both the Same and the Different derive the power to exist. But the Same derives similarity from itself and difference from the Different, while the Different derives difference from itself but congruity and order from the Same.

Plato thinks that this interpenetration of natures leads to the judging and performing of all things by the soul.

Indeed, since the soul consists of Essence, it defines each and every thing; since it consists of the Same, it recognises what is simple; and if something is complex, it recognises the bond by which it is held together and the way in which it harmonises both with itself and with other things; because it consists of the Different, it recognises the diversity present in anything, as well as the conditions under which it is directed into itself or separates itself from all else; since it consists of Stillness, it recognises what sort of things abide within themselves, and how; because it consists of Motion, it recognises the nature of that on which anything depends, as well as the degree of dependence, together with the sort of things it makes and the way it makes them.

Moreover, through Essence the soul gives being to things; through the Same it joins things to itself and to others; but through the Different it separates; through Stillness it confirms them in their own nature and rank; through Motion it moves and causes them to move and act.

For these reasons Plato is not without justification when, in the crafting of the soul, he commingles the natures of all things in a definite proportion. He says that these are mixed together in harmonic proportion. The proportion is not arithmetic, for then there would be an unjust distribution somewhere; it is not merely geometric, for then there would be so much equality in the mixture that it could not harmonise closely with the extreme disparity between bodies. But harmonic proportion, consisting in the similarity of variables, makes the dissimilar similar and joins the unequal through some common equality.

Now this is the quality and function of the soul both in relation to itself and in relation to bodies. For if it acts in harmony with itself, it mixes some otherness with the sameness of intelligence, so to speak, as well as some sameness with the otherness of reason. It does the same in imagination and sense. And if it acts upon the body, it produces difference of motion within a stable order or sameness: this is apparent in the heavens. Again, beneath the heavens, it preserves sameness, by means of continuous order, in the difference of generation. And in both situations it preserves and restores Essence.

This is why God, in composing the soul of the world, uses harmonic proportion, both within the powers of the soul, which forthwith accompany its arising, and within the spheres of the world, which harmonise with the soul. Not only did Plato prove with ratios that such a mixture harmonised with the soul; he also deduced it with inferences carefully culled from the world. For since he contemplated the body of the world, which was placed beneath the soul, was created for its sake, and was ruled, moved, and transformed by it, he judged it to harmonise with nature, so that from the shape of the world, as from an image, we might conceive the form of its soul as a model.

Thus, seeing that the spheres of the world are composed of, arranged, and moved by these proportions, he deduced that its soul was tempered by exactly the same harmonic proportions; so that, just as, according to musicians, harmony flows into the voice from the harmony of the artistic mind, in the same way harmony flows into the world from the harmony of the celestial soul.

But now let us hear Plato himself:

'In the beginning He took a single part of the whole; next, the double of the first part; then, a third part, which was the *sesquialteral* of the second part as well as the triple of the first part; then, a fourth part, the double of the second; then, a fifth part, the triple of the third; then, a sixth part, the eight-fold of the first; finally, a seventh part, which exceeded the first by twenty-six parts.'

That is what Plato says.

Let us therefore set up a triangle at whose apex is unity, from which three numbers flow down each side, even on one side and odd on the other, in such a ratio that on the first side after unity come two, four, and eight, and on the other side beneath unity come three, nine, and twenty-seven.

Thus, to frame the soul, the first part which God took from the soup of natures, if I may call it so, is unity. The second part is two, the double of the first. The third part is three, the triple of the first (unity) and the *sesquialteral* of the second (two). The fourth part is four, the double of the second (two). The fifth part is nine, the triple of the third (three). The sixth part is eight, eight times the first (unity). The seventh part is twenty-seven, the triple of nine, exceeding unity by twenty-six parts.

Within these numbers he subsumed all the harmonic proportions. For in the *sesquioctaval* ratio between nine and eight, he produced a tone harmonising with the nine Muses; in the *sesquialteral* between three and two, the *diapente*, the Venusian grace of the fifth note; in the *sesquitertial* between four and three, the *diatesseron*, the Mercurial nature of the fourth note, which accommodates itself to the harmonies; in the double (2:1, 4:2, 8:4), the *diapason*, the universal absolute melody of the eighth note dedicated to Apollo. In the triple (3:1, 9:3, 27:9) he composed the *diapason diapente*, the Jovial consonance of the eighth note with the fifth; in the quadruple (4:1, 8:2) he produced the *disdiapason*, singing in harmony to Apollo through fifteen notes.

But he found the charm of the third note in the ratios of the *diatesseron*, and the charm of the sixth note in the domain of the *diapente*, so that the roughness of both the second note and the seventh note might be alleviated by the more delicate gentleness of these two notes. For in this way the third note and the sixth note resemble each other in gentleness, just as the second note, which falls away from the first, and the seventh note, which moves down from the eighth, closely resemble each other in roughness.

In the beginning, when he said that God had taken seven parts, he touched upon a mystery both in music and in nature: in music, because all differentiation of the notes proceeds right up to the seventh step, after which the pattern is repeated; and in nature, for two reasons: many things occur in sevens in the natural world, and the other Platonic writers have spoken amply about this; and seven has a unity, which is the link between two trinities, and which, from these two and itself, further unfolds the trinity. In this way, it is a likeness of the universe.

Indeed, because it is distributed firstly into three, Plato commended the number three: I mean, it is distributed into the eternal, the temporal, and the medial.

Under the nature of the trinity things eternal have simplicity in their essence, steadfastness in their power, and reflection in their action.

Within the threefold dimension things temporal have in their turn a compounding of essence, a mobility of power, and a transference of action.

Holding the mean position between these trinities of the eternal and the temporal, the soul makes the seventh degree. It also makes the ninth, and this too is praised here by Plato. I say the ninth, because it has three facets. For it faces itself and also things higher and lower than itself. Now before I return to seven, it will be good for a while to commend three together with nine.

The first trinity of numbers is seen to contain the beginning, the middle, and the end of all things, and alone among numbers contains things indivisible through a certain ratio, since it indicates these single things with single unities.

Moreover, if you are happy to peruse the causes of all things, you will find a threefold nature in causes: for the causes are within themselves; they produce effects; and they fulfil by bringing the created effects back to source. If you go lower and consider the effects, you will likewise encounter a trinity: for the effects are in the causes; they proceed from the causes; and they return to the causes.

If you betake yourself to the soul, which links the highest causes with the lowest effects, you will see it abiding within itself as well as declining to effects and rising to causes.

Now this soul governs the world through a threefold seven: firstly, through the mysterious powers of the seven planets in the heavens, ruling through causes; secondly, through the forms of the seven planets, held within seven globes by the heavens; thirdly, through the gifts of the seven planets, governing all generation beneath the Moon.

Indeed, since beneath the Moon the life-giving light within fire is subject to the Sun, and the burning heat within fire is subject to Mars; and since on Earth the varied surface is subject to Mercury, and the whole mass to Saturn; and since dampness rules in the middle realm, while the airy element submits to Jupiter, the watery element to the Moon, and the mixed to Venus, then productive causes follow the Sun; substances follow the Moon; the fertility of the productive causes follows Jupiter; the fertility of substances follows Venus; and brisk efficiency follows both Mars and Mercury, the first through forcefulness, and the second through adroitness and multifarious forms of power. The abiding continuance of all things is dedicated to Saturn above all.

For the rest, this order proceeds through three sevens from the sevens which are arranged according to the three powers of the world-soul. For within this intelligence is a steadfast circle. It is a circle because it is turned back to whence it came. It is steadfast, because it turns unexpectedly. Beneath this intelligence, as if beneath the heavens, are three powers: universal reason, imagination, life-giving power.

Within reason there are three circles, in some way moving and temporal. The first circle moves from the soul to love the cause, and back again, being mysteriously borne by a natural instinct. The second circle moves from the causes of things to consider effects, and back again. The third circle moves from the more universal forms and ideas to those that are less universal, and back again.

Within the remaining two powers of the soul there are, in all, four circles, also temporal: two in each. The first circle is the natural return to the cause. The second circle is a never-ending orbit that moves from the same forms to the same definite things through definite intervals. By means of this orbit there proceeds the temporal but definite orbit of the configurations in the heavens and of the changes beneath the heavens. Therefore the circle of generation necessarily follows the circle of the heavens, which in turn follows the circle of the soul. The turning of the soul accompanies the sphere of intelligence.

Indeed, if the movement of the soul is diverted far from intelligence, it will at once proceed in a straight line both in its perception and in its action. But because it seeks to find itself again and, globe-like, makes similar revolutions through other things, it is chosen by the higher intellect, which, abiding within itself and turning suddenly towards the cause, bestows upon the soul intelligence with which, as if with an outstretched hand, it holds the wandering soul through its own nature; and it turns its restless movement, naturally more inclined to follow a straight line outside itself, back into an orbit midway between movement in a straight line and motionlessness. Hence the soul goes to return to itself and moves around the deep mind and turns the heavens by means of a similar image.

But I have dealt with these things more fully in the *Theology*.

Let us go back to numbers.

Chapter 34
The main points about the harmonic numbers which lead to the composition of the soul

IN THE EARLIER figure the number one signifies the unity of the soul, supreme simplicity, and the very image of divine unity abiding within itself.

Two signifies the movement of the soul into its nature, which is lower than unity and to some extent multiple.

Three signifies its return to unity, both its own unity and the divine unity.

Four signifies the movement of the soul away from itself and into matter through the four steps of the elements.

Seven signifies its power to govern the elements through the seven spheres of the planets.

Eight signifies its power to govern the planets through the eighth sphere.

Nine signifies the ability of the soul to reconcile the eight spheres into a single form.

Twenty-seven, the highest of the numbers, signifies its fullness, which holds all things in all. For twenty-seven contains the numbers mentioned earlier and is made up of them if they are put in order, as is clear to a mathematician.

It is not beside the point to describe the even numbers and the odd numbers in the figure: through the even numbers the divisible nature of the soul is considered; through the odd numbers, the indivisible nature of the soul; and it is the same with feminine power and masculine power.

There are also gathered together the linear numbers, the plane numbers, and the solid numbers; so that we can see that the soul pervades all, expands in all directions, and fills all completely.

Each side of the figure goes down to a solid number: one side goes down to eight through the even numbers, and the other goes down to twenty-seven through the odd numbers; so that we may consider that the soul completely fills both solids, the compound and the simple.

What the *double*, the *triple*, and the other intervals of numbers, which we have previously mentioned, really mean to themselves within the soul, although so far unknown to the followers of Plato, now needs to be declared, if I may say so, in the following manner:

Take another triangle, with 'Essence' at the summit. Now, on the side where the even numbers were put, let there be 'Limitlessness', then 'Difference' and 'Motion'. But on the side where the odd numbers were displayed, let there be 'Limit', followed by 'Sameness' and 'Stillness'.

Here, indeed, we shall likewise have seven limits, of which the soul can perhaps be portrayed as partaking of reason in relation to itself under the same conditions as those under which the stated limits of the numbers are initially related to each other, so that the soul partakes of proportion in the same way as the five natures of creation and the two elements of the natures (Limit and Limitlessness).

Therefore, for the sake of example, let there be a *sesquioctaval* ratio of essence to all things joined together as one. For the form of all together exceeds the respective qualities of the parts by a single step, as if by a single tone.

Beneath Essence let there be Limitlessness or plastic potentiality. Let Limit accompany this like its own form. And let the ratio of Limit to Limitlessness be double, for the potential must be exceeded by the actual. Let Difference follow the Limitlessness of passivity, and let Sameness accompany Limit. And let this Sameness exceed Difference in a *sesquialteral* ratio. Then let Motion follow Difference, and let Stillness follow Sameness. And let Stillness exceed Motion in a *sesquitertial* ratio. This is what Plato meant when he said that these are scarcely exceeded by those.

If you consider the ratios unfolded here, you will also find *triples* and *quadruples*, as was initially clear in the figure. For you will find that the ratio of Motion to Limitlessness is a *triple*, while that of Stillness to Limitlessness is a *quadruple*.

Moreover, so that we may understand the harmonic proportion of partaking of the soul, not only according to the five natures of all things and the two elements, but also according to their respective powers arranged on seven levels, let us restore the several powers of the soul to the several natures and elements.

Now these are the powers: unity, intelligence, will, reason, imagination, the power to connect, and the power to generate. But we shall join these last two powers together under the single name of nature or life-giving power.

Therefore, if this is agreed, let us compare the unity of the soul with Essence; its will, with Limitlessness; its intelligence, with Limit; its imagination, with Difference; its reason, with Sameness; its power to generate, with Motion; and its power to connect, with Stillness. And let us understand that the ratios between these powers are similar to the ratios mentioned above.

We may say that within our souls there is a double ratio between reason and appetite, a *sesquialteral* ratio between reason and the wrathful element, and a *sesquitertial* ratio between the wrathful element and that of appetite, although some would say that there is a *sesquitertial* ratio between reason and the wrathful element.

If we have said elsewhere that the ratios of things are equal in the soul, we did not mean arithmetical equality but harmonic equality.

Chapter 34*
From the intervals of the spheres Plato seeks the intervals of the ratios between the parts of the soul

JUST AS WE often picture the features of a living shape from the outlines of an image, so from that imaginary countenance of the heavenly soul which we glimpse in the mirror-substance of the world, let us strive to picture its real face.

For just as there are, within the enlivening power, seed-principles and many ratios pertaining to the limbs of the body, and just as there are five faculties within the common sense, so there is, within the soul of the world, an arrangement of the heavenly bodies that is in conformity with both consciousness and nature.

Plato, therefore, thinking that the *double*, the *triple*, and the other intervals described in the first number-figure are found within the spheres, took them back to the parts and powers of the soul, from where they were transferred to the spheres.

For he believed that the distance from the Earth to the Sun was twice that from the Earth to the Moon; that the distance from the Earth to Venus was three times that from the Earth to the Sun; that the distance from the Earth to Mercury was four times that from the Earth to Venus; that Mars was nine times farther from the Earth than the star of Mercury was; that Jupiter was eight times the distance of Mars from the Earth; and that the orb of Saturn was twenty-seven times farther from the Earth than Jupiter was. Here you see, among other things, that the heavier planets of Jupiter and Saturn are both designated by solid numbers.

And if elsewhere I have calculated other intervals based on the view of some Pythagoreans, I consider the Platonic measures more likely.

Through these measures those things can perhaps be understood which are rather mysteriously shrouded in the tenth book of the *Republic* about spheres. Again, through those things which we have

---

* Following the Florence edition of 1496, which assigns the number 34 to two successive chapters. Subsequent chapter numbers will thus be out of step with those of other editions.

dealt with concerning the power of numbers and ratios it is possible to conjecture those things which are implied in the eighth book of the *Republic* concerning the heavenly revolution, numbers, and ratios.

But when in our earlier words we place the Sun next to the Moon according to the Platonic and Aristotelian tradition, do not let the machinations of Ptolemy dissuade you from this view. For the supreme mathematician Geber has investigated all these things and has proved, by the most precise instruments and measurements, that the Sun is next to the Moon.

Chapter 35
How the intervals of the double and triple numbers are filled

AFTER PLATO HAS explained the first figure, which has seven limits and in which the double and triple proportions are contained, he then asks for another figure to be pictured which includes larger numbers, so that when the doubles are filled with *sesquitertials* and *sesquialterals* these medials may also be filled with *sesquioctavals*, so that the spaces of the *sesquitertials* contain a tone.

Let us therefore describe a figure similar to the first, but let us put six at the top, with its double [twelve] far beneath, filling the intervening space with eight and nine. Then let us likewise put twenty-four a long way beneath twelve, with sixteen and eighteen in the intervening space; and in the same way insert thirty-two and thirty-six as means between twenty-four and forty-eight. So far we have dealt with the side of the doubles.

Now let us fill out the spaces of the triples, placing far below six its triple (eighteen) and writing nine and twelve between them. In the same way, between eighteen and its triple (fifty-four) let us put twenty-seven and thirty-six. Finally, let us likewise proceed from fifty-four to its triple (a hundred and sixty-two) through the two mean numbers eighty-one and a hundred and eight.

To return, therefore, to the first 'double' property of this figure, let us consider the two means between six and twelve: eight and nine. Eight is considered the harmonic mean between six and twelve, for it exceeds six by a third of six, and it is exceeded by twelve by a third of twelve. Again, eight is the *sesquitertial* of six, while twelve is the *sesquialteral* of eight. Moreover, the difference between twelve and eight is four, while the difference between eight and six is two. So twelve to six is a double ratio, just as four to two is. But in what we have said the harmonic proportion is apparent.

Let us also compare nine to six through the *sesquialteral* ratio, and nine to twelve through the *sesquitertial* ratio, as well as nine to eight through the *sesquioctaval* ratio, by which a tone resonates: we shall at once realise that two *sesquitertials* are held together by this *sesquioctaval*: eight to six, and nine to twelve.

Nor is the arithmetic mean missing from these numbers, since nine exceeds six by three, while twelve also exceeds nine by three.

Let us proceed in this way through the same ratios in the following doubles, joining the doubles through *sesquitertials* and *sesquialterals*, as well as connecting twin *sesquitertials* through the *sesquioctaval* ratio.

In the same way it is possible to run through the triples, excluding the tone.

But since the *sesquitertial* ratios are formed not only from two tones but also from the half-tone – the smaller one, which falls just short of the full half-tone – Plato says that a small part is left in the *sesquitertials*.

Furthermore, the meaning of this figure based on the large numbers does not seem to be sufficiently explained by the followers of Plato, and we are not going to explain it at present, except to say that perhaps he places several means – or at least two – between the extremes because he intends it to be understood that within the soul the natures of things and the elements, which regard each other as opposites, in fact restore two qualities to each other; just as when Limit touches Limitlessness it carries off an undefined quality of Limit, and when Limitlessness in turn touches Limit it experiences a well-defined effect of Limitlessness; and moreover, there is a somehow limited Limitlessness within Limit and an indefinitely regressing Limit within Limitlessness itself.

In addition, among the powers of the soul some such means can be contemplated, and the soul as its model has resolved to implant at least two means between things which are far apart.

Now a tone signifies a full movement and beat of the soul both within itself and within the heavens. But a half-tone signifies a slower movement within the elements, falling so far short of the first that it adopts less than half of its perfection.

Finally, the whole of the preceding treatise on harmony seems to indicate a triple concord: that between the soul and the body; that among the parts of the soul; and that among the parts of the body.

Chapter 36
The division of the soul; motion; and time

WHEN HE SAYS that this mixing of natures has been fulfilled in the consummation of the soul, understand that the soul has come forth in such perfection that it has fulfilled its Idea perfectly.

Moreover, the division into length shows that the proper motion of the soul is naturally straight: into sense and into the nature of quickening or moving.

Again, he cuts it into two to show firstly that within the soul the straight motion is twofold (towards sensing and moving) and secondly that the motion from the soul within the body is likewise twofold (uniform and multiform).

But he bisects the two lines to portray the soul; then he turns them back into a curve, indicating that the nature of the soul, being more inclined to move from itself in a straight line, is adapted by God Himself, through the gift of intelligence, to follow a circular movement. I mean two circles: the unmoving firmament, and after the firmament the orbs of the wandering planets. The circle of the firmament really stands for the very nature of sameness and intelligence. But the multiple turnings of the planets really represent the nature of difference and of the lower parts of the soul. But from the inner motion as well as the time of the soul there follow the time and motion in the world.

Among these things he touches upon a few general points which pertain to astronomy: but anyone of average education can easily understand them, and the followers of Plato, both Greek and Latin, deal with them at great length.

Soon there arises the inquiry about the Ideas and natures of the creatures in the world, and we have dealt very thoroughly with these in the *Theology*. Moreover, what is probable in his views on the genealogy of certain deities and daemons is likewise declared in the *Theology* and elsewhere.

But before we proceed any further it would be useful to go back and explain more fully those things which we seem to have touched upon rather briefly at the beginning of this chapter.

Let all the harmonic numbers be set out in a line. Let them be marked all the way along this line. Let this continuous series not be divided laterally, otherwise not all of the numbers will be left on both sides, but let it be divided longitudinally, as rushes are commonly split, so that all the numbers are left in both parts after the division. Let lengths of this kind intersect each other like two lines at their mid-points, making a shape like ✕. Let their heads soon curve, so that each makes a circle; and let these two circles (one inner, one outer) move in opposite directions.

The length signifies the tendency of the soul towards external things and towards movement in a straight line. The bisection of the lines (the centre of the two circles) signifies the wonderful union of the soul with its powers and the spheres. The twofold powers and spheres of the soul (the intellectual and the animal) touch each other in the middle (the intellect), whence they proceed as if from a centre.

And because both powers in their own ways are turned to contemplate or imitate the intellect, they are said to be turned into a circle opposite the first meeting-point. For they first met in the outward movement, to which the turning is opposed. But in each of the circles there are all the harmonic powers, although not in the same way, as was signified by the longitudinal division.

When the *Timaeus* says that both the circles of the soul have been embraced by a circle of sameness, understand that they are contained and ruled by the intellect, which exists outside the soul. In the intellect the circle is still and simple. But both the circles of the soul are in movement.

Now the followers of Plato consider it necessary for the soul to move, since if it is compared to what is above it, the intelligible itself is utterly simple and unified, while the soul is strongly multifarious and, as it were, divided. So the soul, through its very variable division, does not match the intelligible, which is fully united. But it naturally longs with all its being to enjoy the intelligible in its entirety.

So because it cannot attain it with a single effort or in a single moment, at least it can attain it with many efforts in never-ending succession. It therefore gradually unfolds its parts, any one of which is a unity in itself; and it applies itself to that unity now through this part, now through that. For each and every one of its parts naturally desires to move around all the intelligible types. But since each one is composed of three (Essence, the Same, and the Different), it lacks the power (because of its compound nature) to unite with the supreme intelligible and the simple Idea.

For the same reason the soul continually develops each and every part into smaller parts, in order, as far as possible, to touch the individual essence of each part, the intelligible essence; and likewise through the particular intelligible Idea of the part to attain sameness itself; again, through the Different to attain difference.

In short, however you imagine it, the soul for ever turns about an intelligible axis always remaining in the same act, then with multiple acts. That axis is eternity, while this circumference is time, an image, as it were, of eternity. As the soul turns in its orbit, the heavens also turn in a similar proportion and receive their time from its time.

But just as the natural philosophers have sought to discover time through motion, as if time were a part of motion (its continuous nature, its number, or its measure), so the metaphysicians seem to have deduced eternity itself from the continual steadiness and orderliness of movement, ever keeping itself in the same manner, since motion, variable by nature and not being able to obtain the steadfast constancy of order from itself, necessarily moves away from something wholly permanent.

Therefore, just as the irregular movement of lower things is governed by the regular movement of heavenly things, so is that which has no life of its own guided by the living orbit of the soul itself. And in the soul the non-intellectual circle is governed by the intellectual circle, which, being multiple, is itself finally stabilised by the simple insight of the utterly steadfast mind.

I would rather join Plotinus in placing eternity within the act of the first mind, and time within the action of the first soul, than imagine with Proclus two divinities and different substances (eternity and time), the former above the first intellect and the second superior to the first soul.

But we draw the following conclusions from the above order: surely the observance of regular periodicity in the world depends on an unmoving cause; steadfastness and continual revolution depend on the infinite power of their cause; and the difference of restitutions depends on the difference of unmoving causes.

I have written more relevantly about these matters elsewhere.

Chapter 37
The arrangement of the living world through its limbs; the opposite movements of revolutions; and the intersectors of axes and orbits

BEING INCORPOREAL and possessing unlimited power, light fills all things instantaneously without ever becoming tainted. To everything it gives birth, life, movement, and expression. There is thus nothing more divine than this light. It is wholly within the Sun and wholly within the firmament, but in the Sun it is concentrated, while in the firmament it is diffused. It is undoubtedly a property of the celestial nature, though beneath the heavens it is allotted to those things alone which are similar to the heavens.

Yet in addition to this light which is apparent to the eyes there is another light which lies hidden within the whole fabric of the heavens, within the more exalted stars, and within the Moon. Both these lights depend on the intellectual power of the world-soul, but the manifest light depends on it insofar as it is the image of the divine intellect, whereas the unmanifest light depends on it insofar as it has become the living intellect. The manifest light comes from the Sun and passes through all things, and in a similar way the unmanifest light comes from the firmament and passes through all things.

It seems, furthermore, that light is the spirit and image of the world-soul, diffusing the life of the world-soul and its perceptive faculties and its powers throughout all the limbs of this world-being. The head of this being is the firmament, which bears before it the power of this being, together with the sensory and intellectual being, and which moves through all things by means of its starry eyes. Its heart is the

Sun, which holds and unfolds the fullness of its life-giving power. Its liver is the Moon, which spreads its natural vigour through all things.

Now Venus is related to the Moon, Mars to the Sun, and Saturn and Mercury to the intellectual power of the firmament. Just as these last two meet in the visible homogeneous light, as Plato says in the *Republic*, so they agree together in the invisible light, which is intelligence. Jupiter, however, is either like a blend composed of all the heavenly bodies or he resembles the Sun and Moon in nature and imitates them in function. The four elements beneath the Moon are like the four humours of this being.

Through the simple form of the Sun this being calls to mind the divine unity and goodness. Through the single firmament, full of countless stars, it manifests the divine mind, which is indeed uniform but also becomes multiform through the sequence of Ideas. Through the wandering spheres of the planets, and especially through the Moon, it portrays the manifold movements of its own soul. Through the four elements which are subject to generation, it depicts the generative power of the soul.

Plato was bold enough to arrange the world-being in this way, as if it had limbs, for Orpheus, Varro, Plotinus, and Porphyry arranged the world-Jupiter on a principle which, although not exactly the same, was yet very similar. But perhaps it was not uncommon for the followers of Plato to say that the mind is indicated by the firmament; that the deepest reasoning is indicated by Saturn, and general reasoning by Mercury (although both types of reasoning are reflective); that practical reasoning is indicated by Jupiter; that the senses and that bold spirit of wrath which fights on behalf of reason are indicated by the Sun; that the wrath which gives its support to the senses is indicated by Mars; that the nature of ardent longing is indicated by Venus and the Moon (with Venus it is the urge to propagate the species, and with the Moon it is the urge to preserve the individual); and, finally, that the nature of invigorating, which begets through fire, as it were, nourishes through air, imparts growth through water, and maintains through earth, is indicated by the elements.

But you should know for a fact that these powers (which we were ascribing just now to different parts of the cosmos) are more profoundly inherent in the world-soul than in any other souls. We shall speak more fully of this in what follows.

There are, in short, two things which are exceedingly beautiful within the cosmos: the Sun and the firmament. The Sun is the greatest of the stars, and the firmament is the most extensive of the spheres. For we can think of nothing beyond the physical that is more beautiful. For if you imagine a further sphere, one devoid of light, you will certainly not be imagining one that is as beautiful; and if you imagine one that is nothing but light, it will definitely not be more beautiful but will have too much light. You are looking beyond all the light that is already found within the cosmos.

But if the firmament has two opposite movements, it is therefore unnecessary for it to revolve beneath a greater sphere. For it can arrange one movement with its soul and the other with its mind, as Plato indicates in the *Politicus*. Although Plato, Aristotle, the Egyptians, and the Chaldaeans (all of whom assign a single movement to the firmament) are not obliged to postulate a higher sphere or a second mover, Proclus shows in this way that the firmament does not move over the poles of the Zodiac from the west, as Hipparchus and Ptolemy believe. For if this were the case, it would mean that, between Homer's time and that of Proclus, both Ursa and Canopus would have had to shift their positions so much that Ursa would now hardly be seen in Lycia, while Canopus would not be seen at all, since within that period of time the firmament would have turned more than fifteen degrees; but observation showed that Ursa and Canopus always appeared in similar positions during those centuries.

Plato was thus justified in recognising a single movement of the firmament from the east over the north and south poles, with the axis considered to run from the north to the south. The orbits of the planets he considered to turn above these poles and this axis and to move towards the west on a daily basis; but, in a longer movement, to turn back on themselves and go towards the east, though not over the same poles, for opposite movements could not thus occur, but over poles about twenty-four degrees from the poles that have just been mentioned and through another axis intersecting the first axis. The first two poles have an intermediate equinox; the second two have a zodiacal equinox, and yet the arch of the Zodiac itself intersects the equinox through Aries and Libra. Plato seems to indicate intersections of this kind through the shape of the letter ✕ and through the innermost intersection of the soul.

Chapter 38
Right and left in the cosmos; the movements of the firmament, of the planets, and of the fixed stars; the arrangement of the soul

PLATO HOLDS, moreover, that this world-being has a right and a left. The right part in living beings is that in which the ability to move predominates. Therefore, since the firmament is the origination of movement and since by its motion it moves all else from the east, it is properly called the right limb of the cosmos and the right movement from the east. But since the wandering revolution is a movement from a different direction, it is called the left part of the cosmos, and its movement from the west is one that is left and even diametrical, inasmuch as it proceeds under the inclination of the Zodiac on the one hand and across the latitude on the other hand.

Aristotle, in agreement with Plato, called an arising 'right' and a setting 'left'; and the firmament was the cause which ensured that all things persisted in the same state of being, but the principle for the wandering revolution was that all things kept changing. Yet within the world-soul the right is its turning once more towards the contemplation of the divine, and the left is its turning aside to make itself available for what is subsequent to the divine. Its own diameter — and the diameter of all that belongs to it – is the giving of attention. Finally, on account of the opposing movements within the soul, there are opposing movements in the heavens; and on account of the different principles within the soul there are also different powers in the heavens.

Now the opposing movements within the soul are the ones we have mentioned, in addition to those movements which it makes from causes to effects, from universals to particulars, as well as the reverse movements in both cases. But when the firmament catches the remaining spheres in its movement from the east, it represents the intelligence of the universal soul, while it imitates the divine mind and assembles all the other powers subject to it in order to make such an imitation.

Now these lower powers are said to be taken by a movement contrary to the likeness of the planets, since intelligence extends particularly to the imitation of those Ideas which pertain to unity, sameness, and stillness, while the powers subject to it strive most of all to imitate the opposite Ideas of multiplicity, difference, and ideal motion.

The spheres and the stars are invigorated not only by the world-soul but also by their own souls, for if they are distinct one from another in their substances, powers, and movements, and if their life is superior to that of the beings which we know, they certainly have their own particular lives as well as a common life, especially if all the stars and spheres make a lengthy circuit around their own centres.

This is why the followers of Plato think that the stars copy their respective spheres in their nature and shape as well as in making circuits. But just as the stars are turned by the sphere in addition to making their own movements, so are their souls ruled by the very soul of the sphere. And in the same way, the souls of the spheres are appointed by the world-soul.

And just as in the firmament there are vast numbers of living stars around its soul, as around their leader, so in any sphere, in addition to the soul of the sphere and the particular soul of the planet, there are many celestial beings, acting as guides and leaders. These the followers of Plato call angels, daemons, heroes, and human souls which have won the heavenly homeland through their merits. For just as the firmament and the furthest ends of the cosmos are full of their own beings, so the intermediate orbits, too, abound with their own life-forms.

But in the revolutions of the planets there are, therefore, twin leaders, the soul of the orbit and the living planet, although within the firmament there is only one leader of the stars, and that is the soul of the sphere, for the throng that follows – being lower, weaker, and more numerous – seems to be in need of large numbers of leaders everywhere. This situation is so prevalent that beneath the Moon countless divinities, engaged in a variety of functions, are related, as if they were similar to the seven planets, to the seven leaders beneath the Moon.

But let us return to the heavens. Since Plato does not introduce any epicycles or eccentric movements, but does attribute multiple movements to the planets, in addition to the movements of the sphere – movements forward, backward, upward, downward, northward, and southward – we are obliged to say, and his own words confirm this, that the planets have, in addition to the sweeping movement of the sphere, their own free advance through the Elysian fields.

Liquids, of course, passing through other liquids and similar substances, proceed without any impediment, and like makes way for like with the greatest of ease and without any deprivation. In the same way, between the unvarying and utterly circular movement of the stars in the firmament and the highly irregular movements of the elements, the planets pursue their mean course, combining the circular with the straight and rightly linking order with irregularity by being irregular in a regular way.

Aristotle should not object to our view by saying that the full Moon always shows us the same shape, albeit somehow or other in the shade. For the Moon has almost the same shape on all sides and seems to weak eyes to present the same shape, even if it is in some ways no more than similar.

Chapter 39
The great harmony, within the cosmic being, between the soul and the heavens and between the heavens and the elements, in relation to the higher worlds and the orders of divinities

WE NECESSARILY THINK of these four within the world-soul: life, the ability to move, intelligence, and reason; and we likewise think of four in the heavens, as if the heavens were likewise affected by the spirit of the soul from this side and from that.

Thus, from the life of the soul comes the warmth in the heavens; from its ability to move comes flowing moisture; from its bright intelligence comes light; from its intellectual reason, which is turned back within itself, comes circular motion.

There is thus a very close relationship between the soul and the heavens. There is also a close association between the heavens and the elements, for to the elements similar properties are transmitted from the heavens and by the heavens: warmth, moisture, light, and orbital motion. Conversely, within the heavens there are, as it were, elemental properties, which we talk about at some length elsewhere, but this relationship can be observed particularly in the Moon, the lowest of the heavenly bodies, and in the ether, the highest of the elements. For the ether, which is the highest part of the air, receives from the heavens its warmth, its steadfastness, its light, and its circular motion; while the Moon, in its turn, displays the qualities of the elements and, through some degree of solidity, resists the light, as does the Earth. This is why Orpheus calls the Moon 'the celestial Earth'.

Again, through some mysterious difference in density and rarefaction or in brightness and darkness, he portrays water together with air, each with an excess of moisture, although water has dense moisture, while air has life-giving moisture. Furthermore, from the changeability of light he indicates the changes of the elemental qualities; from change of form he determines the transpositions of quantities within the elements and the changes wrought in shapes. For the time being I merely allude to the way in which the powers and the images of heavenly beings are discovered within things composed of water and of earth. For in the third *Book on Life* we have discussed this subject at some length.

In short, this cosmic being, no less than any other being anywhere, is self-consistent throughout all its limbs and joints, for it is divinely tempered by a wondrous harmony. It is also consistent with the intelligible world, which holds the Ideas of all that is in the cosmos. It is consistent, moreover, with the intellectual world, that is, with the order of celestial intellects, in which that intelligible world has manifested the Ideas and forms of this physical world sooner than in this.

Thus the world-deities henceforth lead their combined orders, from the highest right down to the lowest. Within any sphere, therefore, the divine powers – those of Saturn and Jupiter, as well as all the others – are within the intelligible world, the intellectual world, and the physical world. And likewise beneath the heavens there are, around the gods in all places, attendant daemons and particular souls, companions on account of the same qualities and designations.

Hence it comes about, as we often say, that each sphere of the cosmos is, as it were, the whole cosmos, for it embraces all things with a property specific to itself. And this is not without some justification, for within the model Idea of this cosmos all Ideas are held within each and every one of them. From this marvellous harmony of all the cosmic constituents it therefore happens that the movements of each belong to all, that the gifts of those that are higher pour down upon those that are subsequent, and that the prayers of the lower beings arise to the higher beings.

Chapter 40
Those things which come into being directly from God, and those things which come into being through intermediaries; the words of God in relation to the gods; and the providence of the gods

THUS FAR IT HAS been possible for anyone to see that it is from the divine intellect, craftsman of the world, that the souls of the world and the gods, as well as the daemons, all the spheres of the world, and the types of all things, have come forth without intermediate causes.

We have said from the outset that, in relation to the primal matter, there is a variation of understanding among the followers of Plato.

The framer of the world therefore proceeds to direct his offspring – the souls of the spheres, of the stars, and of the daemons, together with the lower orders of angels – to imitate him in undertaking the admixture of all things beneath the Moon, to subject all things to man and, by means of an irrational life which depends partly on them and partly on man's soul, to unite to the transient body the rational soul man has received from the creator.

Now you will note, in the very words of God, that whatever comes into being directly from God is everlasting, while whatever is compounded by any cause is dissoluble, inasmuch as it is a compound, but whatever compounds are produced through the will of God are preserved indissoluble, inasmuch as the unity within them predominates over the multiplicity.

You will also note that when he says that God abides within His habitation as He gives directions, while His ministers follow them, there is no shadow of change within God as He rules and moves the changeable things of the world, although within His ministers providence is nearer to some sort of change.

To put it briefly, you will see that in all these matters there is a wondrous confirmation of that statement found in the words of Moses: 'I AM THAT I AM.'

The Maker of the cosmic deities calls Himself their Father, too, when He makes them, like sons, partakers of His counsel and handiwork. He also calls them the deities of the deities, that is, the deities of the rational souls. The lower divinities not only seek the higher ones through their bodies but also turn to the divine in order that they may one day be received into the number of the gods.

He composes these gods from the intellectual soul, the celestial body, and an intermediate life that flows forth through the soul into a body of this kind. Therefore, since they are compounded of diverse parts, they are in some way subject to dissolution, but in another way they are indissoluble, too, through the skill of their Father, which naturally unites them so harmoniously that their unity and stillness far surpass their composite and changeable nature, and particularly through the paternal goodness which wills that those things which are thoroughly connected should remain indissoluble and that those things which are very close to their totally unmoving cause should have an unchangeable essence. Conversely, that paternal goodness allows those things which flow forth from inconstant causes to be changeable in their essence; and since, in the composition of those things, multiplicity surpasses unity, and movement likewise surpasses stillness, it allows them to be dissolved at some point in time. This is the nature of those things which are compounded by the world-deities and the daemons, unless perhaps these deities and daemons also make something that is everlasting, through some unmoving function bestowed by the Father.

In the first place, that which is in no way compounded is indissoluble, and hence that which is very closely compounded becomes indissoluble; whereas that which is not perfectly compounded, on account of the looseness of its coherence and the disruption in its causes, is dissoluble. Moreover, that great God is immortal who of Himself has eternal life.

In the second place, the immortal intellects derive their existence from that source, being separated from animated bodies and at the same time being allotted a complete life spent in eternity.

In the third place, there arise from that source the immortal, cosmic gods and daemons, who have acquired from that source movement and action that are living, unfailing, and perpetually flowing, but always proceeding in the best possible way.

In the fourth place, individual souls receive immortality from that source, but they receive it within the forms and activities of life which develop alternately for worse and for better.

In the fifth and final place, there are the things that are mortal in all respects, for those things which we have listed after the purest intellects on account of some mortal transition seem to have some element of immortality. Indeed, the words spoken by the Father to the gods and daemons are an outpouring of intelligence and power upon them, that they may, in imitation of their Father, beget and provide for what is lower, partly through the exercise of intelligence and will and partly through the exercise of nature and movement in full obedience to the will.

Lower beings therefore come into existence from the Creator and through the gods and daemons; and inasmuch as they come into existence from Him they have unity and a type-form that is everlasting, but inasmuch as they come into existence through the gods and daemons they have the transient multiplicity of individuals.

The order of the universe requires there to be many things that are subject to dissolution. For it is in this way that the change of forms brings forth countless beings in never-ending succession, and the appointed levels henceforth proceed. For those things which remain for ever are followed by those which endure for all time, and these in turn are followed by those which endure for a very long time. In short, those which exist for all time and are, in fact, everlasting must not be unproductive, and so they produce many offspring, but these, being subject to decline, eventually fall away from everlastingness. Their ruling daemons, being dedicated to different stars and distributed among different elements, lands, peoples, cities, families, and persons, make provision under the authority of the deities that offer a wider kind of providence.

Chapter 41
Man's relationship to soul and body

PLATO SAYS THAT the rational soul of man was compounded by God from the same mixture of things and from the same bowl as was the soul of the world. The bowl represents the actual Idea of the rational life. But he adds that the rational soul was produced from the remains of the earlier mixture, thus indicating that individual lives are inferior to the universal life. God then attaches the souls – that is, the particular orders of souls – to particular stars. He also introduces the conveyances, that is, the ethereal bodies. He proceeds to teach the laws of destiny as the souls are imbued with the shapes of Ideas, by means of which the souls, whenever they turn to themselves, may recognise the causes of creation. But what he says about the fateful descent of the soul and its orbit is expounded elsewhere.

The servants of God then continue to craft the human body, fastening it together with invisible bonds. You should understand these invisible bonds to indicate that the human constitution is so tempered and so similar to the heavens that a departure from elemental qualities is scarcely apparent in it. He then adds that the circuits of the soul are hampered within the mass of the body.

At this point you should remember before all else that our soul and the soul of the world have been composed on a similar principle and that they have similar circuits. He therefore says that there are two reasons in particular why the circuit of intelligence is hampered and the circuit of reason is tugged aside: the first reason is that, until the body is fully grown, the soul is completely taken up with the making of the body; and the second reason is that those things which move the senses outwards have a stronger impact at a more impressionable age and through their novelty they cause the soul to stand in wonder of the physical world. For these reasons, therefore, there is a long period of time in which intelligence deserts its divine function, and rational activity itself, being pulled off course in its consideration of all that is lower, seems to lose its rationality, becoming confused and prone to error.

And so it is in this way that the entire soul becomes distorted and leads a toilsome life, while reason gives way to the senses, just like a man who puts his head, instead of his feet, on the ground and lifts his feet aloft to where his head should be.

What Plato puts forward, however, about the arrangement of the limbs of the body has been dealt with adequately by the physicians. You will particularly note at this point that within the body the head is said to be, not merely the chief, but the whole, for everything else has been added purely to serve the head. From this you will gather that man is born for the purpose of contemplation.

There follows a passage on the instruments of the senses. What is said about sight has been adequately expounded by Chalcidius; and what is said about dreams we ourselves have expounded elsewhere. We have also spoken about sight in our commentaries on Plotinus.

Next for your consideration will be the unwavering view of our Plato concerning causes; and you will see that physical things and their qualities, which are moved and directed to their end, not by themselves but by some non-physical cause, should not really be described as causes but as instruments of a secret providence, while the true cause is the will of providence, which models all things on itself as it deems and perceives to be for the best. This is why Plato declares that the final cause, the cause of causes, is ordained within providence.

He then re-asserts that man is born to contemplate celestial matters, or, rather, to make every effort to imitate the Mover of the heavens Himself. And just as he had said that both sight and hearing have been bestowed on us for the purpose of contemplation and education, so it is through the harmony of the senses that we may also impart harmony to the movements of the soul. He puts no value on the senses, other than those of seeing and hearing, as if they were not conducive to reflection.

Chapter 42
How the world is composed of mind and necessity

AFTER HE HAS TREATED of the model order of the world, which he calls the intellect because it is the image of the divine intelligence, he now treats of the matter of the world, which he names necessity because it has been brought in not for its own sake but as necessary for the final forms, and also because the world, on account of its admixture, necessarily endures some deformity. Hence the well-known statement that the world is composed from the intellect and necessity, that is, from the arrangement of forms and from matter. We can, moreover, understand the word 'necessity' not only as matter but also as its soul in the first stage of its development, considered as formless in the way that matter is. For both soul and matter, in the first stage of their arising, are without form, yet both are ready to receive form through the gift of intelligence, whence the principles of the soul and the seeds of natural forms are poured into them, together with the qualities and forms of matter.

But when he says that the elements existed in some way before the arrangement of the world, understand him to mean certain powers of the elements: powers capable of imparting form within the soul and of receiving form within matter. Again, when he says that matter was tossed about haphazardly prior to the world, you should interpret this to mean that the motive power of the soul, even before the gifts bestowed by intelligence, was able to stir matter, but in a fashion by no means orderly. Furthermore, when he says that the world had been embellished by God after necessity had been prevailed upon, take him to mean that that primal nature of matter and of the soul is considered to be without form and yet it has from the beginning so completely received from God the readiness to be conformable to receiving forms that it is impossible for it to be more ready.

Noteworthy at this point is that distinction by which it is said, at the outset of the book, that the universe had been divided into two, that is, the model and its image, whereas it is now to be divided into three: the model, the image, and matter. It can be seen firstly that the model of the world and its efficient and final causes are, in fact, the same; secondly, that the entire order of the world is not something substantial but is rather the image of the invisible world.

Moreover, because he previously distinguished matter from mind and is now distinguishing it from the image of the mind, we may assume that matter moves forth from God not so much through its own Idea as through the Idea of form devised, as it were, by intelligence, not on the earlier premise but on the later one. Then, from the perpetual transformation of forms, he carefully shows that matter exists, what it is, and how it comports itself; from this he reasons that material forms are, in a sense, deceptive.

Next he rises up, through these material forms, to the true and ideal forms, a process fully and clearly explained in the *Theology*. He has already adduced as evidence the numerous names of matter such as the *invisible type*, the *formless bosom which is able to assume all forms*, *nature*, *power*, the *mother of the world*, the *nourisher of forms*, the *subject*, the *receptacle*, and the *place*. From this name of *place*, however, we can make light of the foolish and even malevolent charge of insanity that was brought against Plato by some Aristotelians, as if he were saying that matter is actually a mathematical point, an accusation very evidently refuted by all the other names of matter.

Finally, the fact that matter claims formlessness for itself argues that it likewise claims unity for itself. For if it is formless it has no distinctions. If it has no distinctions it is one. Yet on account of that same formlessness it does not claim being [*esse*] for itself but rather does it fall away from being. Therefore, since one and being [*ens*] do not equally harmonise with matter, they cannot be the same as each other; but one is higher than being [*ente*], since it extends more widely and especially since one is in harmony with deficiency, whereas being [*ens*] is not. From this fact, too, we reason that matter can be brought forth only from the highest principle of creation.

Chapter 43
Natural phenomena are based on the principles of mathematics; concerning the elements and compounds

BEING NOW ABOUT to demonstrate natural phenomena through the principles of mathematics, Plato gives special praise to the teaching of the mathematicians as the pathway of all liberal study.

It would be a long process now, Lorenzo, to enumerate all those who in our times have embarked on the way of mathematics and have reached the desired destination. We know that Pier Leone of Spoleto has bestowed a great blessing on mathematicians by penetrating the meanings given by Platonists as well as by Aristotelians. In Florence, Leon Battista Alberti, starting from the same disciplines, has published a most beautiful work on architecture. What shall I say of our Francesco Berlinghieri, Niccolò's son? Through the services provided by mathematicians, has he not written outstanding poetry on the subject of cosmography?

But let no one be troubled by the fact that Plato, in the manner of the Pythagoreans, seems to build natural phenomena on the principles of mathematics. For he wishes it to be understood that, by some kind of dissolving process, natural bodies are composed from shapes and numbers as if from limits and not from elements and parts; for natural phenomena dissolve into shapes and numbers as if into their limits. Are not the limits of bodies their measurements and shapes? Are not numbers the limits of shapes?

Moreover, natural types require not only a common subject but also a particular subject. Yet a common subject satisfies shapes, while numbers do not require a particular basis, a common basis, or any other physical basis. From this it is clear that shapes are prior to natural types and that numbers are prior to shapes.

And so Pythagoras and Plato considered there to be a threefold order in the creation: types, shapes, and numbers; and likewise a threefold order among Ideas; so that, within both the creation and Ideas, types dissolve into shapes, and shapes dissolve into numbers. Certain types are somehow in harmony with certain shapes, and certain shapes with certain numbers, which is what the order of creation requires in all respects.

This is why, when they say that the fire-type is composed of a pyramidal shape, that the solid pyramid is formed of four triangles, and that these triangles are established on the numbers four and three, their intention is to show that there is a very similar property that is common to all of these and that it is better for them to be compared with each other than to be composed one from another. For this reason he attributes the pyramidal shape to fire; to air, the shape which has eight faces and which he calls the octahedron; to water, the shape with twenty faces, which he calls the icosahedron; to earth, the shape with six faces, known as the cube or knuckle-bone; and finally, to the whole, the shape with twelve faces.

And he considers the pyramidal shape to harmonise with fire because it is slender and better at cutting than the others are, being made of fewer triangles and therefore being the lightest of all shapes. The cube, by contrast, harmonises with earth, being very solid and stable. The remaining shapes harmonise with the intermediate elements, for they stand at points midway between fire and earth in their relationship to motion and stillness. The dodecahedron, which has twelve faces, harmonises with the cosmos, in his view, on account of the twelve spheres and the twelve signs of the Zodiac.

Euclid demonstrates that, within a sphere, there can be inscribed only five shapes that touch the sphere on both sides [*utrinque*] and have equal lines and angles. These are the pyramid, the cube, the octahedron, the dodecahedron, and the icosahedron. The pyramid has four faces, which are four equal and similar triangles. The cube has six similar and equal faces, which are squares. The octahedron has eight faces, which are equal and similar triangles. The icosahedron has twenty faces, which are triangles that are similar and equal among themselves, that is, they are equilateral. The dodecahedron has twelve faces, which are similar and pentagonal. Only one of these shapes, the cube, has square faces, and only one of the five has pentagonal faces. The other three have triangular faces. Thus, when Plato named the worlds, he made a playful allusion to these shapes.

But he resolves solids into plane figures, and plane figures into triangles, especially those known as right-angled, one of which is the scalene, having all its sides of unequal length, and another of which is the isosceles, which means 'equal-legged', having two sides of equal length. For he considers the equilateral triangle, in which there is no right angle and no perpendicular straight line, to be less suited to producing plane figures.

From scalene triangles he makes the pyramid, the octahedron, and the icosahedron, for the pyramid is composed of four equilateral triangles, any one of which may be divided into six scalene triangles. He makes the octahedron from eight similar triangles, each of which may likewise be divided into six scalene triangles. The icosahedron is formed from twenty similar triangles, any one of which may likewise be divided into six scalene triangles, and so twice sixty scalenes are produced. In this shape there are twelve solid angles, each produced from five planes. But the isosceles triangle is said to be the basic shape of the cube, because four isosceles triangles together complete a square. From six such squares the cube is produced, having eight solid angles, each of which is made of three right-angled planes.

Lastly, he linked the dodecahedron with the cosmos, as I was saying, for twelve arrangements of stars appear in the Zodiac, each one of which is divided into thirty parts. In the same way, within the dodecahedron twelve pentagons may be perceived, each divided into five equilateral triangles, each one of which is in turn composed of six scalene triangles, so that within the dodecahedron as a whole we find three hundred and sixty triangles, just as there are three hundred and sixty parts to the Zodiac.

But he goes on to deal with the movements and effects of the elements; how the elements are distinguished from each other; how they are commingled; the effects produced by this commingling; and the nature of the change undergone by the elements and by their combinations. Here he deals with partial mixtures, with fully complete mixtures, with liquids, with stones, and with minerals.

Yet nearly all of these matters are concealed, in typically Pythagorean manner, under obscure metaphors, though we believe that Plato spoke more openly about them to those who gathered to listen to him and that Aristotle committed them to writing more clearly than anyone else. An exposition of all such matters may be found in Aristotle's books *On Generation* and *On Meteors*.

Plato then deals with the effects produced by the elements on the perceptions of living beings, effects both hidden and obvious. He also deals with the different types of pleasure and pain, which are clearly set out in the *Philebus* and in our book *On Pleasure*. He goes on to speak of the senses themselves and their objects. He distinguishes tastes, smells, sounds, and colours.

Chapter 44
More on man:
how much regard he gives to the soul,
and how much to the body

IT IS WORTH CONSIDERING the importance Plato places on advising us that we should make every effort to know ourselves, to remember that God has committed to our charge everything beneath the Moon, and thus avoid ever subjecting ourselves, out of disregard for our own dignity, to those things that are beneath us. For at the very beginning of this entire dialogue a resolution was made that the whole cosmos should be discussed, right up to the birth of man. Again, in the central part of the discussion, the gods are enjoined by their Father to ennoble man, the lord of all creatures, whom He wishes to be pre-eminent and to be in His image and likeness. Then, after a few interpositions, man is returned to. Finally, towards the end of the dialogue, the resolution that was made at the beginning is taken up once more: to discuss the whole cosmos right up to the birth of man. And at all times it is asserted, just as Moses declared, that man is put first in this divine handiwork, and is also put last, as its summation.

And so now, leaving out other matters, he repeats the divine ordinance in creating man and the compliance of divine ministers in completing this work. And he is not without justification in doing so, for he had said earlier that, of all the creatures on earth, man alone would honour justice and the gods, so that it is in full accord with reason for the gods to have carefully nurtured the birth of man. But, leaving these things on one side, let us expound what follows.

The irrational soul is once more discussed, the soul that is constituted not directly by God but through the subsequent changeable causes and that is subject to the rational soul, which has been despatched from heaven by God. Now the followers of Plato consider that the irrational soul is not so much *substantial* as *accidental*, like an impression made by rational souls, something in which the senses do in fact exist, although they are divided and subject to suffering on account of the various instruments of the physical body.

But the followers of Plato locate the common sense – which is simple and not subject to suffering, and which does not in fact receive the effects conveyed by bodies, as another sense would, but perceives the senses of the irrational soul or, rather, assesses their effects – within the very substance of the rational soul.

In a similar way, they demonstrate that the undivided substance of the rational soul abides within itself and is not entrusted to the head for its support but is, as it were, equipped to act either on its own behalf or on behalf of something similar within its own class.

They also demonstrate that the irrational soul resides in some way within the limbs of the body, and that that portion of the irrational soul which partakes of boldness and wrath is entrusted to the heart, while that which partakes of ardent desire is entrusted to the liver. But you will note the extraordinary view held by the Pythagoreans about this liver: it is such a blend of precise firmness and clear gentleness that, like a mirror, it very easily receives and reflects the images of things. Indeed, just as the strong imagination of a pregnant woman often impresses upon the extremely tender foetus the features of whatever is desired, so a strong idea in the mind, or the imagination of sense, very easily forms the mirror-like nature of the liver. It is upon this mirror that the daemons and gods form images of what is to come whenever the inner being is so deeply at rest that images from other sources are not depicted there.

And so it is that the images of the future that are formed on this mirror are immediately reflected onto the mind and the imagination, but there they frequently get so mixed up with other images that they are not able to presage the future, which is what happens, for example, when the mind, busy with the duties of practical good sense, is pulled hither and thither in relation to whatever needs to be administered, or when the imagination is likewise preoccupied with similar activities. But when the watchful, unbroken, and strenuous roving of reason and imagination comes to rest, the images of the future which fall upon our mirror from the gods are clearly reflected from there onto our faculty of judgement.

To discern what they portend, however, is the function of the man who has acquired the habit of ranging, with good sense and insight, from what has gone before to what follows as a result. Yet this kind of roving hinders the faculty of prophecy, so that it comes about quite rightly that there are some who foresee and others who interpret and expound what has been foreseen.

Plato then goes on to speak of a subject that has been very extensively explored by physicians in relation to the humours and complexions and the miraculous artistry of the human body. But, of course, Bartolomeo della Fonte, our outstanding Orator, felt such admiration for the linguistic deftness displayed by Plato in his description of the human body that he demonstrated in a brilliant address that it was impossible for Lactantius and Cornelius Celsus and even Cicero himself to approach the wonderful eloquence which Plato reveals in his descriptions.

Here we shall consider the religious teaching that nothing more should be stated about divine matters than is confirmed by the divine oracle; that, in the process of composing the human being, Providence followed exclusively the principle of ensuring man's full readiness for contemplation; and further, that, in the production of effects, the true causes are not natural phenomena but the instruments of divine Providence, for the principal cause of individual effects resides in that intelligence which, possessing the principle of the Good, makes all things for the sake of their future appropriateness.

Plato then defines bodily health and sickness. He also distinguishes types of diseases – those that are fevers and those that are not – and he attributes causes to individual diseases.

I have long thought that the main causes are those I have read about in the writings of Galen the Platonist, and I have recently been confirmed in my view by that outstanding physician, George of Cyprus. For in those days when he often came to treat my mother and found me reading those very words, he united the thought of Galen with that of Plato in an astonishing manner.

Chapter 45
On the outward and inward breath, according to Plato and Galen

I SUBSEQUENTLY READ a passage in which Galen, when comparing Plato with Hippocrates, states the principles of the outward breath and the inward breath. He has my approval for saying that when the thorax and the lungs expand like bellows they draw in air that not only cools the heart but also fills the lower chest, which would otherwise be empty and, as might be expected, would now be left with greater capacity. But when the thorax and lungs contract, they quickly emit heat from deep within. These movements, which are to some extent voluntary, he calls the outward breath and the inward breath.

Since, in my view, the rate of breathing is slower or more rapid because the nerves which move the muscles of the thorax and lungs through expansion and contraction have their origin in the spinal marrow, which depends on the brain, it comes about that, through the vital power, voluntary movements, too, follow in due course. He adds that similar movements in the pulse are caused by the movement of the heart through the dilation and contraction of the arteries, which, when dilated, draw the external air into the entire body in order to cool their own hot spirits and also to produce the vital spirit; but when they are contracted, they clear away the murky vapours which have found their way into the spirits. To this movement he rightly applies the name *perspiration*.

Some parts of this whole subject were clearly expounded by our Plato, while other parts were, in a manner typical of him, less clearly conveyed. In this way he seems to have given an occasion for quibbling to Galen, who in other respects is more renowned than anyone else for trumpeting Plato's praises. For his part, Galen holds that after the outward breath described by Plato the inward breath follows without delay. He praises Hippocrates for noting this, but does not at all approve of Plato for failing to observe it.

We, however, have good reason to say that Plato introduced *perspiration* straight after the outward breath to provide the necessary assistance without delay. For as soon as the air is expelled from the lower chest by the outward breath, empty spaces will be created forthwith unless the air which has been taken in from all sides through the bronchi and the other channels fill them at the very moment when they are being emptied by the outward breath. For after the outward breath, the air which is awaited from above through the subsequent inward breath and which is about to fill these spaces arrives too late, being pushed backwards by the contrary movement of the outward breath. For this reason, unless the lower chest has already been filled through *perspiration*, either there would be empty spaces for a while or fluids would rise up as they do in cupping-glasses.

However, I do not give Galen so much approval in this matter as I do when he protects his Plato from the critics who raise objections against him as if he had said that all drink pours through the trachea into the lungs, which not even a drunkard would dream of saying. Now what Plato says is that the lungs are porous, that they are always more ready than anything else to absorb fire, and that they always soak up as much fluid as possible from the whole body. And there are times when they slowly absorb refined drops of drink, like dew, which are held in the mouth for a while, through the walls of the trachea. This, then, is what Galen sanctions, both in principle and from experience, when he says that if you give a thirsty beast coloured water to drink and if you slaughter it immediately afterwards, you will find that its lungs are coloured in like fashion.

Plato, however, frequently makes it clear in his writings that he considered drink not to go to the chest but to flow down to the stomach along with food.

In short, those who condemn Plato because he said that the cause of digestion is fire, which burns instead of providing a measured process of digestion, should remember that Plato did not propose fire itself as such, but proposed a fire that is akin to us, congenial to our spirits, and on good terms with our blood: a fire equipped to achieve the process of digestion.

Galen, however, approves of Plato for saying, in agreement with Hippocrates, that the heart is the origination of the blood-vessels, that is, of the arteries, and also of the blood: not of all the blood, but of the blood which is full of vitality, fast, and hot; and within it he located the faculty of the soul for impetuous anger. But he located the power assigned to lust within the liver, from which the blood flows forth less impetuously, and for that reason the blood-vessels carrying such blood do not beat violently.

However, Galen does not approve of Plato for saying that white phlegm is produced from the liquefaction of delicate, newly-formed flesh; for Galen considers white phlegm to be produced from cold food that has been barely cooked, and he thinks that from liquefied flesh is produced a thicker bile of a colour midway between pale yellow and white, although Plato holds that this bile occurs from flesh which is already liquefied, and phlegm is not produced from solid flesh but from liquefied fatty tissue or something similar. This happens at any time, for he will not deny that phlegm and the other humours are produced jointly from indigestion or burning in the veins.

And Galen has no right to rebuke Plato for saying that natural heat is generated by the movement of breathing, for this is not Plato's meaning. What Plato means is that natural heat is aroused and conveyed by the movement of breathing. Galen also makes a somewhat inappropriate attack on Plato for saying that fire is not perfectly commingled with air in all places inside the body, for elsewhere Plato maintains, not without justification, that there are some places where fire rules over air.

Chapter 46
On the good health and poor health of the body and the soul

NOW PLATO NEXT defines perfect human health as the mutual harmony of body and soul, which he believes is eventually attained when both body and soul are well disposed within themselves and simultaneously enjoy excellent constitution. When I say 'excellent', I mean 'in equal measure', so that the strength of the soul does not outstrip the measure of the body, and the strength of the body does not overwhelm the capacity of the soul.

But before giving his definition of perfect health, he divides the ills of the soul into two groups: those derived from ignorance and those derived from madness. Now he says that there are two kinds of madness: that which is hidden and which consists in a chronic inclination and disposition towards madness, such as an eager tendency towards some disturbance or other; and that which is revealed by some disturbance which has been exaggerated beyond all proportion, as in extremes of greed, pleasure, fear, grief, or anger; or the vapours of the humours, being penned in by the limbs, cause black bile to issue from the combustion of the blood or the bile or the salty phlegm.

Now when he says that no one is evil by choice but by deformed nature and habit, you should understand him to mean that no one who has clearly perceived, at the outset, the misery which depravity brings in its train will voluntarily direct all his desires towards this end. You should also understand him to mean that the natural tendency could not initially be easily restrained through an opposing practice, but once that tendency has been strengthened by daily practice it cannot be in any way rooted out, but it can be pruned back by means of precise teaching and repeated encouragement.

He next teaches the care of both body and soul through the regular movement of exercise: I mean measured exercise and appropriate movement, properly directed to a particular benefit, so that both body and soul, being exercised and nourished, may attain such strength that neither succumbs to the other. Of course, Plato wishes the body to yield to the soul, but not to succumb to it in such a way that it is unable to endure the movements of the soul. He wishes the body to be strong and robust, yet under the control of a soul that is far stronger still.

Next note how much praise he lavishes on exercises, and how much scorn he pours upon the wrong use of drugs. Accordingly, just as he prescribed the exercising and strengthening of both body and soul through appropriate movements, so he advises us to maintain the three powers of the soul – the rational power, the wrathful power, and the desirous power – by means of movements specific to each one. He says that we should frequently nurture the rational power with sustenance, to prevent it from succumbing to the other powers, and that the intellect has been given to man as an inner daemon, for man already has an external daemon. Again, the upright posture of the body is like a tribute to the heavenly posture. He also says that the man who gives excessive nourishment to the irrational powers becomes mortal, as if he is explaining how his words should be understood when he says that man becomes a brute, that is, very similar to a brute.

He adds that the man who feeds his mind becomes so immortal that he lacks no part of immortality. For that immortality is imperfect which engages in perpetual movement, while that immortality is perfect which abides just as it is within that man who lives by intelligence alone and who changes from a man into a daemon. From this it may also be understood that, when he says that man is made into a brute, he does not say that he actually becomes a brute but he is using an analogy.

Moreover, when he adds that females have arisen from males, he may be obliquely referring us to that saying of Moses: 'Eve was brought forth from the man'.

But when Plato says that all the levels of the brute creation have gradually been increased in number by the rather serious fall of the rational soul, understand him to mean that our soul, through its unlimited power to move freely, is able, within itself, to plunge headlong into all the brute emotions and qualities and, outside itself, to be moved, through some divine operation of judgement, from the place of torment among similar brutish elements or their abodes. Again, all the gifts bestowed on lower forms of life are held in full perfection in the soul of man, and the souls of brutes within the very fabric of creation and generation are related to our soul as to their end.

If you accept such a movement of the rational soul into other souls and, conversely, this return movement of other souls back to the rational soul, you will perhaps not be far from Plato's meaning. For he himself, speaking through the person of Pythagoras, appropriately weaves a tale similar to the Pythagorean tales. But to prevent us from admitting these things as historical truths, he speaks of animal transformations just as the poets do. So take these in the same way and complete the book of *Timaeus* with that conclusion which teaches us to worship God before all else, for He has created all that is good through the sheer abundant goodness of providence.

I had decided, Magnanimous Lorenzo, to provide quite short comments here, as seemed to befit the main theme, and to keep many points for the fuller commentaries which we have called *On Timaeus*; but Filippo Valori, that most assiduous of Plato's followers, in whose presence I applied the finishing touches to the complete works of Plato in the countryside at Maiano, has obliged me to give my words unstintingly without further ado. Filippo Valori is the most noble heir of Valorian virtue. I confess that I owe so much to him because he generously nurtures all that is Platonic and all that is outstanding and because he feels a singular love for you and all those who are yours.

End of *Compendium*

The Chapter Divisions of the *Timaeus*
with brief commentaries
as given by
Marsilio Ficino

As far as this point there has been a
Compendium of themes related to the *Timaeus*.
There follow the chapter divisions of the *Timaeus*,
as given by the same Marsilio, together with
the first few words of each chapter
and brief commentaries.

[Translator's note: To relate each of the chapters in this section to the relevant part of Plato's dialogue, Ficino quotes a few words from his own translation of the *Timaeus*. To help the reader of the English translation, the corresponding Stephanus number, given in square brackets, has been added immediately after each quotation.]

Chapter 1: *Review of what was said about the State*
'One, two, three … ' [16e]
Socrates repeats what he had said about the State in the previous day's discussion.

Chapter 2: *A commendation of the State in remote antiquity*
'Listen, then … ' [19b]
Socrates wishes to see the State which has been verbally described alive and active one day. Critias gets ready to relate the account of a similar State.

Chapter 3: *Concerning the Athens of the Egyptians before the flood, and concerning floods in general*
'You speak truly ... ' [21a]
Before the Greek Athens that was flourishing at that time there was an Egyptian Athena. It was in this context that Solon received an ancient account of events that occurred before the flood. Note the world floods and fires, and ancient Athens before the flood.

Chapter 4: *Of the Greek Athens before the flood*
'Then, struck with wonder ... ' [23d]
The Greek Athens before the flood had been founded a thousand years earlier than the Egyptian Athens. Nine thousand years elapsed between then and the time of Solon. The wonderful exploits of the Athenians against the Atlanteans before the time of the flood.

Chapter 5: *Two cities called Athens before the flood*
'These things, Socrates ... ' [25d]
The State described by Plato actually existed among the ancient Athenians and Greeks and Egyptians before the flood. Timaeus, after calling upon the gods, prepares to discourse upon the world.

Chapter 6: *On the origin of the world*
'At the beginning ... ' [27d]
Since the world is in flux, it depends on another principle, which is unmoving; and since the world is very beautiful, it arises from an excellent intellect in the likeness of the eternal model.

Chapter 7: *On the model cause of the world*
'But the principle … ' [29b]
This world is the ever-fluctuating image of its model and of the constantly steadfast and eternal intellect. Principles related to things eternal are indeed steadfast, while those related to things in movement are themselves changeable.

Chapter 8: *On the efficient cause, the model cause, and the final cause of the world*
'Let us say, therefore … ' [29d]
Out of sheer goodness the finest intellect bestowed the finest order on the primordial mass of the world, which was otherwise blindly turbulent, to bring it into a likeness of itself, and endowed it with life and mind.

Chapter 9: *The world is a universal organism*
'Once this has been supposed … ' [30c]
The world is a single perceptible organism which includes all perceptible organisms. It has been fashioned in the likeness of the single intelligible organism which embraces all living intelligible beings.

Chapter 10: *Linking the elements*
'But since … ' [31b]
Fire and earth, being separated from each other by a solid (that is, three-dimensional) and absolute interval, required at least two intermediate elements to link them.

Chapter 11: *The indissoluble world*
'For these reasons ... ' [32b]
There are two reasons why the composition of the world seems incapable of being dissolved: it has been perfectly produced through the harmonious proportion of its parts, and it has been made with perfect physical ingredients in their entirety, with nothing physical left over.

Chapter 12: *Why the shape of the world and its motion are circular*
'To which the shape ... ' [33b]
The spherical shape was the most appropriate for the world, because this shape has the greatest capacity, the fullest equality, and the most complete nature. The world has been made internally harmonious, needing nothing outside itself and revolving ever at the same point, in the likeness of intelligence.

Chapter 13: *The soul of the world is prior to the body and is everywhere*
'But the soul ... ' [34b]
God diffuses the soul of the world throughout the universe from the mid-point of the world – that is, from the middle type in creation – from the centre, from the Moon, and from the Sun. The soul is prior to the body through the level of its power and the order of its origin, for the body clearly depends on the soul. It is right to consider that the world has two particular centres: the Moon and the Sun. The Moon is the mean between what cannot be produced and what can be, partaking to some extent of each; while the Sun is the mean between two sets of five, for above the Sun are Venus, Mercury, Mars, Jupiter, and Saturn, and beneath are the Moon in its elemental aspect, as well as the four elements, if the topmost stratum of air, burning with the motion and light of the heavens, is really said to be fire. The higher five relate to the completion of the forms of creation, and the lower five to materials. The Sun relates to both forms and materials, but the Sun is nearer to the Earth than to the firmament, since the earthly realm requires more of the Sun's blessing than does the celestial realm. From

the Moon and the Sun, therefore, He diffuses all the material gifts that have form.

But we have addressed the principles governing the arrangement and qualities of the planets in our commentaries on Plotinus, where he treats of celestial matters.

Chapter 14: *The composition of the soul*
'From these ... ' [34c]
The soul was composed from the indivisible, unmoving nature and from the divisible, moving nature, as well as from the intermediate essence, with all of these ingredients brought together into a single manifestation through perfect blending, that is, through musical proportion.

Chapter 15: *The shape of the soul*
'But now ... ' [36b]
The soul of the heavens was arranged within its living parts exactly as the heavens, which are its image, were arranged in their parts. The heavens have two axes in the form of the letter ✕, intersecting each other and directed towards four poles. Two of these poles are those of the firmament, and the other two are those of the remaining globes, which do not move in the same way as the firmament. These include the Sun, Venus, and Mercury, and as a group they move identically. The globes of the seven planets have six divisions, just as in the shape of the soul as previously described there are six intervals separating the seven numerical terms. Again, just as there are, within that shape, three double proportions and three triple proportions, so it is within the soul and the globes. This is why it has been said that there are three on each of the two sides, that is, there are three intervals in the double ratio and three in the triple.

Chapter 16: *The body rotates within the soul*
'Therefore, when … ' [36d]
The supreme and totally steadfast intellect created the soul of the world as the best of all moving things. Within the bosom of the soul it brought forth the body of the world, a body in perfect harmony with the soul, revolving in an orbit to match the orbital movement of the soul.

Chapter 17: *The universal orders, the types of understanding, and the spheres within the soul*
'Since, therefore … ' [37a]
Since the soul is harmoniously composed from the orders of all things and since it turns onto itself, it has no difficulty in appraising whatever befalls, directly recognising the forms of events within itself. Within the soul the sphere of Sameness is the intellect, while the sphere of Difference is the imagination. Being a thorough blend of these two, reason generates opinion and belief when it turns towards the imagination, but generates knowledge when it turns towards the intellect. And whether it considers indivisible essences or divisible essences, in both cases it understands the points at which they converge and those at which they diverge, as well as their common qualities and conditions or actions.

Chapter 18: *Motion, stillness, time, eternity*
'Therefore, because … ' [37c]
At the level of the intelligible world, stillness itself resides in unity. In stillness abides eternity. In the perceptible world, its multiplicity is followed by motion; and time, which is the image of eternity, follows motion. In eternity we consider three things in particular: a single act, steadfastness, and total Limitlessness. Time therefore strives to imitate that single One through continuity and a never-ending repetition of its own one; it imitates that stillness through the process of renewal; and it imitates that total Limitlessness through its own unendingness unfolded in orderly succession. That God delights in His work seems

to indicate that He made the world in His own express likeness through an effortless act of will and that His provision for it is made with equal abundance and ease. Plato does not think it is necessary for the heavens and time to have existed for ever or for them to continue for ever, but while one of the pair is present, the other will be, too. For just as three dimensions and a spherical shape are necessary for the world, so is the orbital movement that is produced by the dimension of time.

Chapter 19: *The distinctions of time; the motions of the planets*
'For this reason … ' [38c]
Time indeed follows the motion of the *primum mobile*, but this is distinct from the motion of those planets which are moved by the firmament from east to west, although they themselves move from west to east, for being turned round by their own winding obliqueness, as in a spiral, while wandering in various ways under the tilted zodiac, they turn now to the south and now to the north, now moving forwards and now in retrograde, sometimes further from the Earth and sometimes nearer. As means between the straight motion of the elements and the wholly circular motion of the firmament, it is right that they have been allotted a mean motion, that is, an oblique motion which combines something of the straight motion with the circular.

Those of them which are borne by a smaller sphere return to the same point more quickly, while those borne by a larger sphere return more slowly. And so those which return more quickly to their starting-points catch up with and overtake those which are slower in returning, and they catch hold of them in the way that the Moon clearly catches hold of Saturn. And they do this with that forward motion by which they revolve towards the east.

But anyone who sees only the westerly motion of the spheres, which they make across the firmament (yet does not even look up at their other motion, which is their own), and observes furthermore that in the morning the Moon is conjunct with Saturn in the east, while in the evening Saturn is closer to the west, though the Moon is further from the west, such a person will perhaps think that, in this daily course, Saturn has overtaken the Moon because it is revolving more quickly. This, however, is not the case, for Saturn, in its westward course, has not overtaken the Moon, but the Moon, in its own easterly movement, has with its faster motion gone in front of Saturn. This is why it seemed to be caught by Saturn, while in fact it was catching hold of Saturn.

The Sun, Mercury, and Venus complete their courses in almost the same length of time; but since some of them move more quickly than the others and some move more slowly, it comes about that this one catches up with and overtakes that one, on condition that it in turn is overtaken in its course. The power of Venus and Mercury is said to be opposed to the Sun, because their motion, alternately forward and backward, is opposed to the Sun's motion. The Sun brings forth what is concealed, while they do the opposite. Moreover, being subject to comparison, they restrain the incomparable power of the Sun and subject it to comparison. For Venus is the author of attraction and friendship, while Mercury is the author of proportion and combination.

Chapter 20: *The arrangement of the planets; the Great Year*
'But so that … ' [39b]
The Sun is the principal announcer of periods of time and, on the other hand, it measures the movements of the planets. It infuses all the heavens and the stars with light, I mean, the light which is manifest to the eyes. For these have their own natural light, which is hidden from us.

Indeed, the Moon, mother of generation, is very close to the elements, sharing with them a proportional relationship which is not insignificant, as well as something which is subject to change. The Sun, not having this relationship, is linked to them by the interposition of the Moon. In fact, this father of generation is related to the mother of generation; the primal heat is related to primal wetness; and the illuminator to what is illuminated. Aristotle calls the Moon a second but smaller Sun.

Through the moisture of the Moon the Sun begins the process of generation, and through the moisture of Venus it completes the forms of all that is capable of being generated. It is quite appropriate for such great heat to be the mean between such powerful examples of moisture. Next, through Mercury, put in authority over Venus and being the maker of relationship and complete combination, the Sun accomplishes a perfect blending of forms with forms and of objects with objects. Through Mars the Sun bestows skill in movement on all that has been blended and drives out any excessive moisture. Through Jupiter, which supplies life-giving movements as well, it justly directs and orders whatsoever moves. Through Saturn it grants stability to movements and steadfastness to all that is moved. Through the firmament it brings all this to fulfilment. Through itself the Sun bestows the innermost intimations as well as the external senses. In relation to the turning motion of innermost perception it supplies Mercury as an assistant, but to strengthen intelligence it has Saturn as a companion.

The Great Year starting from the time of the flood will come to an end when the circuits of the stars around the centre of the world and around their own centres are completed and all the stars return to that point of celestial longitude, latitude, and depth from which they began. Many say that it is composed of fifteen thousand solar years. Others make different assertions.

Chapter 21: *Four kinds of living beings*
'But now ... ' [39c]
The four kinds of living beings in this world are outlined in the very Ideas of the first life and the first mind. The stars are celestial deities, composed for the most part from celestial fire as well as from celestial air, water, and earth. Those that are called the fixed stars are positioned in the firmament and its uniform circuit, to which intelligence is related. These, together with the planets and their attendant celestial divinities, are called the celestial deities. Through the beings of air the daemons are denoted, and through the beings of water and earth are denoted both these beings themselves and the daemons which care for such beings.

Chapter 22: *The seven motions in the heavens; the ordering of the stars and the earth*

'But he gave ... ' [40a]

There are seven motions in the heavens: circular, forwards, backwards, upwards, downwards, to the right, and to the left. The spheres have circular motion only. The stars in the firmament make their circuits around their own centres, but in imitation of the firmament, as they turn towards the west, they revolve on a fixed centre. They are also said to move towards what is prior to them, for they are pulled by the sphere. They do not have the other five motions, but the planets have all of them, for they revolve on their own centres but, like a sphere, they turn, on these centres, towards the east. At the same time they move forwards, backwards, upwards, downwards, to the right, and to the left. But those which go on ahead towards the east as their natural destination are said to move in front, while the fixed stars, moving towards the west as their natural finishing-point, are said to advance. Every star, through its rotation about its own centre, imitates the action of its soul around its own mind, but through the pulling power exerted by the sphere it imitates the action of the soul around the higher mind. And just as they always have the same conceptions about the same things, so they always revolve at the same rate.

In fact, it is the uniformity in the motions of the firmament that bestows unity and regularity upon all that is lower. But the multifarious and opposed motions of the planets are conducive to producing, blending, and governing all that is characterised by multiplicity and opposition.

The axis of the world appears like a pole extending on both sides and thrust through the centre like a pivot. Around this the earth is tightly arranged, and present here is the soul which gives life to its celestial body and through this to the earthly body, too, whose living power they call Ceres and whose intellectual power they call Vesta. Vesta is the most ancient of the special divinities and daemons allotted to the remaining regions on this side of the heavens.

The Earth is like the whole world, for in its entrails are contained rivers of water, of air, and of fire; and it holds sway beneath the Moon, just as fire holds sway among things celestial. All things celestial declare the authority of the earthly divinity as they revolve around this pivot. And since stillness precedes motion, the Earth, being steadfast and being a unity from among the first limbs of the world, seems older than the stars which move and which were added later than the primal parts of the world.

Heavenly bodies are either in such harmony that they rise together or they are united as if on a perpendicular plane, and they sometimes obstruct each other so that we do not see them. Whenever they move forwards or backwards, being hidden by the Sun or in some other way, they herald many events once they make their appearance. But the stars indicate many things, yet do not themselves directly cause them. The Egyptians revered a star called Ach, which was not visible for a number of years, and they showed a similar reverence for Sirius, the dog-star of Orion, which appeared at intervals.

Chapter 23: *The genealogy of the gods and daemons*
'Of the others …' [40d]
After the gods that are visible in the heavens there are the invisible gods and daemons in the heavens and beneath the heavens. These are unknown to some, but were known to certain of the ancients who were divinely inspired. The gods and daemons beneath the Moon, being artificers of the world, now have the function of rightly attending to the birth and governance of all mortal creatures. The gods exercise intellectual and universal care, while the daemons have been allocated care that is focused more on individual life. They are distributed, according to their rank, throughout the upper air, the intermediate air, and the lowest level of air. They are, in fact, the natural offspring of the Craftsman of the world, but they have adoptive relationships among themselves, for those that exercise authority over others are like parents.

Just as Phoebean theologians are called the sons of Phoebus, while Mercurial theologians are called the sons of Mercury, so the gods and daemons beneath the Moon are called the sons of the heavens and the Earth, since they are enlightened and guided by the divine nature of the heavens and the Earth (which holds sway beneath the heavens), just as children are enlightened and guided by their parents.

The power in the Craftsman of the world is said to embrace all things and to move the heavens perfectly, but it is the Earth that acts as that which is steadfast. By means of these heavens and this Earth the gods and the daemons are given birth, and they all participate in both the heavens and the Earth. It is also by means of them that they have acquired skill in movement and distinct patterns in their movements. The first they call Oceanus, and the second they call Tethys. Through these they have the seed-principle (known as Phorcis), as well as the power (known as Saturn) to distinguish such principles and the power (known as Rhea) to bring them forth.

Beneath the Moon are bodies, natures, souls, and intellects. Saturn rules the intelligences, Rhea the souls, Jupiter the natures, Phorcis the bodies, and Juno the movements of the bodies. Such names would seem to signify various powers in the divinities rather than differences in their substances. That there are such divinities we have shown elsewhere; for just as there are rational living beings in the first and last spheres of the world, so there are in the intermediate spheres, in accordance with their nature. It is through these beings that gods and mortals, though far apart, are brought together, the changeable is regulated, and the accidental is directed.

Chapter 24: *The gods and daemons which are the servants of other gods in the process of creation*
'After they had arisen … ' [41a]
Although every compound is subject to dissolution, especially in those cases where multiplicity predominates over unity, the will of God keeps from dissolution those compounds in which unity is stronger than multiplicity. To whatever He makes closest to Himself He grants immortality, while through the gods and daemons He begets living beings of mortal nature. But it is He alone who sends the rational soul down from on high.

Now the gods and daemons beneath the Moon appear when they wish. They always possess bodies, but of the most tenuous nature, and they appear when they thicken their bodies and the light; or when they use their special quality to restrict the rays from our eyes or reflect them by their power rather than by their density; or when they bring our inner nature into harmony with themselves through the work of imagination; or when they illuminate and give form to the circumambient air. But perhaps it would not be going against Plato to say that one of the celestials appears from time to time in the form of a new star that portends wonders.

Indeed, the daemons which are the rulers of generation beneath the Moon have celestial bodies that befit them, as well as pure bodies of air, both being everlasting, and these daemons do good and are divine. But beneath them are the daemons whose bodies are made from an airy mixture; they are now like human beings, with bodies subject to dissolution, but they live to a very great age.

Daemons of this second kind sometimes deceive through their appearances, which the first kind never do. Among the daemons that dwell in the airy mixture the theology of the gentiles and the school of Plato number some that are brutes or similar to brutes, daemons that are wild in their imagination and of great strength. For just as the living being on earth is conceivably twofold, consisting of the rational and the brute, so it is considered to be twofold in water on those occasions when Orpheus and the poets sing of aquatic divinities; likewise within the blended air, they judged it probable that, in addition to the daemons living by the light of reason, there are daemons that resemble brutes, wielding their exceptionally powerful imagination to their utmost, so that they frequently move natures through their imagination, just as they move bodies through their own bodies. If this is how things are, we shall number them among those which do not deal with us on a serious basis but captivate children and fanatics with their tricks and games, attempt childish undertakings, and induce terror through ghostly apparitions. They move heavy weights and live for the most part amidst the filth of dark places.

It was my considered opinion that in October of this year, 1493, a daemon of this kind was detected in Florence, in a very ancient, dilapidated, dark dwelling belonging to the Galilea family. It had been molesting the servants for two months, and I thought there were many reasons which showed that it was like a brute, Saturnine, a dumb daemon, and an impure spirit. I therefore gave instructions that, after holy prayers and expiations, the whole house should be thoroughly cleaned, perfumed with selected fragrances, whitewashed, filled with light, and decorated, so that it would no longer be a dwelling agreeable to an unclean spirit; and that all this should be done on the day when the Sun came into sextile aspect with Jupiter, for I had learnt that the daemon had begun to harass the family the previous August, on the very day and at the very hour when Saturn was in opposition to Jupiter. When these directions had therefore been followed, that Saturnine and unclean spirit, which did not find clean, Jovial things to its liking, at once disappeared.

In December the following year a daemon similar to this one was driven out of the home of our cobbler, Francesco, by the power of God through exactly the same observances, which we directed. For men cannot do these things without God. This report is indeed true, but whoever is willing to accept an account of such great import in any way at all is nevertheless not at odds with the truth of theology but with the lower daemons, whether rational or brutish, which have now been sent on their way.

Let us return to the first creators of the pure air. For these daemons, according to Plato, are governed by the gods in the creation of mortal living beings, and at the same time they employ as instruments particular natures and the celestial power implanted in all things. The Craftsman of the world, at the opportune time, delivers to his ministers the rational soul which he has created and which has been presented to a celestial body as to a means of conveyance, in order that these ministers may unite the elemental body with an appropriate life, at first in a subtle way and then in a coarser way.

Plato declares that the rational soul is divine for three reasons: through its command over the body; through justice and the laws; through religion and the contemplation of the divine. But he directs mortal life, together with the body, to be subjoined to these. The soul, being undoubtedly given by God, is both rational and immortal. Life which is divinely infused through the soul into a means of conveyance is irrational but immortal. Finally, life which, through the soul, is diffused by the ministers of God into the elemental body, which is both subtle and coarse, is now both irrational and mortal: it is either destroyed or it is resolved into the lives whence it came forth.

Again, within the rational soul, sense is not subject to passion; it is one, and all are within it. In the life of the means of conveyance, sense is likewise one, but it is subject to emotion; in the life of the coarse body, sense is now divided among the instruments and is subject to experience. That this irrational life of the means of conveyance, together with the means of conveyance itself, is everlasting is stated by Plato whenever he says that souls come down from the heavens to these vehicles with some agitation, are purged of agitation in the lower worlds, and go their way by means of these vehicles.

When the soul makes use of the celestial vehicle alone, it has unbounded life and providence; when it avails itself of the airy vehicle, it has a life and providence that are less than universal; and when it uses the earthly vehicle, it has an individual life and providence.

Chapter 25: *The creation and distinguishing of individual souls*
'Having spoken thus ... ' [41d]
From the same mixture of original elements with which He created the soul of the world, God also created our souls, and He enclosed them in ethereal bodies, and He attached some to some stars and others to others. Those souls which eradicate the agitations of the senses while on earth fly back to their own stars. Those which are overpowered by bestial agitations continue to wander in forms similar to those of brutes, until they return to their stars, being purged once the mind has mastered the agitations.

But let us re-consider these matters in greater depth.

Since all rational souls are harmoniously composed from the general kinds of things and from certain specific powers and patterns, it is not surprising that the differences among souls arise from the fact that such elements are more pronounced in some than in others, and that they are more fully connected in some than in others. Another reason is that Unity, Limit, Sameness, and Stillness diminish at every step, while their opposites – Multiplicity, Limitlessness, Difference, and Motion – increase at the same steps, and thus, through the descent, complete the various levels of souls, which is why some souls are divine, such as the souls of the spheres and the stars, while others always follow things divine, these being the souls of the gods and daemons, which make universal provision in all the spheres of the world.

Other souls do not always follow things divine with such complete constancy, but on occasions, when they are going to make provision for generation, they descend from a higher to a lower level of contemplation, but without being in any way corrupted thereby.

Other souls, in some measure subject to corruption, slip down from there, but do so gently and therefore remain in the process of generation for but a short time.

Yet other souls, being subject to more serious corruption, are therefore slower in returning to the celestial realms.

There are also different levels of intelligence among rational souls, for there are all the mean points between the two extremes, that is, between the pure intellects, which always understand all things simultaneously, and the brutes, which, of course, review nothing at all with any kind of intellectual reason.

The first souls, however, embrace with a single glance all that can be embraced. The second group of souls comprehends fewer things, and every succeeding group likewise understands fewer and fewer, until we reach those daemonic souls which with a single look observe one thing, yet perpetuate rational intelligence in an unbroken, definite sequence. Finally, among the rational souls there are those which pursue one thing in particular with a single consideration and even, from time to time, refrain or strongly withdraw from intelligence.

There are further differences which occur among souls, for by the work of the Craftsman some souls were made suitable for some stars from the very beginning, and other souls for other stars; that is, souls themselves were made suitable for the stars, while their means of conveyance were made suitable for their bodies and movements. They equal the stars in number, but not on a one-to-one basis, for with every successive level the power diminishes in each one individually, while the number, in compensation, increases collectively. They are therefore equal in number because there are as many stars as there are types of rational, daemonic, and particular souls, but there are more souls within any one type of particular souls than there are souls allotted to the daemonic type; and all the souls which, throughout any sphere, are henceforth endowed with the property of that star and are named after it, vary among themselves according to how many powers there are within that selfsame star. They are also said to have been made equal to the stars in number, that is, similar to them by numerical proportion, for they have all been produced from the same types of harmonic proportion.

Now you should understand at this point that the stars are not only those that are visible but also those that are invisible, both in the heavens and beneath the heavens; for all are rulers of the world universally. They have bodies that are hidden from our eyes, bodies that are celestial, round, and shining. That our souls, endowed with a similar body, are like the stars is what Plato relates in the tenth book of the *Republic*. But to the extent to which God gave the soul a celestial means of conveyance, He brought no part down from the heavens in order to compose it, but He created the means of conveyance separately and specifically for the soul, to be equally everlasting with it, in order that the immortal soul might be linked to the mortal body by the immortal body: by the celestial, immortal body, I say, linked most closely to the airy body with its greater resemblance to the heavens, a body which is indeed mortal but which is endowed with a very long lifespan. Through this body the soul is linked to an earthly body of shorter duration.

Through its own essence the soul is above fate, that is, it is above the natural sequence of inconstant causes; but through its celestial conveyance it is within fate, and in all other respects it is under fate. Although some souls fall into the process of generation, they always maintain the natural property of their own star to some extent; but those which are said to be scattered onto the Earth have been made ready for the terrestrial divinities after those in the heavens. Particular souls, which find it difficult to accomplish all the requirements of contemplation in conjunction with the duties of making provision and raising offspring, are considered to practise each activity in turn, but the first one for the longest time.

All these souls are thought to descend to such things at least once in the Great Year, for otherwise they will never descend any more, but different souls quite often resort to different things; and it is quite common for those souls which take pleasure in exploiting their lawful position and their freedom of movement to be entrusted to the lower guardians, but less common are the souls which are more steadfast by nature and which are devoted to the higher stars and deities that are most strongly related to contemplation.

It is also thought that many souls, loftier than human souls, are perfected by the heavens, arise into the air there and enter into beings which live longer and more happily than we do, before finally returning in the same way to their own stars. However, they return more quickly to the same star than our souls do to the same intelligible and to precisely the same level of blessed contemplation. But when they have slipped down to our bodies, then they are said to pass into brutes.

Proclus explains that the rational soul never becomes the life of the body of a brute, but he says that, through a degree of compassion, it is in some way bound to the soul of a brute which has been brought down from above. This is perhaps similar to the explanation we often give when we say that the daemons do not in fact miraculously insinuate themselves into our bodies but enter our imaginations through their own imaginations. However, he rightly rejects the suggestion that the form of the brute body arises from the nature of the rational soul, just as no creature is derived from the nature of another creature, and no tree comes from the nature of another tree.

In short, the life-force in human nature moves only in the direction of the human, rational type and form. It is not fundamentally transformed as a result of changes in life-style. The only form on Earth equipped by its own nature to serve the rational soul is that which is restrained and upright, with tongue and hand as ambassador and minister to reason. No movement towards any other form on Earth comes to the aid of the imagination or nature. If it were otherwise, the rational soul would exist in vain, having no place where it could function and no place for repentance.

Chaper 26: *How souls are distributed among the stars and are then joined together on Earth*
'When these to those … ' [42d]
When God fitted the souls to the stars in the firmament and gave them instruction, He distributed them, at fixed intervals, among the planets, whence they might fall on occasion into the elements, when the remaining gods would temper the elemental body with the souls and insert irrational life, like a bond, between the elemental body and the souls.

Chapter 27: *How the daemons bind the souls to the bodies*
'And to these, indeed … ' [42e]
Because God abides in His own stillness while making provision, His ministers proceed in a definite sequence. The souls which have been received through divine agency make use of a body and a spirit exquisitely tempered on an ineffable principle, but in the regulation of its assemblage the circuits of the soul – that is, the intellect and reason – are impeded inasmuch as the soul is not turned upon itself and, while the lowest parts of sense dominate the soul, the being strays about upside down, with his head – or reason – on the ground. When it is said that our body is held together with numerous invisible pegs and knots, you should understand that the finer parts are infused by the coarser parts through an arrangement affecting the smallest details, to produce a perfectly complete creation, whereby the body, being moderated through some celestial resemblance, is prepared for the celestial soul.

The exposition given by Proclus is that the irrational soul is made together with the body, while the rational soul enters the body, but does not do so until the foetus is completely disengaged from all paraphernalia and virtually ready to move forward to serve the sublime soul with all its faculties brought to fulfilment.

Just as the soul and body are joined together so that neither fully masters or contains the other, because the soul does not transform the bodily nature into something different, and the body does not impair the nature of the soul, the soul does not restrict the body in its movements, and the body does not prevent the soul from rising up from time to time. On the other hand, the soul checks the body from unexpected disintegration, and the body keeps the soul from unencumbered understanding. The body generally draws the soul downwards by some force, while the soul buoys the body upwards.

Chapter 28: *The disturbances and difficulties experienced by the soul in the body*
'But when ... ' [43b]
When the soul enters the body, it is greatly disturbed for a long time, for it makes a sudden descent from a level that is full of light to a level that is dark and very different, into a body which is totally foreign to it, from calm watchfulness to sleep that troubles it with manifold dreams, which are continually aroused and provoked by the need for nourishment and sustenance, by the ebb and flow of matter, and by the passions related to the senses, as well as by novelties which induce a benumbed sense of wonderment for quite a long period of time. A distorted condition is thus formed, which would then hamper reason itself for a long time, if reason were in fact awake.

A disposition both hostile and unpropitious to whatever is divine affects both the circuits of the soul, that is, those things which stand apart from matter are so different from material items that whatever relationship the power of the soul has with the former it cannot have with the latter. Therefore there are deemed to be two powers that are related to these two: in relation to those things which stand apart from matter there is the intellectual principle, or that which creates knowledge through its intelligence; in relation to material things there is the imaging principle, which is like the handmaid of the senses and the mother of opinions. These are known as the two circuits.

The first is the circuit of Sameness, and the second is the circuit of Difference. The first is said to be hindered or bound or restrained by bodily misfortune, and the second is said to be pulled off course by it; for the first, belonging to things immaterial but being enslaved by things material in this life, deserts its function by and large and is therefore said to be restrained from acting, but not pulled off course so as to go astray, while the second is indeed pulled off course by means of false opinions. For we are unable to form correct opinions, and we have no access to right knowledge. Therefore, since disturbed imaginations arise, bringing in their wake false opinions and distorted ways of living, it has been said that the circuits of the soul are twisted from their true shape and forward movement.

You should understand here that the harmony of the soul conflicts not with that harmony which is wholly incontestable within substance but with that which is required in actions. You should also understand that excessive feelings within the body can hamper the rational movements of the soul, while feelings that are moderated neither hinder nor initiate, for once the riots of the body have been quelled the intelligence requires a discipline of instruction which will proceed by steps.

In infancy, as in sleep, there is very considerable exercising of the imagination as it follows the dispositions, services, and functions of the body. The needful work of growth – a work quite removed from intelligence – is also undertaken. Hence the action of intelligence and reason is in the main set on one side for a long time while the mighty causes of the disturbances eventually withdraw their power, and then the right vibration of intelligence and reason is struck up, especially when instruction is also being given. But if a wrong disposition has persisted to the very end, the mind is said to be crippled and maimed: crippled, because it is moved by sense alone, with reason in second place; and maimed, because it does not use the wings of intelligence. But to move to the lower world, that is, to the invisible world, is to be suspended in the air, as if in some kind of purgatory, where the transition into beasts is held in abeyance.

Chapter 29: *Contemplation and the pre-eminence of the head*
'But these things, indeed … ' [44c]
If man is considered to have been created for the purpose of contemplating, then his head, in which flourishes the spirit of life and which is the instrument of contemplation, is his principal part and is almost the whole of the man, the other limbs being like servants conjoined to the head. The head is like the heavens in serving reason, which has two circuits that are similar to the revolutions in the heavens. The various instruments in the face serve the senses and reason; the others uphold and carry the head, prepare food for it, grasp, and walk.

Man is a creature to be wondered at, being composed from the immortal and the mortal, for it was necessary to have here a creature who would worship the gods, a creature midway between the highest beings, which are immortal in body as well as in soul, and the lower beings, which are transient in both respects, a creature who is mortal in his body but immortal in his soul and who, for these reasons, not only descends to the Earth but also, while here, would subsequently imitate the contemplation of old as well as divine providence.

In brief, man is the whole world: through his intellect he resembles the firmament to some extent; through his reflective reason he resembles Saturn; through his practical reason, Jupiter; through his expression of both, Mercury; through his senses and imagination, the Sun; through his wrathful tendency, Mars; through his strong desires, Venus; through his invigorating nature, the Moon; through his means of conveyance, the heavens; and through his tangible body, the elemental realm.

Chapter 30: *Concerning sight, the eye, light, and images*
'But of all …' [45b]
The airy spirit, the instrument of the senses, is solar by nature. Its principal property is one of radiance, especially in the eye. Wherever its ray, flying forth with greater purity through the pupil, mingles with a similar external light within that part of the air in particular to which it is directed through the gaze, there it mingles thus with this light into a single type, and if it encounters anything which offers any sort of

resistance it is reflected straight back to the spirit and thence to the soul, and it renews its own receptivity to sight.

When it is constricted at night time, the spirit moderates and quietens its own movements, and dreams thus arise: faint dreams are born from faint movement, while many violent dreams are born from movement that is intense and vigorous. But these are to be found at a slightly deeper level.

Democritus, Heraclitus, the Stoics, and many Aristotelians and geometricians, together with the followers of Plato, think that vision is produced at a distance by a spirit or ray which darts forth from the eyes. We have given our assent to this, in company with Plotinus; and now we join the astronomers in re-affirming it. When the astronomers regard the Moon as comparable to the stars of the firmament and carefully reckon it to be in a straight line beneath one star in particular, they are revealing the trick played by ordinary sight.

Therefore let there be three stars in the same aspect of a sign which appear to our eyes as if they were arranged in a straight line, with the central star having one on its right and another on its left, and with the Moon perpendicularly beneath the central star. However, let three eyes that are far apart from one another observe from the Earth that conjunction of the Moon. Then the eye that looks up at the Moon diametrically, that is, in a straight line overhead, carefully calculates the Moon to be beneath the central star. But the eye that looks up obliquely from the left will see the Moon beneath the star which is shining to the right of the central one, since it is possible for the visual ray to reach there only when it is directed in a straight line, for otherwise it would break or, as I might say, be slanted. However, the eye that has looked up at the Moon from the right transfers it to the star on the left of the central star. This is similar to what happens to us with regard to many phenomena.

In this situation the astronomers relate the ratios of deceptive perspective to the rays which dart forth from the eyes. The natural fire of our body arouses heat, particularly in the vital spirit, and light in the airy spirit. This light it gathers together more fully within the eye as if within some translucent jelly whose fluid is very bright and whose membranes are thin and transparent yet strong enough to keep the light intact. Through the more substantial pupil an extremely clear ray shoots forth, whose single source was in a single nerve within, connected next by two small nerves to the two eyes. Now these small nerves, curving beneath the membranes and going through the thick fluids of the eyes, finally reach the pupils. The light, therefore, being kept intact by these little nerves and breaking forth with greater clarity through the narrow apertures of the pupils, immediately returns to a single ray (just as it began from a single ray) as soon as it has flashed out into rays on this side and on that, for the rays naturally unite into a single common ray, since the eyes, being united in their origin, turn this way and that way with an equal and like movement, performing these actions easily on account of a substance which is oily, smooth, and soft.

That a single visual ray is produced is not only evident from this common point of origin and matching movement but is also clearly confirmed by the fact that, whenever its unitary nature is split by a particular rolling of the eyes or by a compacting of the rays, whatever is presented appears to us as double. This illusion, of course, arises from the fluid and also affects the pupil, which sometimes divides. In the meantime these things confirm that sight is produced by the flying movement of the rays.

Yet it is impossible for our ray to move outside and to perceive at a distance unless it unites with the external light which comes to our eyes through a cone and to which our ray, making its way particularly to that point to which it is directed through the gaze, as though through an instrument or reinforcement, keeps on moving until it strikes something which is to some extent unyielding and which it itself resists. Then the ray, meeting this surface, becomes diffused or, with remarkable swiftness, as if in a moment, speeds off in different directions and is strongly affected by its quality. Within this kind of resistance, dispersal, and conditioning there occurs immediately the effect of sight, which happens when the ray is moved to and fro by these things and when this vibration gradually extends as far as the spirit of frontal vision.

In this way, if the nerve that is stretched out receives an impulse at one point, the impulse passes immediately to the whole nerve. Indeed, the stronger the ray becomes, the greater is the resistance offered by more solid objects, and the ray which now proceeds to the substance of the object will thereby perceive with greater certainty. But when the ray has been weakened by a longer journey, resistance will be offered not only by a thick mist but also by a thin mist and even by the air itself, and the ray, remaining caught there in whatever way it may be, surveys more distant objects in the form of their images spread out thus far by means of the light, and so it is now under an illusion.

Some followers of Plato think that vision at least is effected in this way, whether the faculty of judgement be accomplished externally or internally. Others think that, in addition to this kind of vibration, the shape of the object which is naturally implanted in the senses is aroused from here by the senses, and that this arousal constitutes perception. There are some who think that, besides this, the vibrating ray reaches as far as the eye, and there are others who think differently. More extensive treatment of this subject appears in the short commentaries to Theophrastus (*On the Soul*) and to Plotinus.

But some of Plato's followers, such as Democritus and Empedocles, found that the images of natural objects are not only formed by rays of light and the breath of life but are also composed of matter, for they flow forth through the channels of bodies and they preserve, for a certain time, not only the quality of the body but also its shape; and they work mysteriously upon a nearby person's spirit and imagination, especially if the imagination is weak and similarly fashioned. Such activities are particularly detected and noted by diviners.

Images formed by rays of light are touched upon by Plato in the *Timaeus*, the *Sophist*, and the seventh book of the *Republic*. These images have such tenuous essences that they are unable to reveal themselves openly to the sight except in reflective bodies. Being uniformly established, renewed, and illuminated, they receive a certain primordial power and the measure of the form from which they have come forth. Density is required to prevent an incoming appearance, falling upon an extremely tenuous object, from quickly passing right through it, and to prevent the non-formation of a single image from multiple effluences; but softness is also required to prevent roughness itself, with its mixture of peaks and troughs caused by its unevenness, from having to be constructed for the image.

There is also a requirement for splendid brilliance, so that the image, which would otherwise have a tenuous form, may become clearly visible, for in this way even the tiniest specks in the household air are commonly observable in the sunbeams coming through slits and cracks: specks which would otherwise be hidden from our eyes on account of their tenuous nature. The light has such a strong affinity with a mirror that within the mirror itself the rays of visible light, the images produced by the rays, are not even broken but they at once grow so strong that the light, being thus immediately intensified, illumines the wall opposite, and the visual ray not only sees the mirror but also, being strongly intensified thereby and as if darting forth from the eye once more, reaches things which are out of sight of the mirror and looks around. And the ray-formed image of the object, being brought thus far by the mirror and being enfolded by the rays, is now unfolded here in its pristine form and is perceived.

Now our ray-formed images come into being in mirrors from a combination of the general light and the form of the body which is conveyed by the light. But different appearances are produced by differences in mirrors, and angle and position play their part. In a plane mirror the right-hand side of the image corresponds to our left-hand side, and the left corresponds to the right, for the likeness, being prevented from further movement by the interposition of the mirror, turns back to face us, just as men, standing out of sight and speaking to you, have their right side in front of your left, and their left in front of your right; and in a similar way the visual ray is directed from our right to our left, and from our left to our right.

And if the mirror has a curved form, both its raised edges change the images at both sides, and they change the incoming visual rays in the same way, so that there is a reversal and transposition from the right of the mirror to the left of the mirror, and, conversely, from the left to the right. The earlier order being hereby reversed, the right of the image is now opposite our right, and the left is opposite our left. But if a rectangular mirror with raised edges is put before us on its side, with one of its raised edges at the top and the other at the bottom, it will show the images upside down, for the upper raised part will deflect the upper part of the image (and likewise the ray that is directed thither) to the lower raised part, and, conversely, the lower raised part will drive the lower parts of the image (together with the ray that is directed thither) to the upper edge.

Thus, since the visual ray that is directed towards a mirror is turned back from it and sees in front of it very many objects in accordance with the equal angles of incidence and reflection (as they are called) and at the same time reaches their images in the mirrors, why does it not seem to itself to behold two images with regard to the same thing? This, of course, is because it is deceived by the perfect likeness of the image in relation to the object. It is further mistaken when it thinks that an object is exclusively in the mirror when it sees the image of the object, although some say that certain images are not reflected from mirrors.

However, as Iamblichus and Priscian explain, Theophrastus, in his book on the soul, is in agreement with Plato, and Proclus demonstrates this in the sixth book of the *Republic*. But we deal more fittingly with this in the commentaries to the *Sophist*.

Chapter 31: *The final cause is the highest. The aim of vision*
'And these ...' [46c]
Natural qualities are not the causes of the creation, but are instruments of active providence, which directs all things towards an end that is both definite and good. And so the aim, for the sake of which the eyes have been made by divine agency, is the knowledge and imitation of the celestials, and philosophy is the best gift of the Godhead.

Chapter 32: *The aim of hearing*
'The voice, too ...' [47c]
The cause of the voice and of hearing is its divinely ordained aim: speech and discipline and the moderation of the movements of the soul.

Chapter 33: *The composition and originals of the world*
'So far, the works ...' [47e]
The world is composed of intelligence and necessity, that is, of formal order and material substance. The four elements are not its originals, for prior to the elements there are matter and, to some extent, the form into which they dissolve. Prior to these two are the divine and efficient cause, the model, the end, and the seed-principles of all these, within nature itself.

Chapter 34: *The first matter*
'But this ...' [48d]
From the mutual, repeated, and constant interchange of the elements with things elemental, two conclusions are demonstrated. The first is that a single, shapeless, and everlasting matter underpins all these as the support of fluid forms. The second is that such forms are not true substances but are the images of true substances or Ideas.

Chapter 35: *Matter and material forms*
'Three things at present ...' [50c]
The divine intellect is the father of the world, and matter is the mother of the world. The glory of the world is the divine offspring in the womb of matter. That matter may readily bear all forms and clearly reveal them, she herself must needs have no form of her own. For if she did, either she would not receive the other forms or she would bring them into disorder. The forms of the elements and of things elemental, being imperfect, depend on something external, that is, they depend on the specific Ideas of the divine mind.

Chapter 36: *Ideas*
'But concerning these ...' [51b]
Intelligence, proceeding on definite principles, being well-founded, and corresponding to little else on account of its vast superiority, is different from opinion or imagination, which is the uncertain, wavering, and common handmaid of the senses. To the same extent things imaginable are excelled by things intelligible, which are their ideal principles. And so the intelligibles have a truer essence than do perceptible forms, an essence which is so different that the fire here does not match that remote fire in nature, but merely in shadowy likeness and name.

Chapter 37: *A consideration of matter*
'The third kind ...' [52a]
Since learning usually comes about through some form and therefore surmises rather than understands that formless matter is always directed towards something with form, the mind, busying itself with material forms, is deceived, as in a dream, as long as it thinks that such forms, which are but images of true substances or Ideas, are the true substances themselves. Ideas are not in the object and, unlike material forms, are not blended together.

Chapter 38: *Chaos*
'Finally, these ...' [52d]
Just as, through some original order, formless matter is considered to be prior to formed matter, so matter that is not yet formed and set in unseemly motion through the intellectual soul of the world is considered to be prior to matter that is beautifully formed and guided through the same soul, which God has now endowed with intelligence.

Chapter 39: *How shapes are the beginnings of bodies*
'Firstly, because ...' [53c]
Solids resolve into planes. Planes resolve into triangles, for the triangle is the first of the shapes formed from a number of lines. But the triangles that are better fitted for making compositions are the isosceles and the scalene: the isosceles in which one angle is a right angle, each of the other two being half of a right angle. The scalene has a right angle, but the other angles and lines are unequal. Six scalenes comprise an equilateral triangle, and make three twos when viewed from any one of the sides.

Chapter 40: *How shapes are assigned to the elements*
'But that which ...' [54b]
On account of its inequality the scalene belongs to fire, air, and water, which are called unequal on account of their changeability. On account of its greater equality the isosceles is inclined towards the more stable earth. The three elements just mentioned easily interchange with each other through their common fluidity, but through the harshness and compactness of earth it is very difficult for them to interchange with earth or for earth to interchange with them. For while earth seeks a centre it shuns company. In the same way, it is very difficult for natural black bile to interchange with the other three humours. Saturn, lord of earth, does not mingle in the heavens; it is the same for the Saturnian and melancholic on Earth, and the same holds true for the Jews, as they are subject to Saturn.

Chapter 41: *Confirmation of what was said earlier concerning shapes*
'There will certainly be ...' [54d]
Fire is matched by the tetrahedron, with its four faces; air is matched by the octahedron, with its eight faces; water, by the icosahedron, with its twenty faces; and earth, by the cube, which is endowed with six faces. In the tetrahedron each solid angle consists of three plane angles, which equal two right angles. Two right angles are seen to follow immediately after the most obtuse angle, because if you continue to increase this angle you will soon reach a plane into which a line dropping perpendicularly produces two right angles. The shape which has eight faces, each an equilateral triangle, is compatible with air. In this shape, wherever four triangles meet at the same point, one solid angle is produced from the four plane angles; and there are six solid angles in the whole figure.

When you have marked out a scalene triangle within an equilateral triangle by dividing it from the top, understand that the longer side of this scalene, that is, the side above the right angle, has a power three times greater than that of the shorter horizontal side which contains the right angle. For if you set up a square on the longer side and a separate square on the shorter side, the first will be three times the second. The hypotenuse, that is, the line drawn under or subtending, is that which is produced sideways, as it were, from this side to that, and it is opposite the right angle, making the other two angles acute. And it is not less than double the side in length, for it equals the whole of the side of the first equilateral triangle. The short side is half of this. But if a square is made from the line drawn beneath, it will be equal to the two squares which are formed from the longer side and the shorter side. This is a discovery made by Pythagoras.

Enough of mathematics for the present. More is given in the *Compendium*, from which an able person will easily understand everything else.

Chapter 42: *The five shapes of the world. The distribution of the shapes through the elements*
'There is also a fifth …' [55c]
Since, in addition to the four shapes assigned to the four elements, there is a fifth shape attributed to the heavens, it seems that any one of these five parts may be called the world, especially as all of them are, in their own way, within each of the others. Earth is predominantly solid, thick, and unmoving. Fire, by contrast, is extremely rarefied, sharp, and fast-moving. The intermediate elements have moderate qualities in comparison with these two. Their shapes, which are somewhat similar, seem to be adaptable to each of the others.

Chapter 43: *The unchangeability of earth and the interchangeability of the elements*
'From all …' [56c]
Earth is quite unchangeable, and when it seems to be eventually reduced into the other elements – for example, ash under the power of fire or sand under the power of water – it returns to itself. When water is reduced into air, it doubles its bulk on account of its rarefied nature, and the same happens when air is reduced into fire. But the opposite happens in the reverse process: fire halves its bulk when changed into air, and air does exactly the same when changed into water. But since air is closer to fire in rarefaction than it is to water in density, air requires greater bulk and stronger compression for water to be

condensed from it; but this kind of deviation is counterbalanced by another, for air is closer to water in inertness and softness than it is to fire in sharpness and forcefulness.

Chapter 44: *The interaction of the elements*
'Finally ...' [56e]
A portion of fire attacks a portion of air in order to make it similar to itself. If this portion of air has low resistance, either it takes refuge in its own element or it turns into fire, seeks the location of fire, and no longer suffers at the hands of fire. The same principle holds true for the other elements.

Chapter 45: *The generation of forms within the elements*
'Bodies ...' [57c]
Within the four types of elements many kinds of seed-principles have been sown by divine agency, and it is undoubtedly through these seed-principles, assisted by the motion of the heavens, that the various forms of creation take their birth within each element and from the diverse intermixtures of the elements.

Chapter 46: *Why this acts upon that*
'In itself ...' [57e]
Why this acts upon that and attacks it is not on account of equality but on account of inequality, that is, dissimilarity of quality and difference of power. Fire is universal, for since it is the most tenuous and the most nimble it easily penetrates a coarser mass under the driving impulse of the heavens; and again, by springing back and following its engulfing nature as it penetrates, it increases in size.

These matters are treated in greater detail in the commentaries on Plotinus concerning matters celestial, but since the heavens are fire you will be able to conclude that its nature is universally celestial.

Chapter 47: *Metals*
'After this ...' [58c]
Flame is the intermediary between charcoal and light. Ether is the upper air. Earth that is well mixed with a great deal of fluid generates metal. On account of the abundance of fluid the metal melts under the penetrating power of fire. Through scarcity of fluid a stone does not do this. Air gathers with the fire in the melted metal. The fire leaves the metal more quickly than the air does, but eventually the metal, abandoned by them both under the pressure of coldness, is gathered back into itself.

Chapter 48: *The origin of gold*
'From these ...' [59b]
Gold is perfectly commingled. In the veins that produce gold which is somewhat less pure it is adamant, being lapis lazuli when it is less stable and copper when it is dirtier; and because it is dirty and badly mixed it breaks up into verdigris.

Chapter 49: *Hail, and suchlike*
'Other things of the kind ...' [59c]
The power of fire and air makes water less dense and carries it upwards. Here it is violently compressed by the cold, and in the same way things made of fine particles are squeezed out by the pressure: hail is formed in the air, and ice is formed on the Earth; but when there is less pressure snow forms in the air, and hoar-frost forms on the Earth.

Chapter 50: *Gums*
'But when ...' [59e]
There are four fiery types of fluids from plants: castor-oil, catapucia, gum, and the oil of its seed.

Chapter 51: *The production of stones*
'But of the earth …' [60b]
When water is compressed by frost, and earth is at the same time forcefully joined with the water, air being the bond between them, then stone is formed, but not if fire is present in great abundance. If fire, brought under the compressing power of frost, heats the fluid moderately and makes a perfect mixture, it will produce rather beautiful little stones.

Chapter 52: *Salt, potash, liquefaction, solution*
'But when …' [60d]
When fine earth mixed with a little fluid is compressed by cold and also scorched by heat, salt or potash is produced. When the earth in these mixtures far exceeds the water, they do not melt; but when the converse holds true, the poorly compounded mixtures are dissolved by water, the better compounds are dissolved by hot air, and the best compounds are dissolved by fire.

Chapter 53: *The effects of heat*
'So far, these …' [61c]
We observe that fire is hot because it creates violent divisions, which it effects on account of the fineness of its parts, the efficacy of its power, and the violence of its movement. This is indicated by its pyramidal shape made of equilateral triangles in which all the angles are acute.

Chapter 54: *The effects of cold*
'But the opposite …' [62a]
If cold fluid that is watery and somewhat earthy and thick reaches us, it puts to flight our own fluid, which is somewhat airy and fine, as if they were opposites. And so, to prevent the channels from becoming immediately empty, that thick fluid enters the narrow channels, and

because it has difficulty in moving through the impenetrable passageways it twists them, especially as it constricts our previously rarefied fluid and forces it into a confined space. And so it puts pressure upon it, while it itself is drawn forcibly and against its will to the entrance, with resulting numbness and trembling.

In brief, we judge something to be cold, not because it is ready to penetrate and dissolve, but because it has the power to deaden and compress. Trembling and numbness occur when the spirit, being forced into a confined space by the cold, is striving to expand once more.

Chapter 55: *Hard effects and soft effects*
'But hard …' [62b]
Something is said to be soft if it does not resist the touch, and hard if it does resist. Something hard is steady and dense; but a cube, with its six square faces, is steady and is similar to the earth, while the other elements and the things in which they are predominant are said to have triangular faces and are thus less steady and more yielding.

Chapter 56: *Why earth does not depart from its central position*
'But that …' [62c]
Earth never naturally departs from the centre of the world, because this alone is what it naturally seeks. Again, since the parts of the heavens are concave and similar to each other, they are equidistant from the centre. Earth is either opposed to them all equally or compatible with them all, or it is opposed to some of them or compatible with some of them. And so, choosing or shunning none of them in preference to the others, it has the same relationship with them all in respect of distance and intimacy.

Chapter 57: *Up and down in the world*
'If anyone in this ...' [63b]
Up or down in a spherical world is not in accordance with the principle of the world but arises from some comparison of small parts in relation to each other when they are moved by some power. Anyone forcing flames to move downwards will bring down a quite small flame more easily. If he is making clods of earth go upwards, a smaller one will go up more easily. For in both cases there is less resistance to that which is applying a weaker force. In the first case it will be seen that the greater the flame the lighter it is, while in the second case the larger the piece of earth the heavier it is.

Chapter 58: *Roughness and smoothness, and the location of the senses within us*
'Of these, therefore ...' [63e]
Something rough is hard and uneven, while something smooth is compact and even. The really earthy parts within us are scarcely affected by external things and report to the senses but little, if any, change, while the fiery and airy parts are very easily affected and are very ready to make their report, and the watery parts are between the two extremes.

Chapter 59: *The five senses; pleasure and pain*
'Moreover, what ...' [64c]
Sight and touch are very different from one another. Hearing tends towards sight, and taste towards touch. The sense of smell holds the middle position. Now the higher senses easily yield to whatever moves, and they have obtained a motive power that is quick and smooth in operation. This is why their perception is sharp, but they register little pleasure or discomfort. The lower senses, on the other hand, do not yield so easily to change but they have been assigned a forceful motive power; and for this reason their perception is blunter, but they often feel greater pain or pleasure. Indeed, the forceful nature of their perception obstructs the judgement made by the sense. The

intermediate sense, however, adopts a moderate stance towards all these things. When movement away from the natural condition is slow and easy, it does not entail obvious pain, but pain arises when this movement is sudden and sharp. When the return to the natural condition is sudden and full, it fills us with obvious pleasure, and the converse also holds true.

Chapter 60: *The senses and flavours*
'Now the common ...' [65b]
The channels proceeding from the tongue to the lower chest are open, so that the finest part of sweet flavours may bring immediate and full refreshment to the vital spirit of the heart, while the coarser part of those flavours, through the digestive process in the belly and the liver, refreshes the natural spirit. A pungent flavour and a sour flavour dry up and contract the tongue with their roughness: the former more so, the latter less. A bitter flavour and a salty flavour wipe the tongue clean: the former more so, the latter less. A sharp flavour warms and divides and goes upwards. An acid flavour penetrates with its slippery fineness and mingles with the humours: encompassing the coarser humours with the finer ones, it produces swellings. A sweet flavour – warm and moist – soothes the tongue, being well-suited to its nature. The Peripatetics of former times held that the power to taste had its root in the heart. Within these limits, taste is performed by the tongue.

Chapter 61: *Scent, and the sense of smell*
'Around the nostrils ...' [66c]
The very deep veins which serve the sense of smell do not have a full correspondence with the elements, even if the elements are thoroughly mixed. For they are rather constricted in the proximity of water and earth and anything in which these two predominate; but they are more dilated in the proximity of fire and air and anything that has the same rarefied nature, although they do have a closer correspondence with some volatile exhalations which waft up from easily dissoluble compounds, being coarser than air but finer than water. These,

therefore, the sense of smell distinctly detects, not perceiving them as complete forms or types and mixtures, but as mingled vapours of no clear variety.

In brief, smell has two main causes: the vapours of air and the fumes of water.

And since odour is coarser than air, when we draw in air through the mouth, the compressed air, flowing out quite liberally through the nostrils, does not allow any approaching odour to come in. Smell particularly affects those channels which run from the top of the head to the navel, and that is where the sense of smell is employed.

Chapter 62: *Hearing and sound*
'The third, moreover …' [67a]
Sound is a vibration of air, flowing through the ears into the veins that proceed from the head to the liver, and this is how hearing occurs. A swift movement strikes the hearing strongly with a high note, while a slow movement soothes it with a low note.

Chapter 63: *Sight and colours; the arrangement of the senses*
'There follows the fourth …' [67c]
Colour that is full of light is the object of sight. Colour is a variable participation in light, according to the nature of whatever is on the surface of the body, flashing out and being in harmony with sight. The transparent nature of sight is not moved by anything equally transparent unless this is coloured in some way; but it perceives anything more transparent than itself, that is, anything bright, as well as anything that is less transparent than itself, that is, anything opaque. Indeed, anything that gathers the sight is said to be black, while anything that disperses the sight is said to be white. An object that is fiery or really bright scatters the sight and melts the eyes. The fiery force, thoroughly blended with the airy force, produces something bright and gleaming. If water is mixed with these two, the result is red, but brightness compounded with red produces reddish yellow. All other things are obvious.

Let us end our words on the senses as follows:

The Peripatetics of former times said that sight and hearing have their source at the top of the head; smell, in the middle of the head; taste and touch, in the heart.

The later Peripatetics located all the powers of the senses within the heart.

Galen joins the followers of Plato in thinking that each sense has its root in the head.

And, according to Plato, sight is produced in the head alone; hearing extends its movement and effect as far as the liver; taste, to the heart; and smell, to the navel. Touch is produced throughout.

The words used earlier, however, — 'anything less transparent' or 'anything more transparent' than the functions of sight – may also be explained as 'more rarefied' or 'denser', the former with its scattering effect to produce white, and the latter with its gathering effect to produce dark colour.

Chapter 64: *The causes of the differentiation of forms lie with the gods, but the preparations are in the mixture*
'But if anyone …' [68d]
To know the causes for there being, under one universal form, so many kinds of forms, each with a great number of types, is the province of the world-framer alone, with whom reside the principle and authority of this unity and this number.

   The diverse mixtures of elements and compounds seem to be the causes that are necessary and preparatory to ensure that multifarious types are able to present themselves to us under a single kind of form. But the causes of this precise number lie particularly with God: the efficient cause is His power; the model cause is His multiform intelligence; and the final cause is His goodness, which wills there to be as many forms in the world as there are Ideas within itself, so that the world may be perfect and may convey the divine goodness. But, to achieve this, He seems to have ordained elemental mixtures as being necessary for the types.

Chapter 65: *What God does through Himself, and what He does through other agencies; the twofold soul within us*
'Just as …' [69b]
God formed matter that would, of itself, be perhaps shapeless and certainly misshapen, and He applied order to it. He alone made all that is everlasting. He accomplished the transient by means of celestial causes. He Himself created the rational soul. But the celestial beings created the irrational soul, which, within us, depends generally upon the heavens and individually upon our rational soul. It is said to be mortal because its actions are mortal and concern mortal things alone; and it does not exist for ever through its action, although it always abides within the power of the rational soul.

Chapter 66: *The twofold soul; the powers of the soul; the principal limbs*
'For the rest …' [69d]
The irrational soul is to some extent like an activity of the rational soul, the brilliance of the rational soul reflecting in a particular body as in a mirror. This brilliance is certainly quite dependent on our moon-like soul and on the sun-like soul of the Sphere.

Now it is quite clear that the rational power performs its work in the head; the wrathful power, in the heart; and the desirous power, in the liver. The wrathful power, being nobler, is located closer to reason. The heart is the origin of the very fine veins which dilate in the liver and of the very fine blood which is designed to generate spirit. The heart itself, the creator of spirits, is the origin of the arteries through which spirit flows, but the arteries spread throughout the lungs. The lungs, like sponges, soak up fluid and draw in air to cool the fire of the heart.

Chapter 67: *The liver, images, presentiments, and daemons*
'But since …' [71a]
On the liver – as if on something compact, soft, and bright – images are reflected from the powerful activity and disposition of reason and imagination, which is exactly the effect made by a pregnant woman on

her unborn child and is also frequently the effect produced by the daemons which devise portents for her.

The power of desire, being granted to the liver as if it were quite removed from reason, was destined to have movements that would never have conformed to reason if God had not supplied the liver with its own sweetness on the one hand and the bitterness of gall on the other. For that power, being far removed from reason, would be too hasty one moment and too sluggish the next if sweetness did not oppose the rage and bitterness oppose the sluggishness. Indeed, it is frequently the case that the noble spiritedness of the wrathful nature, aided by the bitterness of gall, contends on behalf of reason with the enfeebled softness of passion and idleness.

Chapter 68: *Prophecies*
'But what ...' [71e]
The author of prophecy is not God in conjunction with our reason, but God alone, once the habitual excursions made by our reason come to an end, for these excursions confound the divine manifestation within us.

Indeed, it is by divine agency that images are impressed upon the liver, and from here they are reflected onto the mind if it is properly unoccupied. But to discern the meaning of these images is the function, not of the person inspired by them, but of the wise and prudent man.

Chapter 69: *The amazing function of the spleen*
'Next to this ...' [72c]
As the spongy nature of the spleen absorbs the thick blood, it purifies the liver and is thus conducive to prophecy and joy. In this way it resembles the kidneys, which, being dry, absorb the internal oiliness and render the spirit clear and capable of understanding. Hence divine utterances through the kidneys often signify understanding.

Chapter 70: *The principle of the abdomen and the intestines*
'What, therefore ...' [72d]
When natural things and natural principles are mingled with those that are divine, they are not directly proclaimed to be so unless divine authority gives its seal of approval. Now the lower abdomen has been added so that any superfluous food that we have consumed may not remain in the upper parts, or waste or destroy its inherent qualities; the intestines, for their part, have been rolled back upon themselves to prevent the food that would otherwise flow down too quickly from obliging us, like geese, to quite forsake contemplation on account of a perpetual deep hole.

Chapter 71: *The three spirits and powers; the origin of the genitals*
'Of the bones, however ...' [73a]
The soul reproduces life from itself as its own glory and extends it into the body which is now appropriately equipped; and this life is held by spirits as if by chains. These spirits become established in the principal parts of the body. Indeed, the vital spirit thrives in the heart, while the natural spirit flourishes in the liver, and the life-spirit is active in the brain. These parts of the body, together with the spirits, are made from seminal matter. This is called the primal marrow, which is why the three principal parts are also called marrow, being hardened forms of it. And the marrow found universally within bones is of a similar origin.

Those three spirits spread from those three parts to permeate everything, which thereby comes under their rule. Triangles and rectangles are the principal components of composite figures. They are said to be gentle or easy, because they easily cohere to constitute planes. Matter and form, likewise and in the manner of rectangles, that is, on a right basis, are the elemental principles that have been established by divine agency and are perfectly ready to unite. In the same way, on account of correct inter-connections, they are in perfect readiness to provide the composition of all bodies.

Finally, living seminal matter is produced from those very subtle elements that lend themselves most readily to a combination where there is a preponderance of air, together with retentiveness and fertility, and where the celestial power brings all things to perfection.

From this are made the brain, as the spherical instrument of reason, as well as the heart and liver as the round yet somewhat elongated instruments of the wrathful and the desirous.

In the writings of physicians the bones and sinews are also called seminal parts. But this is certainly not true of the flesh, for it is in a state of continual ebb and flow, as are the humours.

Chapter 72: *The composition of bones and marrow*
'But bone itself ...' [73e]
In the composition of bones there is a preponderance of earth but very little impurity. There is also marrow, a denser portion of the seminal matter, acting as the catalyst for other things. There are equal measures of fire and water, but they are so perfectly commingled that it is difficult for them to be dissolved. Bones are thus very resistant to decomposition. From the concave bone of the head the whole structure of the bones acts as a protection for the marrow and the seminal parts of the body. The marrow in the neck is also thought to contribute in large measure to the preservation of the living spirit. The bones are not made to be continuous or uniform throughout the body, but they are variously shaped by means of joints, thus ensuring that the limbs are flexible.

Chapter 73: *The nature of sinews and flesh*
'But having thought ...' [74a]
Now sinews are made to bind the bones together at the joints; but flesh is made soft, moist, and warm. With its softness it protects the bones and sinews from external knocks and prevents the internal organs from being struck by the bones; with its moisture it protects the body from heat; and with its warmth it protects it from cold. In contrast to the flesh, bone is hard, dry, and cold. Sinew is of medium density, cold, and somewhat moist. Some saltiness has been given to the constitution of the flesh so that it neither dissolves through excessive softness nor putrefies; but it has not been given to the sinews, and thus they are prevented from becoming too dry and unsuitable for bending.

Chapter 74: *Natural ability and strength*
'These, therefore ...' [74e]
The nature that is related to spirit, sense, and constitution is predominantly airy, but it has been granted a measure of fiery vigour. It is therefore subtle and fine. In contrast to it, there is the nature related to the denseness of bones and to the bulk of flesh. And so, in that body and in that part of the body where this nature waxes, the first nature wanes; and that seed or that part of the seed which combines with the one does not combine with the other.

But since God made man for contemplation, his natural ability is greater than his physical strength. If you look to this end, you will put the brain before the heart; if you love the bodily form, you will do the reverse. The end, however, should be put before the form.

Chapter 75: *The composition of the head*
'Besides, our ...' [75d]
The right use of speech is as excellent as the consumption of food is essential. To provide a fleshy covering for the head it was necessary for the seed-matter from which the head and brain were to be produced to be thick, and hence it was that the spirit, too, had become thick, and also that the close texture of the head, which restrains the exhalation of vapours, had darkened the spirit. In the process of procreation, whatever was drier was gathered together from all the flesh that was in any way seminal, in order that it might give more secure protection to the skin of the head without adding much weight. But fluid, gushing through the joints near the neck, dilated this skin. However, the joints attached to the head are of various kinds, to enable the head and the jaws to perform a variety of movements; and where potential movements were in greater opposition, more joints were made; where the opposition was less, fewer joints were made.

There are, of course, different muscles in the head, in the face, and in the various parts of the neck, just as there are in the rest of the body, to enable opposite movements to be made.

Chapter 76: *The skin of the head, and hair*
'All this ...' [76b]
God, making convenient use of the nature of our warmth, which seeks what is above and is easily able to penetrate in all directions, made holes in the skin of the head and through these holes removed the fluid which the warmth carried with it. In fact, the finer fluid vanished, while the thicker fluid settled as a deposit. It was gathered by the cold of the air into hair, which is harder than skin on account of the external cold, the hair, I say, which, as thick as one of the apertures and as long as its vigour permits it to grow, is spread as a light covering over the head. And to make the hair hard there was no need for the fluid in the brain to become more resistant to sensations; in fact, it would be quite inappropriate, as the hair is sufficiently hardened by the external cold.

Chapter 77: *Why the limbs are so arranged; change*
'But those ...' [76d]
The arrangement of the limbs is as God decreed it would be, in accordance with the ideal model and for the sake of the best end, and this is the main cause for it, but a subordinate and accessory cause contributing to this effect is considered to be the nature of the active or material substance. Yet since God foresaw that some members of the human race would be women and that others would be like brutes, He made some limbs softer and others harder, so that some would be more suitable for one function and others for another function. Anyone who would wish for a different explanation should remember that Plato often plays the part of a poet.

Chapter 78: *Nourishment and plants*
'But since ...' [76e]
The burning heat of the heart and spirit, in which the life of the body precisely consists, would quickly melt and dissolve the body if certain parts of the body had not been made to absorb fluid from outside. Now the fruit of plants has been provided for nourishment of this kind. Plants have life and some dull sensation which in some way

registers what happens to them but which is unable to appreciate the qualities of the perceptible world. Indeed, plants have a natural desire of this kind, through which they are strongly attracted to moisture and warmth.

Chapter 79: *Mainly on the channels and sinews of the head*
'Since all these ...' [77c]
Beneath the nape of the neck appear two quite wide channels containing the central backbone and the genital marrow, which are led off from there and which moisten everything. These and other channels, going in different directions, enclose the head on all sides; but those on the right side of the head open out from there and extend to the whole of the left side of the body, while those on the left side of the head are transferred to the right side of the body, for it is in this way that the connection between the head and the whole is made tighter and the flourishing power of sensing that is within the head is easily spread from each side of the head to fill the entire body. But the sinews do not move down with this kind of crossover and interweaving.

Chapter 80: *Spirit, heat, movement, digestion, veins, arteries*
'What from the smaller ...' [78a]
Natural heat finds its kindling material within the heart, as does spirit, the blood-infused vapour produced by this heat from the finest part of the blood; and both the heat and the spirit pervade the entire body with astonishing efficacy and subtlety. Because the spirit is life-giving and is produced by the opening and contracting of the heart, it circulates perpetually, moves to and fro through all the passage-ways, continually engenders heat through its movement, and conveys the heat throughout the body.
It heats the nourishment in the stomach, breaks it down, digests it, and conveys it to the liver, where it digests it further into the bloodstream. It then matures the blood within the veins, conveys the matured blood to the limbs and imparts nourishment there through a process of individual distribution.

Through the arteries and veins the spirit, together with the heat, passes into the whole body. It fills the veins with the thicker blood, and the arteries with the thinner blood. In both veins and arteries the spirit is within the blood. In the veins there is a great deal of blood but very little spirit, and this is the natural spirit. In the arteries the blood is scanty but the spirit abounds, and this is the vital animating spirit. The veins and arteries are all interwoven and resemble a circular net or tangle. One web, in which there are a great many arteries, extends from the mouth to the chest; its two ends, brought close together, are attached to the nostrils. The web in which veins predominate goes from the mouth to the abdomen and spreads into all the cavities of our body. The web that extends throughout the body contains a great deal of air and fluid; it keeps the vital heat within the boundaries of the body. Through these conduits, as it were, the hot spirit flows continuously to and fro, kept in circulation by the incessant movement of the heart. It manifests in the pulse, and it conveys the blood and the nourishment.

Chapter 81: *The function of the lungs and of the outward and inward breaths*
'But let us see ...' [79a]
Through their movement the lungs expel the warmer vapours and draw in the colder air to cool the inner fires. The breath emitted through the mouth drives away the cold external air that is close to it and regularly carries with it the internal air. And so, to ensure that the chest does not happen to become empty, the external air finds its way into us through any channels; and since the air is in turn expelled from the body or leaves it in some other way, we are obliged to take it in again by breathing through our mouth and nostrils.

Chapter 82: *The outward and inward breaths*
'All of the whole ...' [79d]
For us, there are two breathing cycles that occur unceasingly: the universal and the particular; for the hot air that is confined in the veins along with the blood seeks greater space, and so, looking for the airy

element that has an affinity with itself, and at the same time turning towards the sphere of fire that is similar to itself, it always breathes out through the whole body. To ensure, therefore, that the body is not left empty, the circumambient air flows back into us from all sides and, being straightway heated, it once more seeks the world outside. Conversely, the cold air outside seeks the most inward parts. Through a similar kind of reciprocity, panting produces a particular cycle, breathing out hot air and breathing in cold air, while nature providentially shuns a vacuum in all situations.

Chapter 83: *The movements of nature which prevent a vacuum*
'But, indeed, the causes …' [80a]
Air very quickly escapes from cupping-glasses which have been heated, and therefore, to prevent the occurrence of a vacuum, the air that is deep within us moves into the cupping-glass and draws with it the moisture and the skin.

If you place one end of a tube in water and the other between your lips, then the more air you draw in from the tube, the more water you will suck up, so that a potential vacuum is forestalled. To some extent this is the same principle which enables little children to suck milk.

Once you have thrown a pebble, not only does the force you have expended propel it, but the air, too, quickly follows from behind, so that the space from which the pebble moves is not left empty.

In a similar way, once you have expelled the vocal air through singing, the faster the air moves forward the more quickly does the air behind follow to prevent the occurrence of a vacuum.

If you breathe simultaneously into two tubes – one of them being a narrow tube and the other having twice the diameter – a quick movement giving a high note will be produced from the first tube, while a slow movement giving a low note will be produced from the second. That fast movement through the air will exceed the slow movement both temporally and spatially. And so, unless the slow movement catches up with the fast movement, there will be a vacuum between the two. To prevent this, therefore, nature slows down the fast movement and at the same time speeds up the slow movement, so that at the point where they are able to touch each other a single movement, as it were, is produced from both of them, and similarly, from the preceding high note and the subsequent low note there arises a single harmony, while both notes continue to sound in exactly the same way at the limit of their range.

Chapter 84: *What marvels happen in opposition to a vacuum; digestion*
'The same principle is …' [80c]
When water is once drawn up through a tube, the rest of the water follows in an unbroken sequence, to prevent a vacuum.

On a similar principle, when wind which has been confined by clouds together with oppressive heat has been driven downwards, it is followed immediately by the astonishing violence of a thunderbolt.

A magnet and iron are naturally affected in such a way that they react strongly upon each other, giving off heat and energy, by which the air, being driven from both sides towards them both, is first of all forced into a confined space between them but soon escapes into unrestricted space. To prevent a vacuum, therefore, the iron is moved to fill up the air immediately. The magnet is not moved, because, acting quite strongly upon the iron, it has set in motion the air that is next to the iron and has forced it out. The same thing happens with amber in relation to chaff.

The incessant movement in the innermost parts of our bodies produces heat and conveys it, to digest and refine the nourishment before transporting it to the limbs; and on account of the different mixtures and the different degrees of digestion it imparts different colours to the fluids and limbs. It makes the blood red on account of the heat, which is moderately dominant in it, and the fluid is thereupon purified and fully digested.

Chapter 85: *Outflow and inflow; growth and diminution*
'But the way …' [81a]
The subtle elements take refuge within us partly by choice and partly because they are drawn towards the grosser elements. In the same way, things that are fiery within the blood are conveyed to the fiery parts of our body, the airy to the airy, the watery to the watery, and the earthy

to the earthy. And so whatever has departed is now restored to us: if more, the body grows; and if less, the body diminishes.

Chapter 86: *The structure of our body, as it were by means of triangles, its duration, and its dissolution*
'Therefore, the recent …' [81b]
The mathematician first resolves a solid into planes, then a plane into triangles that are usually equilateral, having no right angle, and thirdly into right-angled triangles, which are the first basic elements of such shapes.

In the same way, the doctor divides the body first into parts such as the entrails, the head, the arms, and the legs, then every portion of these, as far as is possible, into its constituents, such as the bones, the sinews, and the flesh – these are like the secondary or equilateral triangles — and thirdly, each of these into the four humours, like those primary scalene but right-angled triangles. But in all the compounds the parts, like the secondary triangles, are strongly related to the whole, whereas the primary triangles are the elements, the elemental material, and form.

The body of the young child is very tender, because it is composed of tender seed and of milk; and yet it has that very strong structure by which the four humours, the constituents of the principal parts, the bones, the sinews, and the flesh are all inter-connected. Since this inter-connection has been forged only recently from the life of this world and the power of the heavens, it still preserves and maintains strong contact with the energy of this world and of the heavens. It is by this power that it directs the different types of nourishment to the appropriate parts of its own body; but, growing weak in the course of time, it does not so much subdue the nutrients as become subdued by them, and yet it grows weak insofar as the primary proportion of its parts comes to rely more and more on the other parts and on the whole, and as the primary proportion of the whole comes to rely more and more on the heavens.

Now these inter-weavings, mixtures, and proportions are called the bonds of the soul, because they have been forged by the universal soul and the individual soul and because they seem to keep the enlivening soul, which is inclined towards a body, within the body which is thus affected and, as it were, in agreement. When these bonds are finally loosened, the soul ceases to enliven the body, which is, so to speak, no longer useful. Such a change of abode, which occurs gradually through a single, lengthy, and natural process of unfastening, brings no distress to the soul and no torment to the body.

Chapter 87: *The humours, the limbs, the veins, and the arteries*
'But diseases …' [81e]
Each of the four humours is composed of the four elements, but bile is described as fire because most of it is fire. In the same way, blood is called air, phlegm is called water, and black bile is called earth. But first of all within us there is the blood that grows strong from the true initial digestion which takes place in the liver through heat and moisture: this blood is the chief friend of life. It is also abundant and contains the other humours. From it the other parts of the body are nourished, and from it arises spirit. But the way it is produced from the elements is said to be different from the way the limbs are produced, for the forms within it remain separated as the four elements; but this is by no means so within the limbs, where the elements are quite thoroughly mixed.

To maintain a good bodily condition, so to speak, eight parts of blood are required, together with four parts of phlegm, two of bile, and one of black bile. Again, to make the blood perhaps one degree warmer and moister, or perhaps to make it just a little warmer, the bile needs to be three degrees warmer, and the phlegm three degrees wetter, for this seems to be how the moisture of phlegm and the heat of bile are related to the temperature of the blood.

The thicker blood is found in the veins, the thinner blood in the arteries. The fine phlegm that is indispensable to us flows beneath the blood in the veins for the purpose of moderating or refreshing the blood. Red bile, like thin blood, flows to the same place, and black bile, like salt of tartar, will remain there, too. Now all these things are needed in the blood, to maintain its proper balance and to provide nourishment for the parts that are akin to them. The thicker phlegm is found at the base of the abdomen; yellow bile is found in the gall bladder; and black bile, which disagrees with the blood, is found in the spleen: all of these, too, have their respective uses.

And so, insofar as the body abides in its original condition, which is natural to it, in accordance, that is, with the quantity and quality just described, and insofar as everything is in its proper place, it enjoys good health; but otherwise, it certainly does not.

Chapter 88: *Veins, capillaries, sinews, marrow, and nutrition*
'When, clearly …' [82c]
Throughout the body, capillaries are connected to the sinews from the veins. Through these capillaries the blood that is fine yet viscid flows from the veins for the purpose of renewing the sinews. But the softer constituents in this blood abound and soon overflow, to be condensed into flesh. Again, the fatty, more viscous constituents that are more than the sinews and flesh require make cartilage. When some dry, viscous substance is still left over, it nourishes the bones. Finally, because it is within all the bones, like a very fine, very soft oil and very similar to the first seed, it is called triangular, or elemental. And it flows through the narrowest apertures of the bones and, once within, congeals into marrow. This marrow softens the hardness of the bones; sometimes it renews the reproductive seed, and sometimes it refreshes the principal limbs; either it flows out through the middle of the bones or it seeps out through the holes in the bones.

Chapter 89: *How bad humours are produced*
'But the bad things …' [82e]
A natural movement occurs when moisture, issuing from the veins, condenses into flesh, but it is unnatural for flesh to relapse into moisture, to flow back into the veins in its dissolved condition, and, infecting the spirit and the blood with its rottenness, to produce bitter bile, acidic or salty phlegm, or black bile from yellow bile.

Chapter 90: *The production of bad humours*
'For the portion ...' [83a]
Old flesh, that is, the flesh that has been used up in the limbs and is sometimes dissolved by some kind of external heat and taken back once more into the veins, being black through heat and bitter through heat and decay, cannot be digested once again in the veins; but one part of it turns from bitter to sour when the sharp parts contributing to the bitterness have been dissolved, and black bile of this kind within the veins is contrary to nature; the other part does not suffer dissolution but undergoes some mixing with the blood. And in this way it is made somewhat red with the bitterness, but at the same time it is made dark by the bilious colour, and the result is thick bile.

But when the new flesh, that is, a part of the fourth distribution assigned to the flesh, quickly dissolves, perhaps through any external heat of generation, it flows back into the veins as yellow bile, and if it ferments once more it becomes black bile or green bile.

Chapter 91: *The different ways in which bad humours are produced*
'Blood, moreover ...' [83c]
If the fine part of the blood sinks down in a putrefied condition, there is no taste and no serious illness. If the thick part of the blood, which is said to be the natural black bile, dissolves through putrefaction, it is more serious and generates sour phlegm. If it becomes warm, it produces salty phlegm.

Sometimes the more tender flesh – the part of the blood required to produce flesh – having more moisture than is required by the flesh that is to be renewed, putrefies in the veins as a tepid warmth stirs up maximum moisture and fills them with wind and bloating. From this is produced phlegm that is white, viscous, and sweet, fine phlegm being produced every day, and while it oozes out through sweat and tears after being thoroughly mixed with the blood, it has a salty or bitter quality, for it is readily subject to heat on account of its fineness.

Chapter 92: *Bad humours, diseases, and fevers*
'And these …' [83e]
When he says 'any flesh' he means either solid flesh or its fatty tissue, or the matter that seems to be prepared for this. When a part of the flesh that is further from the sinews is slightly weakened, it is easily renewed; but when a deep part of the flesh in contact with a sinew suffers, then the sinew, which connects the flesh to the bones, dries up and also suffers.

However, the flesh becomes utterly languid when the nourishment conveyed to it by the veins is so earthy and dry that it is not fit for flesh or sinew; as a result, even the bones become extremely dry, and the weakened flesh is, as they say, regurgitated back to the veins. Sometimes the tiny holes in the bones become compressed or blocked, so that they can neither emit the heavy exhalations nor admit the nourishment. Thus a bone which lacks moisture and is consequently devoid of both natural and external heat, having putrefied, will relapse into flabby material like flesh that has been, as it were, overcome. But this, as we have said, flows back to the veins.

This is quite a serious condition, but it becomes very serious when the state of the marrow which is inside the bones or the state of some principal limb becomes weak through excess or deficiency or poor quality. So far, consumptive fevers have been pointed out, which at their first appearance quickly destroy essential moisture from the veins as if by perspiration. At their second appearance they heat and destroy the essential moisture that is close to the limbs; and at their third appearance they destroy the very substance of the limb. And on recurring, they destroy flesh at their first appearance, sinew at their second appearance, and bone and marrow at their third appearance.

We have also pointed out the putrefying fevers which are associated with the consumptive fevers and are subsequent to them.

Chapter 93: *Diseases arising from an impediment in the spirit and the act of breathing*
'The third after these …' [84c]
The heart is the main source of the spirit, which is the quintessential exhalation of the blood. But the lungs are the receptacles of the attendant spirit, which is the breath. In the lungs there are tubes, and if

these are blocked the internal fire is not given out and the external cold is not taken in. Deep sighs and fevers follow. But since the mouth and the nostrils are meanwhile striving strenuously to breathe in more air, and yet the air, being moderated on its journey, cannot make its way into the passages that go down to the chest, that is, it cannot make its way into the arteries and veins of the network and cartilage which separates the parts pertaining to the spirit from the parts that are natural, the person therefore breathes in and tosses about in a sweat, frequently driving the fever into the spirit, and this fever is called ephemeral.

Chapter 94: *Wind, the gut, and colic*
'Frequently, too …' [84e]
Within the wider channels in the flesh, wind is often produced from a modicum of heat and a greater quantity of fluid. Not being easily able to break out, it troubles us with colic, but it is more excruciating when there is inflation within the actual channels of the sinews and the nearby veins, for then, on account of the continuity between the sinews and the veins, it contorts the front and back of the body simultaneously. It is a wretched disease, to be terminated by fever alone, either with life or to the limit of life.

Chapter 95: *Diseases and pains related to phlegm*
'But white …' [85a]
If phlegm that is white and sweet thickens and becomes swollen from trapped wind, it causes serious distortions in the intestines and other internal organs. If phlegm that is finer is driven towards the skin by heat, it discolours the skin with white spots. If phlegm that is more viscous mixes with black bile and is taken up by the heat to the front parts of the head, blocking the channels of the brain and checking the movement of the vital spirit, it causes epilepsy: less serious if it occurs only in sleep but more serious if it also happens during the hours of waking. Sour phlegm produces rheum that upsets the stomach, whereas salty phlegm produces rheum that is harmful to the chest.

Chapter 96: *Pains and diseases related to bile and blood*
'But whatever ...' [85b]
If pungent bile finds its way to the skin, it causes red swellings, but if it is confined in the internal organs it produces hot abscesses and fevers that are very similar. If it becomes thoroughly mixed with the fine blood in the veins, it sometimes oozes out from the veins, together with the fine blood, and trickles into the capillaries, which are like fine veins and which are inter-connected, in all parts, with all the veins and the sinews, being made for this purpose, so that through their narrow passage-ways they can absorb the finer blood and convey it, drop by drop, to other parts of the body. If this were not the case, blood of this nature, flowing away through the rather scattered passage-ways of parts of the body, would suffer or cause destruction. The thicker blood, too, being forced out through narrow channels of this kind, becomes thinner and purer, and flows around with less encumbrance. If the capillaries are tensed, the fluid of the blood is pushed out forcibly; if they are relaxed, it is squeezed out more gently. Therefore, when the bile, flowing forth from the veins or oozing out from parts of the body, becomes mingled with the pungent blood and flows with it into the capillaries, it is firstly compressed, as it were, by their narrowness, produces tremors, and distorts the capillaries, and secondly, if nature prevails, it is gradually forced out in the form of exhalations, discolorations, and sweat, or, if nature is overcome, it harms the marrow and the principal parts of the body, which are the bonds of the vital soul. Alternatively, if nature prevails in part and at the same time is overcome in part, it flows out in different directions through the remaining internal organs and causes hot diseases and fluxes.

Chapter 97: *Types of fevers and humours*
'When therefore ...' [86a]
When the humours are inflamed by the putrefaction in the veins, there also occur the fevers which we call putrid, not those subsequent to consumption, but those prior to it.

If the fever occurs through an excess of fire, that is, an excess of the most pungent bile or blood heated through being near to the pungency of the bile, it is incessant, and it maintains the same uninterrupted course.

If the fever is produced by an excess of air, that is, an excess of slightly thicker blood, it, too, causes continuous distress, but sometimes it is less aggressive and then it appears to be interrupted in its course.

If the fever occurs through an excess of water, either this is thick phlegm and is a daily burden, although it seems to become lukewarm within some six hours, or it is very thin phlegm which combines fully with the bile: it does not allow the bile to escape, but retains it and causes it to decompose, the result being tertian fever, which varies according to the balance in the mixture. Some consider tertian fever to result from pure bile, while Plato relates it to the first type, judging that, if the bile is pure, it will rage deeply and continuously, like fire.

Finally, the fever that makes a rather slow attack from black bile recurs on the fourth day, being positioned, of course, at the fourth level of the elements, just as fever from water recurs on the third day, being placed, as it were, at the third level of the elements. Fire is in constant movement in the world; less commonly do gales rise up into the air; floods recur at even greater intervals; and earthquakes recur very infrequently. The same applies to the fevers associated with the elements.

Chapter 98: *Mental illnesses and delusions; marrow and seed*
'But of the soul …' [86b]
Mental illness is of two kinds: ignorance and madness. Madness is also of two kinds: the first type is concealed, a state of body and spirit which is somewhat inclined to madness, that is, to some uncontrolled disturbance; the second type is obvious, being induced either by quite violent disturbances or by exhalations of black bile. From the burning of blood or bile or salty phlegm this black bile falls upon a perverse state; the decline occurs not so much through a choice made by the primary will as through a tendency of nature, through irregularity of upbringing and custom, and through ignorance. However, this tendency could have been eliminated from the beginning, and the condition can to some extent be moderated.

There is an ancient secret: in the channels of the bones, as if in some highly fortified shelter, the treasure of life is preserved, that is, the marrow, consisting partly of the primary seed, which is like leaven, and partly of the purest constituent of everyday food, the constituent that is very similar to the primary seed. From this marrow a drop is distilled, to ferment the seed which will make its way to the testicles. And when there has been no nourishment for a long time, some moisture oozes from it to refresh the principal parts of the body. But generally the reproductive seed that remains from the fourth stage of digestion is infused, like marrow, into all the parts of the body.

Imbalance of combination, humour, and exhalation can be injurious to the power and living spirit of the brain which serve the temperament, or to the vital spirit which is in harmony with the spirited nature of the heart, or to the natural power of the liver which complies with natural desire. In the first of these conditions the imbalance produces delusions, forgetfulness, or dullness; in the second, ferocity or timidity; in the third, a state that is either wayward, difficult, and sad, or else incoherent and delicate.

Chapter 99: *How the strength of character and physique should be tempered to suit the life*
'But of these …' [87c]
It sometimes happens that, from the horoscope and from the influence of the heavens, the living spirit, which is there to serve the imagination and temperament, is robust, while the body is weak. On the other hand, it often happens that the physique is robust, but the spirit is weak. Of course, individual upbringing and training can strengthen either of these.

If the spirit is in some way made impetuous, it undermines the weak body through its violent movements. Conversely, if the body is made stronger either by nature or by practice, it completely masters the spirit through its vigorous movements and makes it weak.

In brief, health of body and health of mind cannot co-exist unless they both harmonise with each other in due proportion, whether this be a natural state or whether it be attained through practice.

Chapter 100: *How temperament, simultaneously with the body, is to be nourished and kept in constant movement*
'Finally, together with …' [88b]
We should sensibly nurture both body and soul with appropriate nourishment and exercise, thus causing them to grow and become stronger. By regulating the body with gymnastic exercise, the soul with philosophic exercise, and the spirit – the link between soul and body – with music, we shall regulate both body and soul simultaneously. We are completely changed by all that surrounds us and all that is taken within, through the strength of the impulse and through the efficacy of its qualities. And so, to avoid succumbing to these influences in a merely passive way, we must constantly resist them by striving to regulate our own movements, thus imitating the universal nature of the world, which revolves in unceasing movement.

Chapter 101: *Types of movements, drugs, length of life*
'But of all …' [89a]
The best movement is that by which everyone moves himself, imitating the intelligence and life of the world in which we live and move and have our being. An inferior movement is that by which one is moved as if by another and external mover, while still moving oneself to some extent. The worst movement, however, is when one has taken in a violent moving force, such as a drug, oneself being quite inactive under the power of this force.

A particular duration of life has been assigned to the horse, another to the goose, and a third to man. Again, a particular length of life has been allotted to one man, and a different length to another man. In fact, our triangles, by which are meant the principal constituents of our body, or the four humours, together with the respective parts and qualities of each seed-part and the seed-parts themselves, came together from the very beginning as the result of a particular mixture and temperament and an amazing inter-relationship, under the regulating power of both the seed and the heavens and all their interactions and inter-connections. In one person this happens more intimately, more favourably, and more strongly than in another person, and for this reason it lasts longer. The tempering of the first spirit, too, relates on the one hand to the parts of the body and on the other hand to the moderating influence of the heavens, but most of all to the way of life.

And so, if such proportion, such tempering, such harmony flourishes within and is, from the outset, such as can last for a hundred years, it promises the new-born child a hundred years ordained by destiny, that is, a hundred natural years. It will also guarantee the continuance of such a life, provided that no violence, howsoever inflicted from without, cuts it off. Diseases, too, arising both from the body and from the heavens, have their natural course and should therefore not be thoughtlessly provoked by drugs, lest nature grow weary and the diseases change irreversibly into something worse.

Chapter 102: *The three powers of the soul; the head; the daemon; contemplation*
'And concerning the common …' [89d]
It is right to promote the three powers of the soul – rational, wrathful, lustful – through their respective types of exercise. This is particularly true of the rational power.

Now the mind, which is the highest point of reason, acts as a daemon within us. Just as the Framer of the world has Himself given us a rational soul from the heavens, so He has made provision for the head, which is celestial and similar to the heavens, to serve reason, so that, as the other powers of the mind serve reason, in the same way the whole body serves the head. Indeed, the human body seems to be simply the head of the human soul, while the other parts are like props and conveyances and servants subjoined to the head as tools for the human being.

Reason herself proclaims her own divinity when she recalls us to the divine. But, most importantly, she shows herself to be immortal when, united with the mind as with her daemon, she contemplates things divine above all else.

Through its intelligence the soul of the world makes a very simple circuit around the higher Ideas, but through its reason it makes a complicated circuit around similar forms of Ideas that need to be expressed in the world, and through its motive power it turns the spheres of the world in manifold ways. Similarly, our soul, which once worshipped things heavenly, embraced, in its joyful contemplation, divine Ideas and cosmic forms and all things heavenly and, with its spherical and celestial means of conveyance, displayed an orbital motion. But later it came down into the human head, to use it as its instrument, for of all our parts the head is most congenial to it. At this point, however, it ceased its pristine revolutions. Yet we have the power to take them up again, in this very life, or at least to imitate them, by contemplating and venerating the higher powers, just as we did formerly.

In this way, the soul, being rendered somehow similar to the blessed, will be blessed in the present life, and, inasmuch as it will one day be fully similar, it will be fully blessed in the life to come.

Chapter 103: *The reproductive parts and the transmigration of souls*
'But now …' [90e]
The reproductive seed and member seem to be like a living creature inserted into us, a creature that has, as it were, its own life, for it is perceived through its own movement and its rebellious principle. Since it is vigorous and full of spirit, it possesses an abundance of life and sensation, so that through it another living being may be generated.

But, most importantly, it is to this member that the spirit flows from the very marrow of the spine, whence there trickles, at the same time, a marrowy drop, as the fermentation of the whole seed. But the tube created for the outflow of this drop is joined at its end to the urinary tract; although a little higher it is separate, as if there were two tubes. The urinary tract, which goes downwards through the kidneys to the bladder, is said to make its way somehow from the lungs for the following reason, as I understand it: the heart and lungs are particularly dry, the heart because it is very hot, and the lungs because they are very porous and extremely close to the fire. This is why they directly absorb most of the fluid from the entire body. And so nature ensures that what we drink has no possibility of flowing out with the urine unless it is left over after the lower parts of the chest have been thoroughly soused.

That his additional words about transmigration into beasts are figurative and allegorical will be understood by anyone who has observed how lightweight are the reasons given for this kind of transformation by a man who, in all other respects, is so firmly grounded.

It will also be remembered that Timaeus himself, who is speaking here, clearly denies, in his book on the nature of the world, the occurrences of any such transmigrations. And so the Platonic view may be that, although rational souls do not cross over into bodies that are other than human, they seem to transmigrate into as many types of beast as there are brutish dispositions and practices among human beings, for the human race is so extensive and varied that it may, in some way, appear to embrace, in the human character, angels, daemons, men, birds, fish, wild beasts, tame animals, and snakes.

But unless you expound these matters allegorically in this way or in a similar way, you will be obliged to declare that there is only one type of soul here, and that this is the human soul, which acts in one way in one set of circumstances and in another way in a different set of circumstances. Plato and Timaeus, however, enumerate many types, and even kinds, of soul here from the beginning, and they affirm that the rational souls come down from the Maker of the heavens, while the irrational souls are generated by the heavenly powers.

NOTES TO THE COMPENDIUM

Compiled by Peter Blumsom

Chapter 1: *'Just as Plato devotes his energies…'* [Page 3]
In Renaissance times it was generally assumed that Timaeus of Locri, was the original Timaeus of the dialogue. He was, in fact, born several centuries later, but he did write a work, *De Mundo*, which was based upon the original *Timaeus*.

Chapter 3: *'After the arrangement and concluding speech …'* [Page 5]
Although written many years after *Republic*, *Timaeus* was composed as if to follow on the next day.

Chapter 6: *'After Porphyry, let us listen to his disciple, the divine Iamblichus, whose words are fully confirmed by Proclus …'* [Page 8]
The following speech, ending with *'but rather do we fall back to their opposites'* is based upon that of Proclus in his own *Timaeus Commentary*, 1, 209-213.

'However, the supreme purpose of this worship …' [Page 10]
The reference in this paragraph is to Plato's *Laws*, 716d.

Chapter 7: *'Thus whatever is considered to be above the soul always is and never becomes.'*
Refers to Plato's *Timaeus*, 27e.

Chapter 8: *'All the followers of …'* [Page 13]
Ficino talks more on 'action, power and essence' in his *Platonic Theology*, I vi 4.

'But in order …' [Page 14]
Republic, 505a; *Parmenides*, passim; *Sophist*, 244b-245e.

Chapter 11: *'But to what I am now calling matter Plato, in the Philebus, gives the more extensive name of Limitlessness …'* [Page 18]
Philebus, 23cd.

Chapter 12: *'Anyone who might reproach Plato ...'* [Page 20]
Genesis, 1:2.

'In the same way ...' [Page 20]
The Pythagoreans considered **6** to be a perfect number in that it was the sum of its factors: **1 + 2 + 3 = 6**. It was also unique among perfect numbers in that it was also the product of its factors: **1 x 2 x 3 = 6**.

Chapter 14: *'Again, as I have said ...'* [Page 22]
Plato discusses this in the myth the Stranger relates in *Statesman*, 268d.

Chapter 15: *'He therefore made the world ...'* [Page 24]
Compare *Timaeus*, 29e-31d with *Genesis*, 1:31.

'And because beauty ...' [Page 24]
Timaeus, 30c.

'Yet when he says...' [Page 24]
St John, 1:4.

Chapter 16: *'Plato shows next ...'* [Page 25]
St John, 1:1.

'And it is not right to dream up numerous worlds...' [Page 25]
Timaeus, 33b.

Chapter 17: *'Although they call some of these numbers square ...'* [Page 26]
Epinomis, 981c.

Generally in Pythagorean number lore, **3** as a male number is considered 'fixed', whereas **2**, a female number, will be cast as 'wandering'. This will be relevant when the Lambda diagram is considered.

For a discussion of **5** and **6**, consult Ficino's *Philebus Commentary*, Book 2, Chapter 2.

'The result is that after the number two...' [Page 27]
Genesis, 1:1–2:3.

'But if you return ...' [Page 27]
This refers to the elements as explained in *Timaeus*, 31d.

Chapter 18: *'This why Plato ...'* [Page 28]
Timaeus, 31e. See also the notes to Chapter 19.

NOTES TO THE COMPENDIUM

Chapter 19: *'We have stated elsewhere ...'* [Page 29]
Normally Ficino refers to longs (linear) as 'rectangular numbers' with sides of unit difference, e.g. **6 (2 x 3)**

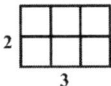

and retains the term 'oblong', for rectangular numbers with sides of more than unit difference, e.g. **15 (3 x 5)**.

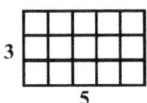

'Take the first two plane numbers ...' [Page 30]
To a Pythagorean a plane number is one that can be arranged, as those above, in rectangular form (length x breadth). The intermediary was mentioned in the last chapter. If we take two numbers, say, the squares **4** and **9**, we may place between them the geometric mean **6**, which, as an intermediary, has something of both of them: **4** (2 x 2), **6** (2 x 3), **9** (3 x 3). The Pythagoreans would have liked to represent this visually in the following way:

'Next take the first of the solid numbers ...' [Page 30]
Following the same reasoning, a solid number is one that can be arranged in three dimensions (length x breadth x height). Some numbers were regarded as both solid and plane numbers; for example, **12** can be arranged as a plane, **4 x 3**, or as **2 x 2 x 3**, which would be solid. As the purest form of plane is the equilateral or square, the purest solid will be the cube. It is a fact that, although there is only one intermediary, or geometric mean, between two consecutive squares, there are two between two consecutive cubes. Take the example that Ficino gives: two cubed and three cubed. This is how it would be arranged as a continuous geometric proportion:

   8 (2 x 2 x 2), **12** (2 x 2 x 3), **18** (2 x 3 x 3) and **27** (3 x 3 x 3).

But looking at this in the Pythagorean way, we get:

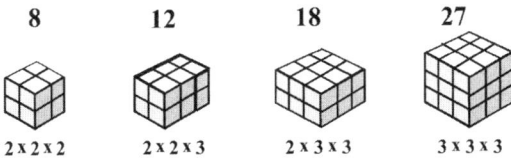

'Again, by numbers he indicates ...' [Page 31]
The three means are discussed in the notes to Chapter 30.

Chapter 20: *'But more of these things elsewhere ...'* [Page 32]
In this and the following paragraph Ficino is introducing the *tetractys*. This literally means 'four intervals' and was used by the Pythagoreans to signify how the whole of reality could be seen in the fourth triangular number.

Tetractys

```
         O  ——— 1 point
        O O  ——— 2 line
       O O O — 3 plane
      O O O O — 4 solid
```

This ancient abacus device was constructed from an array of pebbles placed in the sand as a pattern of contemplation. Many things could be 'calculated' from it. Our word 'calculate' originated from the Greek *khalix* – 'a small pebble'. Ficino's Pythagorean sources stretch far into antiquity. One is reminded of Jacob's sojourn 'in a certain place': '... and he took the stones of that place and put them for his pillows, and lay down in that place to sleep. And he dreamed, and behold a ladder set up on the earth, and the top of it reached to heaven: and behold the angels of God ascending and descending on it.' *Genesis*, 28:11-12.

Chapter 21: *'Again, if I did not fear prolixity ...'* [Page 33]
This is summarised in the *Timaeus Commentary* of Proclus, 2,162.

'Again, they maintain ...' [Page 33]
Timaeus, 29a.

'They also say ...' [Page 33]
Timaeus, 30cd.

Chapter 22
The main idea of this chapter is that when two plane forms 'touch', for example, two circles, then, as no material is involved, no solidity can be involved. Therefore they may be comprehended by a single mean (see chapter 19). However, when two material circles touch, solidity must be involved, and two means are needed to comprehend them: one for the form itself, and a second for the material involved.

Chapter 23

'Now the natures of all these are said ...' [Page 35]
Perhaps this and the next paragraph can be understood according to the figure for Chapter 19. Between fire and earth there are two means (as all the elements must be regarded as 'solid' in some way). Let's say that fire, as **8**, is fully itself and completely nimble (2 x 2 x 2). Earth, as **27**, is fully itself, yet completely blunt (3 x 3 x 3). Air, however, as **12** (2 x 2 x 3), is near to fire in nimbleness, having two powers of 2, yet falls short on account of possessing a single power of 3. Likewise, water, as **18** (2 x 3 x 3), having two powers of 3, is less nimble than both fire and air. Yet its single power of 2 stops it from being as blunt as earth.

'But musicians are not allowed to go beyond the fourth ...' [Page 36]
In this case the fourth is describing the ratio of the double octave. Greek musical theorists considered it unseemly to exceed the range of a double octave, which was the musical compass of Pythagoras' Immutable System, the fulfilment of Greek scale theory.

Chapter 24: *'The Hebrews will give their strong support ...'* [Page 39]
Genesis, 1:1-10.

'And so on, together with Heraclitus and Empedocles ...' [Page 39]
In Fragment 118, Heraclitus says, 'A gleam of light is the wise soul, wisest and best.' Empedocles states, 'But the benevolent flame (of the eye) happened to obtain only a slight admixture of earth.' – Fragment 85. Also Ficino talks on the same subject in his *Platonic Theology*, V iii 19-21; VIII xiii 1; and XVI vi 5-6.

'We shall end by declaring ...' [Page 40]
Genesis, 1:1; *Timaeus*, 31b.

Chapter 25: *'But let us not be troubled ...'* [Page 40]
On the movement of the heavens see Aristotle, *On The Heavens*, 269^a 10.

Chapter 26: *'But somewhere, universal fire ...'* [Page 42]
See Ficino's *Platonic Theology*, I ii 3.

'The heavens are indeed the true fire ...' [Page 42]
Aristotle, *On The Heavens*, 269^a 10 and 270^b 20.

Chapter 27: *'Now when he has dealt ...'* [Page 44]
This paragraph on formless matter refers to *Timaeus*, 48e – 51b.

'But since there is a double order …' [Page 46]
The two references in this paragraph are to *Timaeus*, 30b and 36de. Ficino may also have in mind the double account of the creation in *Genesis*, the second 'order' beginning at 2:5.

Chapter 28: *'Firstly, we think that the number five accords …'* [Page 47]
The first even number is **2** and the first odd, **3**. The Pythagorean mathematicians did not consider **1**, or the monad, to be a number, in this primary sense.

The five natures are first fully disclosed in *Sophist*, 245d. In *Timaeus* Plato overtly uses only three: Essence, Same and Difference.

See also Proclus' *Timaeus Commentary*, 2, 126-7.

'For five is the perfect mean of ten.' [Page 47]
See Theon, *Mathematics Useful For Understanding Plato*, 2, 44.

'For these reasons …' [Page 47]
Ficino partly follows Proclus in his *Timaeus Commentary*, 2, 160. Firstly, the Demiurge bases the SUBSTANCE of the soul upon the blending together of Essence, Same and Different. Secondly, this substance is ordered by number in the manner of musical ratios and proportions which is the HARMONY OF THE PARTS. Then he is concerned with the FORM of the soul, to which the visible cosmos is gathered, that is, the two circles of the Same, which becomes the fixed stars, and the Different, the latter being connected within the former, and sub-divided to form the planetary paths. Then the soul is imbued with power, the POWER of life, and from this living power the MOTIONS of the cosmos itself arise.

'Indeed, the followers of Plato …' [Page 48]
The three primary natures mentioned here are also dealt with by Proclus, *Timaeus Commentary*, 2,127.

For *'the principles of all the* things', see *Timaeus*, 41e.

'Indeed, when he calls the soul …' [Page 48]
The reference here is Plato's *Phaedo*, 92de. But the seemingly different view is put in *Timaeus*, 35a.

'For when he says "living" …' [Page 48]
Timaeus, 33b and 36c-e for *'the body of the world'*.

'Now power and action …' [Page 48]
See Ficino's *Platonic Theology*, I iv 1.

NOTES TO THE COMPENDIUM

'But above these five natures…' [Page 49]
Philebus, 23c.

'The triangle is like the soul …' [Page 50]
This paragraph is also dealt with by Proclus in his *Timaeus Commentary*, 2, 123-5. Ficino deals with it himself in *Platonic Theology*, XVII xi 12.

Chapter 29: *'But since those things which are perceived …'* [Page 52]
This 'musical harmony' described by Ficino is introduced by the numbers and subsequent musical ratios in *Timaeus*, 35b. The way sounds affect the senses is described at 80a, and the subsequent contemplation of their harmonious beauty at 47c.

'Moreover, those things related to sight …' [Page 52]
In *Timaeus*, 46e, Plato describes how the beauty of the cosmos is relayed to us by the power of sight, and at 67c he concentrates of the operation of sight itself.

'Moreover when Plato represents the Maker of the world …' [Page 52]
The Orphic hymns were collected around the second or third centuries AD, but were probably part of an already existing oral tradition, in the same way that English folk songs had existed for centuries before Cecil Sharp began collecting them towards the end of the 19th century.

Orpheus sings of Apollo, the leader of the Muses:

> 'Th'immortal golden lyre, now touch'd by thee,
> Responsive yields a Dorian melody.'

The Ancient Greek Dorian mode was considered by Plato to be the 'true Hellenic mode': *Laches*, 188d.

Chapter 30: *'They call the sound fit for melodies the phthongus …'* [Page 54]
According to Ptolemy, the *phthongus* is a distinct and continuous musical note.

'Furthermore, resonances of strings …' [Page 54]
Music historians and commentators have never completely agreed on the notes of Hermes' (Mercury's) mythical lyre. Most believe it to have four strings, but there is no absolute consensus as to what their notes were. Ficino seems to favour the Dorian Melody described by the Orphic Hymn, for a reason we will soon discover.

As can be seen, the lyre covers a four-note interval called a tetrachord. This tetrachord was to become the building-block of all Greek scale construction, and is still used today for the same purpose.

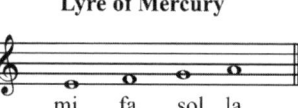

Lyre of Mercury

mi fa sol la

I have used tonic sol-fa to enable those who cannot read music in order that they may appreciate the sounds.

The connection between Terpander, an ancient musician, and Orpheus and is mythological. Terpander is alleged to have discovered the head of Orpheus floating in a river (some say in the sea). It had been severed in a savage encounter with a group of Thracian women, who were jealous of his powers to commune with nature through his music. Terpander realised that the head of Orpheus was still singing and somehow it was able to communicate the sacred laws of music to the musician. From this encounter Terpander was able to construct the first Greek scale, based upon the lyre of Mercury, and known as the System of Terpander.

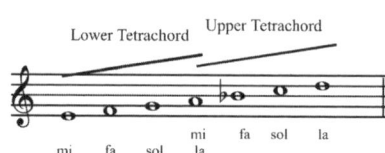

System of Terpander

Lower Tetrachord Upper Tetrachord

mi fa sol la   mi fa sol la

This, above, is the scale described by Ficino in this paragraph: '*two tetrachords united through seven strings.*'

Lycao appears to be a pseudonym for Pythagoras, who also came from Samos; and it was indeed Pythagoras who had the good sense to amend Terpander's scale so that the extreme notes formed an octave. This, however, necessitated inserting a tone between the two tetrachords in the following manner:

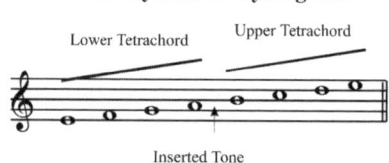

Lesser System of Pythagoras

Lower Tetrachord Upper Tetrachord

Inserted Tone

This was called the lesser system because it covered only a single octave. In Chapter 23 it was mentioned that the full range of Greek music covered a double octave. This is referred to in this paragraph when Ficino writes: '*in the four tetrachords joined together and consisting of fifteen strings ...*'

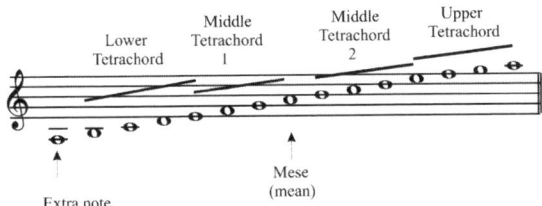

Greater System of Pythagoras

Note that Pythagoras did not merely add an octave above the original. In fact, he connected a tetrachord of the Terpanderean type both above and below the original octave. But as this gave only fourteen notes, he added an extra note at the bottom – *proslambanomenos* – to give the whole ranging scale a strong foundation by completing the double octave, and also because it provided a middle note (*mese*) to the whole system. This scale was an exceedingly subtle construction, retaining its Orphic tradition but at the same time making it a useful proposition for practising musicians. The testament to its success is that it has retained its character for two and a half thousand years, remaining a recognisable basis of the modern diatonic system (to be found on the 'white keys' of every keyboard instrument). Every note of this scale has a Greek name, and we will meet these in Chapter 32. For now, because of its importance, I have been content to just supply *mese*.

'Equal proportion, they say ...' [Page 54]
From here, until the end of the chapter, Ficino is explaining number theory but at the same time informing us how this affects musical harmonies. When necessary, music notation will be used, but it should be noted that none of this is musically complicated. Far from it: it is the simplicity that Ficino is constantly trying to convey to us.

The harmonic numbers that Ficino uses to measure musical intervals have little to do with conventional music terminology, such as perfect fifths and major thirds, etc. They belong essentially to the Pythagorean tradition and describe the vibrational frequency of the various pitches involved. Ficino himself did not know this. How could he have done? Frequency was only scientifically demonstrated in the

17th century. He also shared the notion with the Pythagoreans that there was a direct relation between the tension applied to sounding strings by weights, and the pitch the string expressed. Here the mathematics was incorrect, but it was not proven until about fifty years after his death. Divine Providence therefore stepped in to prove the Pythagoreans right after all, even though for the wrong reasons! All the numbers therefore are correct in Ficino's Commentary, but instead of thinking they apply to weights we simply take them to express rates of vibration.

Ficino's task for the rest of this chapter is to study number harmony in preparation for studying musical harmony. There will be more about both in the 'Soul Numbers' section which follows these notes.

After expounding the relative virtues of the three different kinds of harmonies, *multiples*, *superparticulars* and *superpartients*, we come to the paragraph beginning:

'Again, the double arises from the very proportion of equality.' [Page 56]
Here he is inviting us to consider both the numbers and their musical implications. What he means is quite clear from the notes:

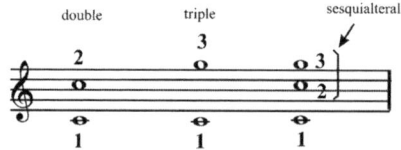

The term *sesquialteral* (one and a half times as big, or 3 to 2 in Greek terms) strictly belongs to number harmony rather than to music, but in Chapter 32, we shall learn the musical terms for such ratios. Nevertheless, it is important to study these harmonies through music, as they become more meaningful when linked to musical sound.

Then Ficino goes on to describe the arising of the *sesquitertial* (one and a third times as big, or 4 to 3):

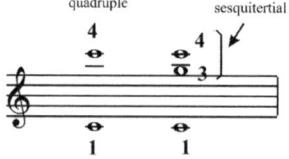

'Thus all the others are brought back to the double.' [Page 56]
Ficino is drawing our attention to the harmony of the double, especially regarding music. He uses the term, *diapason*, which is special to

music. Its Greek meaning is 'through all'. But why should 'two' be 'all' when it seems the least of multiples? Once more we must turn to music for our answer, where we see that the octave is, in one respect, the first step from one to two, but for another more profound reason it is also the last step, for beyond the seven notes contained within the octave they begin to repeat at higher pitches – no new notes are added. This needs to be remembered when dealing with music and its numbers. Ptolemy, in his *Harmonics* Book 3, alluded to this fact when he called the *diapason* the WHOLE PATTERN or *idea* of melody. That is why he made a distinction between *di okto* or 'through eight' and *diapason*, 'through all'.

'However, before I take harmonies any further ...' [Page 56]
Proportion arises from the equality of ratios, but sometimes Ficino uses the term to describe a single ratio.

'Proportionality is defined as the mutual likeness ...' [Page 56]
He tells us of the two kinds of proportion: continuous and discontinuous. Continuous uses only three terms or limits, where the middle term or mean is compatible with both extremes. His example of **2** to **4** and **8** to **16** is not the best, because in fact these numbers do seem to provide a continuous geometric progression. **2** to **4** and **3** to **6** is a clearer example, as these terms cannot be connected except through the similarity of ratio. He makes the point also that the mean arises in three different ways.

'The arithmetic consists in the equality of number.' [Page 57]
The most simple way of approaching the three types of proportion is, again, through the concept of equality. These can be intuitively illustrated.

In the Arithmetic proportion the differences are equal. **5** is the arithmetic mean between **3** and **7** because it creates equal differences of **2**.

Arithmetic proportion and mean

3   5   7
  2   2

Geometric proportion is founded upon equality of ratio. 2 to 4 shares the same ratio as 4 to 8, which is 1 to 2.

Geometric proportion and mean

1 —— 2
2   4   8
     1 —— 2

The harmonic mean strikes a balance between the two. The mean cuts the extreme terms in such a way that the differences are in the same proportion as the extreme terms:

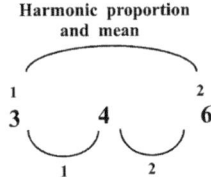

Harmonic proportion and mean

So the harmonic proportion has a portion of the Arithmetic, which Platonists consider the mean of the material body, and a portion of the Geometric, which is known as the proportion loved by the gods, and by Zeus in particular. This is why the Harmonic is associated with the soul, which mediates between the divine and material worlds.

'Take two, four, and eight ...' [Page 57]
Ficino is revealing here the special symmetrical properties of Geometric Proportion. First he examines multiples, where the guiding ratio is a multiple. This occurs in the progression **2, 4** and **8**, where the ratio is the multiple, **2:1**. Then he gives the example of **4, 6** and **9**, where the ratio is *superparticular*, that is 'containing a part in addition', that is one part of the denominator, **1 ?** in this case.

However, there is a certain obscurity in the next paragraph, where he denies the same property to *superpartients*. These contain more than one part in addition, and are therefore farther removed from unity. However, the reason why the *superpartients* lack symmetry in the case Ficino cites is that they are arranged in an arithmetic progression, which has no true proportion. Yet if we employ the same *superpartient* progression of **5** to **3** (one whole plus and two parts of three) in a geometric progression, say, **9, 15** and **25**, we find that it suddenly has full symmetry (**9 x 25 = 15 x 15 = 225**). Was this an oversight on Ficino's part, or did he want to show the asymmetry of the arithmetic mean? Unfortunately, we may no longer ask him!

Chapter 31: *'But in case someone says ...'* [Page 59]
A *'common note-form'* refers to the fact that when two or more notes are sounded together carefully they are heard not separately but as one harmonic interval.

'For the same reason ...' [Page 60]
The reference here is to *Psalm* 119:103.

'The physicians maintain ...' [Page 61]
Timaeus 80a.

Chapter 32: *'Nor was he said to be able to divide the tone into two equal half tones…'* [Page 61]

If we think, in the Greek way, of a tetrachord comprising the notes **E, F, G** and **A**, (or **mi, fa, sol, la**) from **F** to **G** and from **G** to **A**, we have whole tones, both of the ratio **9:8**. This leaves the interval of **E** to **F** to complete the tetrachord. Plato called this a *limma* or 'left-over'. Two such *limmas* fall short of the whole tone by what is known as the Pythagorean comma, a very small interval. As Ficino, who has committed himself as far as possible to simplicity, is not offering a detailed analysis in his commentary this is probably not the place to go into the exact detail. Proclus, however in his *Timaeus Commentary* (2,179) fully investigates the whole question.

One can obtain an intuitional view from the Lyre of Mercury:

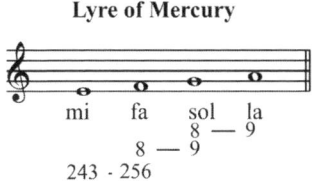

Plato was not happy with the interval 256/243 because it is *superpartient*; hence the rather dismissive description: 'left-over'.

'The first of these harmonies, the diapason …' [Page 62]

In this and the next two paragraphs Ficino introduces the musical intervals of the *diapason*, that is, the double ratio, the *diapente*, which is equivalent to the *sesquialteral* numerical ratio, and the *diatessaron*, equivalent to the *sesquitertial*. Today we call the *diapente* the perfect fifth, and we call the *diatessaron* the perfect fourth.

These intervals should be known musically. The *diatessaron* is a Greek term meaning 'though four'; and that is an apt description:

(Note that the numbers refer to the ratios involved in producing the notes, based on vibrational frequency.)

Next he looks at the *diapente*, or 'through five':

diapente

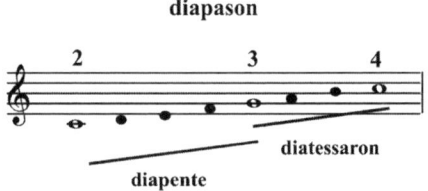

'Then he observed …' [Page 62]
Putting these intervals together, Ficino observes that they complete the *diapason* or octave.

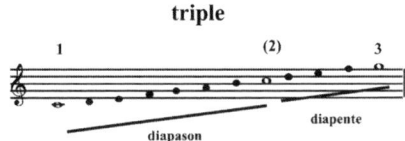

'But from its triple appearance …' [Page 62]
Next, to form the triple harmony, all he has to do is to add a *diapente*, or perfect fifth, to the *diapason*, giving an interval through 12 notes:

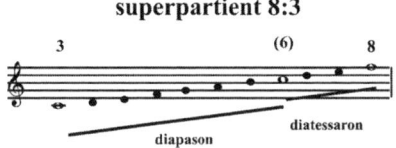

'However, it is not a triple if …' [Page 63]
Now Ficino lets us know that if we add a *diatessaron* to the *diapason*, the result will not be a multiple, or even a *superparticular*, but the less unified *superpartient*.

superpartient 8:3

Note that the **1** of the unison has moved to **3**, revealing its incompatibility with unity. However, it should be noted that on this point Ptolemy was in disagreement with the Pythagoreans and defended the **8:3** interval. Ptolemy declared it absurd to claim that an interval can be made discordant merely by adding the perfect interval of an octave to it? If **4:3** sounds concordant, so should **8:3**, which shows that even with the ancients all was not harmonious on these matters.

In this paragraph Ficino also makes the important comparison between the *diatessaron* and the *diapente*. He says that if **4:3** and **3:2** shared common denominators we would have **8:6** and **9:6**, and so their difference would be **9:8**, or a whole tone, which is, in fact, the case.

'But the sesquitertial ...' [Page 63]
Ficino says that if we wish to remain in contact with unity in our harmonic progression, the correct placement of the *diatessaron* is above the triple, where it completes the quadruple harmony, beyond which Greek theory says we should not proceed.

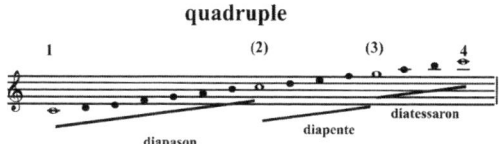

Observe that again we have a fifteen-note array, as in the Pythagorean system, although the placement of the intervals is more modern than Greek and is based on the major scale rather than around the ancient Dorian mode.

'But for the sake of melody ...' [Page 63]
Ficino shows that by generating intervals beyond the double octave, *superpartient* intervals immediately begin to arise. Although the additional interval of **5:4** is lawful (being *superparticular*), at the same time the *superpartient* **5:3** is inadvertently produced:

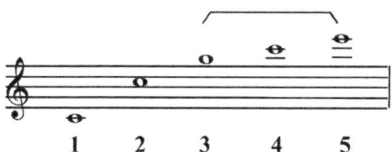

Indeed with this addition of 5, two *superpartients* appear. (The second the readers can supply for themselves.) But it is interesting that no *superpartient* can occur within the quadruple.

'But so that we may not go beyond ...' [Page 63]
Simple calculation shows us that with the addition of two *sesquitertial* harmonies (remember to multiply), **4/3** x **4/3** gives **16/9**, which clearly falls short of an octave by an eighth (numerically) and at the same time is unpleasant to listen to.

'The first and lowest note …' [Page 64]
One should not be confused by the fact that the lowest pitch of the Scale of Terpander, that is *hypate*, translates as 'highest', and *nete*, the highest pitch, is called 'lowest'. The note-names indicated the position and function of the strings on the lyre. For example, *Lichanos* simply refers to the note struck by the index finger.

'Moreover, if we make a comparison …' [Page 64]
There were two contrasting views of how the planets were linked to musical notes. In this paragraph Ficino refers to the version expounded by Nichomachus of Gerasa in his *Manual of Harmonics*, Chapter 3. In the next paragraph he describes the earlier and more authentic version given by Plato in The Myth of Er, *Republic*, 617ab.

'The ancients counted three harmonies.' [Page 65]
These refer to the three ways the middle notes are arranged within the tetrachord, which were, for the Greeks, the foundation of scale construction; only the diatonic remains today as the basis of our modern music system. The other two are very strange to modern ears, and their descriptions, *chromatic* and *enharmonic*, bear no relation to the modern musical terms of the same names.

'Now many related subjects…' [Page 65]
Here Ficino refers to the long letter that he sent to Domenico Benivieni under the title, *The Principles of Music*, which is no less than a complete treatise on music, and should be read in conjunction with this commentary. It can be found in Volume 7 of *The Letters of Marsilio Ficino*.

Chapter 33: *'And so within this division …'* [Page 66]
Timaeus, 34b-35a.

'For these reasons Plato is not without justification …' [Page 67]
In this and the following two important paragraphs Ficino compares the three types of proportion to see which is closest in nature to the soul itself. The candidate is found to be the Harmonic, as it partakes of both the absolute proportion of the Geometric and the lack of proportion of the Arithmetic. See Ficino's *Platonic Theology* III ii 5 and also compare Proclus' *Timaeus Commentary* 2, 198, where the Harmonic Mean is related to justice. See also 2, 273 and 2, 317.

'Now this is the quality and function of the soul …' [Page 67]
How the soul reasons is dealt with by Plato in *Timaeus*, 36e-37.

NOTES TO THE COMPENDIUM

'But now let us hear Plato himself.' [Page 68]
Timaeus, 35b.

'Let us therefore set up a triangle …' [Page 68]

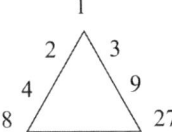

This triangular array is generally known as the *Lambda* after the shape of the Greek letter Λ. As Ficino hints in the previous paragraph, the *Lambda* was not specifically mentioned in *Timaeus*, but it is probable that it was known and used as a diagram in the Academy. It is traditionally attributed to Crantor (335-275 BC), one of the following generation of Academy members.

Ficino talks more on these numbers in his *Platonic Theology*, XVII ii 11.

'But he found the charm of the third note …' [Page 69]
Here is a possible representation of this intriguing paragraph:

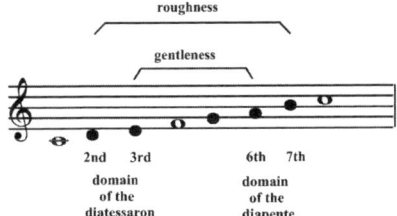

The 3rd and the 6th notes (**E** and **A**) are traditionally considered harmonious when played with the octave notes, whereas the 2nd and 7th (**D** and **B**) are very dissonant when sounded against the octave notes.

'Holding the mean position …' [Page 69]
Both the temporal and eternal worlds are trinities, with the soul as a single intermediate entity between to give sevenfoldness; but if we grant the soul as a trinity, we have ninefoldness.

'Indeed, since beneath the moon …' [Page 70]
Refer to Ficino's *De Numero Fatali*, chapter 12.

'Within reason there are three circles …' [Page 70]
Refer to Ficino's *Platonic Theology*, IV i 19-22.

'Indeed, if the movement of the soul …' [Page 71]
Refer to Ficino's *Platonic Theology*, VI xii 13-15.

Chapter 34: *'Take another triangle ...'* [Page 72]
See Michael Allen, *Nuptial Arithmetic*, p.96 n.4.
Ficino is describing what seems a new paradigm of his own. Professor Allen calls it a 'metaphysical triangle'. Here is an attempt to reconstruct it:

```
                    9
              sesquioctaval
                    8
                 Essence
                   /\
                  /  \
    1 limitlessness / double \ limit    2
                /          \
    2 difference / sesquialteral \ sameness  3
              /                \
    3 motion / sesquitertial   \ stillness  4
```

Ficino seems to be using the *Lambda* as a model as he seeks to combine, in a harmonic way, the metaphysical forms previously mentioned. Down the left side, which in the Lambda is a 'two-ing', he unfolds the inferior aspects of soul, whereas on the right, the side of 'three-ing', the superior aspects show themselves. He also portrays each matching set of elements as a harmony, perhaps a musical harmony. At the apex there is Essence, but, as Ficino explains in his *Philebus Commentary* (Book 2, Chapter 2), Essence may relate to single entities in all their infinitude, or it may relate to Being itself.

He also says that the Five Natures would be six if we were to include true Being, but that Plato excluded true Being from the definition of an entity because the fact that it IS an entity already involves its existence. THAT a thing is, is not the same as WHAT a thing is. So Being is not involved in the definition of anything, and this is why, Ficino tells us, Plato only gave five and not six natures.

However, it may well be that by linking essence to the *sesquioctaval* interval (**9:8**), he requires this diagram to show this differentiation between universal and individual essence. Proclus was fond of comparing the sesquioctaval ratio with the nine Muses and the eight Sirens. (See Proclus, *Timaeus Commentary*, 2, 208 and 210).

Perhaps Ficino also contemplated such a relationship between them, with the Sirens representing the visible universe and its beings, and the Muses extending into the invisible realm of true Being, where they choreograph the dance of the spheres under the divine tutelage of Apollo.

Chapter 34★: *'For he believed that the distance from the earth ...'* [Page 74]
These distances between the planets are attributed originally to Porphyry.

NOTES TO THE COMPENDIUM

'Through these measures ...' [Page 74]
Ficino's first reference in this paragraph is to the Spindle of Necessity, which Plato expounds in the Myth of Er, *Republic* 617c. It is the first known attempt to construct a model of the cosmos, and because of its reference to the song of the Sirens originated the notion of 'the music of the spheres'.

The second reference is to the mysterious Muse-like utterance at 546a-547a. Ficino was so impressed by this passage that he composed nothing less than a complete commentary upon it: *De Numero Fatali*.

Chapter 35: *'After Plato has explained the first figure ...'* [Page 75]
In this and the following paragraphs Ficino explains how the original *Lambda* figure was converted from numbers to music. Previously the numbers had arisen only in the form of Geometric means. Now it was time to insert the other two means essential to the structure of music, namely, the Arithmetic and the Harmonic. First, dealing with the first octave (on the left side of the Lambda), the insertion of twin means compelled the simple 1:2 relation to increase to 6:12, that is, avoiding fractions, as there is no sound to part of a vibration.

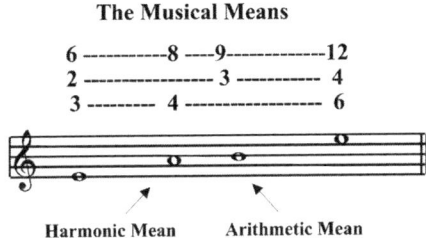

The Musical Means

6 ---------8 ----9------------12
2 ------------------ 3 ---------- 4
3 -------- 4 ------------------ 6

Harmonic Mean   Arithmetic Mean

Anyone who understands music might begin to understand how deeply it is founded on these means.

The right limb of the *Lambda* was also subjected to the same insertion of the Arithmetic and Harmonic means, in the following way:

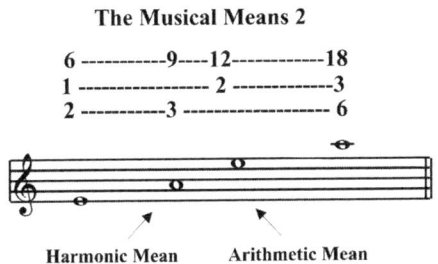

The Musical Means 2

6 -----------9----12------------18
1 ------------------ 2 -------------3
2 ---------3 -------------------- 6

Harmonic Mean   Arithmetic Mean

Because the intervals are larger on the right side the numbers and note-spacing reflect this fact.

Ficino does not write any musical notes himself, but I have confined the pitches to the Ancient Dorian that Plato regarded so highly.

Now to complete this diagram the means must be distributed by multiples down to the 'solid level'.

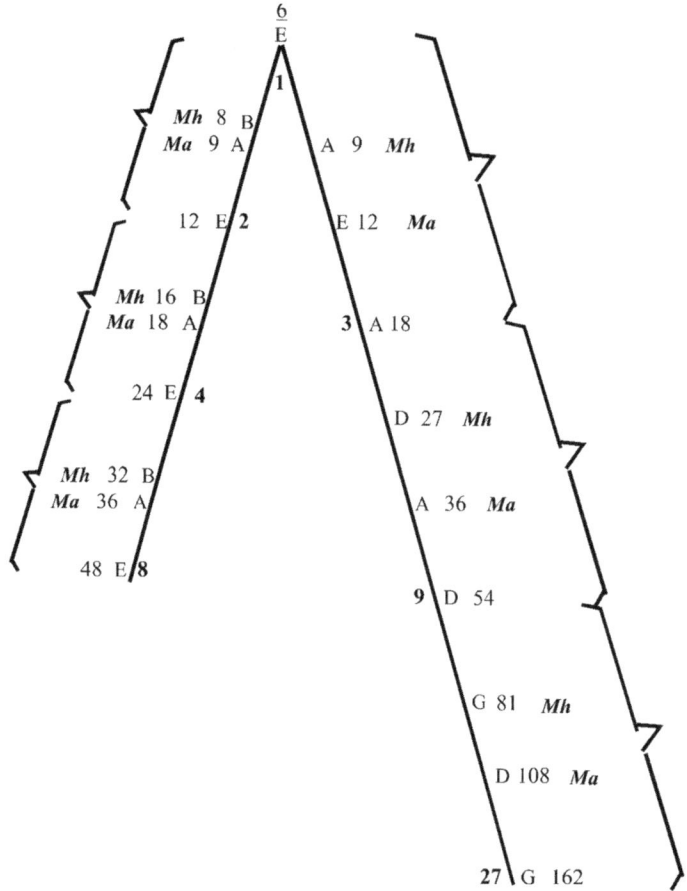

It is worth looking again at the way the Arithmetic and Harmonic means divide the octave. We should bear in mind that the octave notes belong to the Geometric progression, which is apt, for, according to Ficino's hypothesis, the ratio **1:2** (or **2:1**) has a simplicity about it that you would expect from the godly realm.

So all three means are partaking, each in their own way, to form the structure of music. It is interesting to note that although the two lesser

NOTES TO THE COMPENDIUM

means of the Harmonic and Arithmetic are not true proportions, they find a proportionate symmetry in their interaction within the octave. We can study this by simply looking at the number ratios.

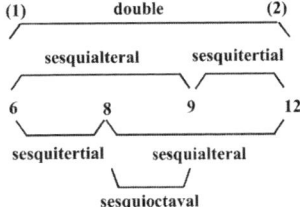

Looking at this diagram, known to the Pythagoreans simply as *The Proportion*, one can begin to appreciate the deep bonds that hold Plato's harmonic cosmos together. The *sequialteral* (**2:3**) appears twice, as **6:9** and **8:12**, and the *sesquitertial* (**3:4**) as **6:8** and **9:12**. The *sesquioctaval*, which forms the apex of Ficino's diagram of Chapter 34, is clearly seen here as the difference between *sesquialteral* and *sesquitertial*. The ancient theorists found much to contemplate in this diagram.

'*But since the sesquitertial ratios ...*' [Page 76]
Having established *sesquitertials* which form the numerical basis of the *diatessaron*, i.e. **3:4**, it becomes possible to fill these by employing the method established in Chapter 32, that is, by using two whole tones and a *limma*. The *limma* is the only interval that has not been generated lawfully according to the means, another reason for Plato's disapproval. (See the notes to Chapter 32.)

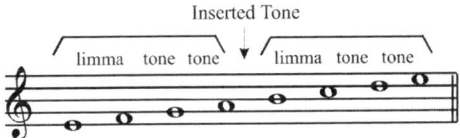

So Plato, working as far as is possible within the confines that he has set himself (using only the numbers 'one', 'two' and 'three' mentioned by Socrates at the outset of dialogue), has established 'the true Hellenic mode'.

'*Furthermore, the meaning of this figure ...*' [Page 76]
Ficino is possibly alluding to the fact that, in *Timaeus*, Plato himself never found it necessary to proceed beyond **27**. The *superpartient* nature of the *limma* may have made him doubt the usefulness of the high numbers that it provided. Again, once the octave had been established

on the left limb of the *Lambda,* the subsequent octaves add nothing new. This had been made clear by Ptolemy. None of this, however, deterred those who followed Plato, such as Adrastus, Severus, and Proclus. They established that the presence of the *limma* compelled the octave numbers (1:2) to expand to 394:768, and, in the opinion of Severus, when the whole *Lambda* of over four and a half octaves was filled in with numbers, it began with 768 and concluded with 20,736. Some modern musicologists, including Professor Ernest McClain in *The Pythagorean Plato*, offer a robust defence of this high number, stating that it was EXACTLY what Plato intended.

Chapter 36: *'When he says that this mixing of natures …'* [Page 77]
Having dealt with the first and second stages of Soul's creation, that is, Substance and Harmony of Parts, he now proceeds to Form: in other words, the overall shape of the Soul. The *"natures"* that the God has kneaded together are Essence, the Same, and the Different. From this arises the extremely vibrant 'soul-stuff' which is shaped into something like a long baguette. This is the completion of Substance. It seems as if the soul-stuff longs to connect everything to everything, reflecting its own components, but it is not until it receives numbers, harmony, and proportion that it has the means to do this. In this chapter we have reached the stage when all this has been accomplished, and Soul is ready for the third stage of its creation. It is to be given a Form. The description he gives of this is easy to follow and ends with the invisible model of the cosmos, which, were it visible, would look like this:

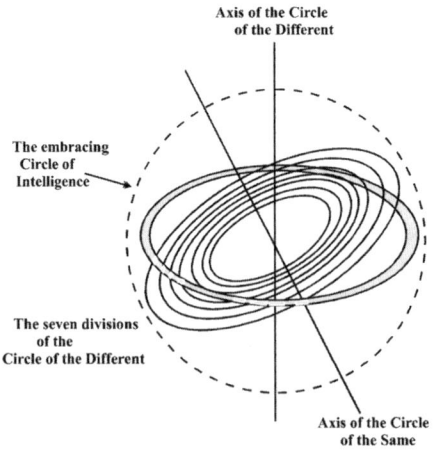

'When the Timaeus *says ...'* [Page 78]
The idea of a third circle is not overtly mentioned in *Timaeus*, but at 35 Plato says, 'And He compassed them about with a motion that revolves in the same spot continually ...' The idea of what Ficino calls *'a circle of Sameness'* seems to have arisen with Chalcidius, a fourth-century Christian. F.M. Cornford was minded to agree with him. In spite of Ficino's description, he is not saying that this embracing circle has been formed from the soul-stuff, but that it is of the intellect, and totally motionless and immaterial.

'In short, however you imagine it ...' [Page 79]
Refer to *Timaeus*, 37d.

'I would rather join Plotinus ...' [Page 79]
Compare Plotinus, *Enneads*, 3,7,1-15 with Proclus, *Timaeus Commentary*, 3, 17.

'I have written ...' [Page 80]
Ficino, *Platonic Theology*, II vi 8 and XI vi 1-17.

Chapter 37: *'Being incorporeal and possessing unlimited power ...'* [Page 80]
This and the following paragraph refer to *Timaeus*, 45b-46c.

'Now Venus is related to the Moon ...' [Page 81]
The comparison between Saturn and Mercury perhaps refers to *Republic*, 616e- 617a.

'But if the firmament ...' [Page 82]
In *Politicus* (which we call *The Statesman*), 269c, the Stranger relates a myth which tells of two opposite motions of the universe, one under the hand of God, in the golden age, and the other when the universe moves under its own energy rather in the fashion of a great clock being wound up and then let to run. Both Proclus and Ficino consider that instead of being sequential, these two movements take place at the same time. Also see Proclus, *Platonic Theology*, Book 5, Chapter 25.

'Plato was thus justified ...' [Page 82]
See the diagram in the notes to Chapter 36. Here Ficino describes the variance of the axis of the zodiacal path, including the planets, from the equatorial axis of the fixed stars. Known as the *ecliptic*, it was said to have been discovered by Anaximander, the pre-Socratic philosopher. Milton gave a Christian turn to the Platonic interpretation in *Paradise Lost*, Book 10:

> Some said he bid his Angels turn ascance
> The Poles of Earth twice ten degrees and more
> From the Sun's Axle; they with labour pushed
> Oblique the Centric Globe.

This happened as a result of man's disobedience, which led to his expulsion from Eden.

> ... else had the Spring
> Perpetual smiled on Earth with vernant Flowers,
> Equal in Days and Nights ...

Here we have an interpretation of Same and Different identical to that found in the pagan world.

Chapter 38: *'Plato holds, moreover, that this world ...'* [Page 83]
Refer to *Timaeus*, 36c.

Regarding the status of 'right' and 'left', see Proclus, *Timaeus Commentary*, 2, 258; and on the inability to discriminate right and left, *Timaeus*, 43e.

Chapter 39: *'Thus the world deities ...'* [Page 86]
See *Phaedrus*, 246d.

Chapter 40: (In this chapter Ficino is commenting on *Timaeus*, 41ad)
'To put it briefly ...' [Page 87]
Exodus, 3:14.

Chapter 41: *'Plato says that the rational soul of man ...'* [Page 89]
The 'bowl of the world' and the 'laws of destiny' can be found at *Timaeus*, 41de; these laws from the God himself should not be confused with the less lofty instructions given by the Fates to the embodied soul for its next life, as told in Myth of Er, *Republic*, Book 10. The descent of the individual souls is chronicled in *Phaedrus*, 248a-249c.

'At this point you should remember ...' [Page 90]
This passage at *Timaeus*, 44c can be seen as the natural event of childbirth, where the innate understanding of the individual soul becomes confused.

'And so it is in this way ...' [Page 90]
Timaeus, 43a-44b.

'What Plato puts forward ...' [Page 90]
Timaeus, 44d-45a.

'There follows a passage ...' [Page 90]
Timaeus, 45b-46a.

'He then re-asserts that man ...' [Page 91]
Timaeus, 46e-47e

Chapter 42: *'After he has treated of the model order of the world ...'* [Page 91]
In the Myth of Er (*Republic*, Book 10) Necessity is portrayed as the fearsome goddess who presides over the Three Fates. Ficino in a moral essay 'How False is Human Prosperity' (*Third Book of Letters*) shows how, under her fateful rule, man becomes selfish and pursues worldly desires. Only the intervention of Divine Providence can save him from his fate and lead him to true philosophy. In *Timaeus*, a 'scientific' myth, the subject is treated somewhat differently. Necessity is no longer addressed as a goddess, but is a kind of inchoate force in nature that stops it descending into complete formlessness, yet also will not let it rise above itself. Ficino's description as 'the soul of matter' is both poetic and apt. In *Timaeus* the role of Providence is taken by Intelligence (*nous*) which prevails upon Necessity to bring forth a result better than she would wish.

'But when he says ...' [Page 92]
Ficino seems to be saying that even before Soul had been fitted to the material world (*Timaeus*, 36de), it still had an influence upon it. Remember the words of Timaeus at 34de; 'God did not, of course, contrive the Soul later than the body'. Nevertheless, Ficino explains that its influence was constrained to that of a mere partial 'stirring' until that moment when the two were fitted in the correct way, i.e. 'centre to centre'. Hence the statement at 30a, where Timaeus describes the universe 'in a state not of rest but of inharmonious and disorderly motion'.

'Noteworthy at this point ...' [Page 92]
In this and the following paragraph (related to *Timaeus*, 48e-50a) Ficino differentiates between the world of Becoming - mentioned at the beginning of Timaeus' speech as in opposition the world of Being – and the prime matter that he is now offering as a third permanent state. Until now Plato has been content to allow 'becoming and

'matter' to coalesce as in some way a twofold, but now it is required that we see them as distinct states. Yet, as Ficino observes, if we extract 'becoming' from matter we are left with an almost ghost-like *'image of the world'* – somewhat similar to the grin of the Cheshire cat! It is this ambiguity that renders the existence of the third state so obscure, and in Christian terms, so controversial. After all, in *Genesis* there is no mention of anything preceding the creation of Heaven and Earth. This is possibly why Ficino is keen to explain that 'matter' in its pure state also comes from God.

'Next he rises up, through these material forms …' [Page 92]
Ficino has dealt with this process at various places in his *Platonic Theology*, most notably throughout Book I, which is devoted exclusively to it. Plato himself discusses it at *Timaeus*, 50c.

Chapter 43: *'And so Pythagoras and Plato …'* [Page 94]
Here Ficino describes the inter-connectedness between the traditional element types and their solid shapes. Empedocles had been convinced that the elements, which he called 'roots', formed the unbreakable foundation of the material world. Plato, however, held that each of the four element types was related to its own unique shape, in the form of a three-dimensional figure with a regular face. Each face could again be broken down into triangles, the most simple of planes. It was at this stage that the shapes were dissolved into the soul's harmonic numbers, thus establishing the vital connection between the realm of intelligence and the world of body. There is an interesting and provocative account of this whole process in *The Cosmology of Plato*, pp 210-239, F. M. Cornford.

'That is why, when they say …' [Page 94]
Here are what Ficino calls the *shapes*, pyramid, etc., each of which accepts the quality of its according element:

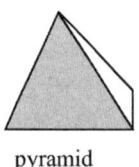
pyramid
(fire-type)

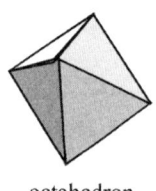
octahedron
(air-type)

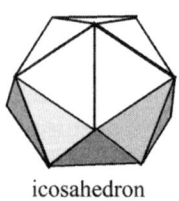
icosahedron
(water-type)

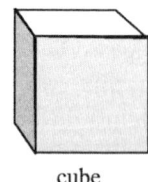
cube
(earth-type)

NOTES TO THE COMPENDIUM

He wants us to hold element and the shape as distinct, for the shape is the work of reason, originating in number itself and able to be dissolved back into number, whereas the qualities, without reason's guidance, he describes in his *Platonic Theology* as *'crippled', 'scattered through the breadth and depths of matter, plunged in the stream of Lethe (forgetfulness)'* – I iii 16.

'Euclid demonstrates, ...' [Page 94]
In this and the two following paragraphs he demonstrates the process by which the gross forms may be *dissolved* into simple numbers. He looks at the faces of all the regular 'solids' and notes that they are composed of two types of triangle: the scalene and the isosceles. The scalene triangle is one with unequal sides. Of the countless varieties he chooses the half equilateral triangle (shaded here).

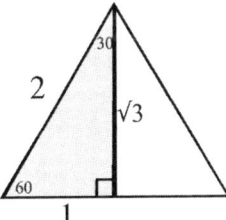

scalene as a half equilateral

He uses this to compose the regular faces of the fire, air and water shapes, which are all equilateral. However, he does not subdivide into two scalenes, as above, but into six as shown below.

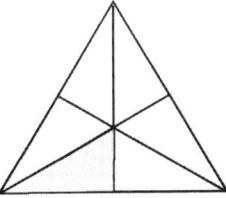

The reason for this is possibly to create a great variety of triangle sizes for different kinds of materials. See *Timaeus*, 57cd and Cornford's *Cosmology of Plato* pp.228-239.

The other triangle is the isosceles triangle, which is half a square, as can be seen shaded in the diagram below.

ALL THINGS NATURAL

isosceles
within the square

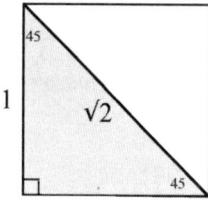

This he used to compose the face of the cube, not as above, but in a double subdivision, as below.

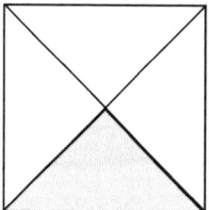

'Lastly, he linked the dodecahedron ...' [Page 95]

When Ficino talks of the pentagon being composed of equilaterals, this is clearly not the case. This does not affect his assigning it to the 12 signs of the Zodiac, but he cannot make a case for it being subdivided into 360 parts. The pentagon is indeed composed of 5 triangles, but they are certainly not equal-angled, being in fact isosceles, as the centre angle must be a fifth division of 360, and is therefore 72 degrees, leaving 54 degrees for each of the side angles. Only an equilateral may be subdivided into six equal scalenes, whereas this isosceles may be divided into only two.

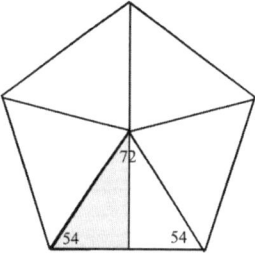

Perhaps this was the reason why Plato himself no more than inferred that 'one other construction, a fifth, still remained, and this one the god used for the whole universe, embroidering figures on it.' *Timaeus*, 55c. Here is that figure:

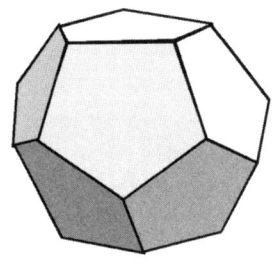

dodecahedron
(cosmos)

'Yet nearly all of these matters are concealed ...' [Page 95]
Aristotle, *On Generation and Corruption*, (*passim*, but particularly Book 1, Chapter 8 and Book 2, Chapter 3).

'Plato then deals with the effects ...' [Page 96]
Timaeus, 65b-68d.

Chapter 44: *'It is worth considering the importance Plato places ...'* [Page 96]
Socrates' resolution, *Timaeus* 19b-20c.

'The irrational soul is once more discussed ...' [Page 97]
Timaeus, 86b-87b.

'But the followers of Plato ...' [Page 97]
Ficino, *Platonic Theology* VII ii 1.

'They also demonstrate ...' [Page 97]
Timaeus, 71ad.

'And so it is that the images of the future ...' [Page 97]
Timaeus, 71e-72b.

'I have long thought ...' [Page 98]
Aelius Galinus, known as Galen, AD 129-199 (or 217). A Roman philosopher of Greek origin and the most accomplished physician of the Roman period.

Chapter 46
'Now Plato next defines ...' [Page 101].
Timaeus, 87c-89d.

SOUL NUMBERS

AS NUMBERS OCCUR frequently in the Commentary, it might be useful to add a short note of guidance on how they work, especially with regard to musical harmony and its attendant ratios. The easiest way to understand Ficino's use of what we might call 'soul numbers' is to see them as representing rates of frequency.

In my note to page 54 I explain that these numbers, though all correct, were wrongly attributed by the Pythagoreans to string tension rather than to the relative speed of vibrations between musical pitches. This latter fact was unknown until Marin Mersenne's discovery a century or so after Ficino's death, and though Ficino followed the Pythagoreans in this, had he known the truth he would have embraced it wholeheartedly, as the sympathetic communication of vibrating strings had always fascinated him.

The numbers that Ficino employs in the Commentary take two forms. First there are the number relationships themselves, for example *sesquialteral* or 3 to 2, lit. 'half again'; and then there are their musical equivalents, in this case the *diapente*, an interval 'through 5 notes' which is, in modern terminology, a perfect fifth. So this is the harmony that arises when two sounds vibrate at a ratio of 3 to 2 with each other – the greater the frequency, the higher the pitch of a note. As we are not assigning anything but pitch to the numbers it is immaterial whether we call it 3 to 2, or 2 to 3.

Ficino's great insight was that by linking the numbers so closely to music it was possible to lend them an added significance that we would fail to perceive in the numbers alone. For example, the *double*, or 2 to 1, becomes charged with meaning when we consider it to express the musical octave, for the octave is not merely the first step from unity, but in a way it is also the last. It is a fact that beyond the octave lies a mere repetition of the notes which have already occurred within the octave interval. Every musician knows this is so, and a glance at any piano keyboard, with its recurring pattern of octaves, will also verify the fact. So when the *triple* arises, it merely duplicates above the octave that note that is already contained within it. Therefore as numbers increase beyond the octave they are also exploring within the octave itself, which is an extraordinary fact. It was this that prompted Ptolemy, the great Greek astronomer and musician, to remark that the diapason, 'through all', was the *idea* of all octaves – that there is nothing beyond this first great step from one to two, which holds the inner *form* of the whole cosmos. The task of the harmonic numbers of the *Lambda* is to actuate at all levels, i.e. from point to solid, this mighty *form*.

Finally, it is up to individuals to discover for themselves the beauty and full implication of these numbers of the Soul.

GLOSSARY

Aliquot part – see **Numerical Ratios**.
Ancient Dorian Mode

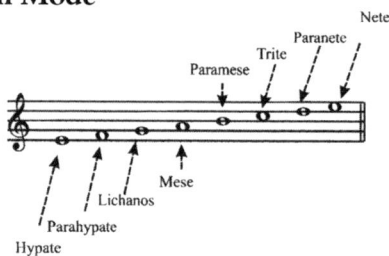

This is the mode that Plato called 'the true Hellenic mode'. There has often been confusion regarding these note-names. As with the modern guitar, the lowest string on the lyre has the highest pitch; so *hypate*, or 'high', refers to its position on the lyre, not to its pitch. In the same way, *nete*, or 'low', refers to its position as the bottom string, even though it has the highest pitch. *Parahypate* is the note 'next to hypate', and *paramese* the note 'next to *mese*'. *Lichanos* indicates that this string is plucked by the forefinger, and, *trite* is the third note from both *mese* and *nete*. Although *mese* is not the middle note of the eight-note scale, it adopts the central position in the full fifteen-note double octave referred to by Ficino in Chapter 30 (note to page 54).

Chromatic – A tetrachord consisting of two semitones and a minor third. (See **Diatonic** for more information.)
Diapason – see **Musical Intervals**.
Diapente – see **Musical Intervals**.
Diatessaron – see **Musical Intervals**.
Diatonic – Ficino refers to this as one of the three 'harmonies'. The harmonies are the three methods by which the ancient Greeks divided the tetrachord, a four-stepped part scale from which all the larger scales were formed. The steps of the diatonic are semitone, tone, and tone. These three methods were called the 'three genera'.
Diesis – see **Musical Intervals**.

Different, The – see **Five Natures of the Soul**.
Disdiapason – see **Musical Intervals**.
Double – see **Numerical Ratios**.
Enharmonic – A tetrachord consisting of two quarter tones and a major third. (See **Diatonic** for more information.)
Equivox, equison – see **Musical Intervals**.
Essence – That which renders a thing distinct from all else. See **Five Natures of the Soul**.
Five Natures of the Soul – These are the five natures that every individual entity or individual soul possesses. It must have an 'essence', and this essence must be the 'same' as itself and 'different' from all others. It will possess the 'stillness' to remain itself a certain term and it will either have 'motion' in itself, or a 'motion' passed on to it from another. These natures are described in Plato's *Sophist*. In *Timaeus* only the first three are mentioned overtly, whereas stillness and motion are implied.
Four Complexions – (correlated to the humours): ruddy, thin, corpulent, sallow.
Four Dispositions – (correlated to the humours): happy and generous; ambitious; sluggish and pallid; introspective (melancholic).
Four Humours – blood, phlegm, yellow bile, black bile.
Four Virtues – wisdom, courage, temperance, and justice.
Harmony – The relationship of things, numbers, and musical sounds, when brought together as a whole. It has two main conditions: concord and discord. As Harmony is ruled by Unity, there is a constant tendency to resolve discord to concord and thus bring it closer to the One.
Hypate – see **Ancient Greek Dorian Mode**.
Lichanos – see **Ancient Greek Dorian Mode**.
Limit, limitless, and a **mixture** (or **combination**) of these two are those three states that are most universal. Only the **One Itself** precedes them in Being. They permeate the numbers of the Lambda. Plato's *Philebus* is the main source for Ficino when he discusses these. (See **Five Natures of the Soul**.)
Limma – See **Musical Intervals (Diesis)**.
Model – In *Timaeus* the model for the Cosmos was the world of *forms*. As he fashioned this world, God had in mind the other, finer world as a kind of 'blueprint'.
Mese – the middle note of the scale. (See **Ancient Greek Dorian Mode**.)

Motion – see **Five Natures of the Soul**.
Multiple – see **Numerical Ratios**.
Musical Intervals
  Diapason – 'through all the notes' – the Greek term for the musical interval of an octave.
  Diapente – 'through five notes' – the interval of a perfect fifth.
  Diatessaron – 'through four notes' – the interval of a perfect fourth.
  Diesis – a small interval that is similar to a semitone, having a musical ratio of 256:243. Plato called it a **Limma** or 'left-over' because it was what remained when two whole tones were extracted from a perfect fourth.
  Disdiapason – a musical interval of two octaves.
  Equivox, equison – different voices or sounds sharing in (equated within) a single harmonic ratio.
  Unison – a single sound. (See **equison** and **equivox**.)
Numbers
  These are numbers seen in the Pythagorean way. The Pythagoreans were most interested in the special characteristics of numbers.
  Circular – these are numbers which, no matter how many times they are multiplied by themselves, always reappear in the last digit: e.g., no matter how many times 6 is multiplied by itself, the total will always contain 6 as the last digit of the total: 6 x 6 = 36; 6 x 6 x 6 = 216; 6 x 6 x 6 x 6 = 1296, etc. 5 is another well known circular number.
  Harmonic – the number ratios which are related to proportion and are relevant to music.
  Linear – these are prime numbers, for they cannot be formed into planes or solids: that is, as they can only be divided by themselves and unity, they contain no breadth.
  Plane – any number that has at least two factors can be arranged as a plane.
  Plane numbers are of two types:
  a) square, which have equal sides (equilateral)
  b) rectangular, which have two unequal sides, for example (6 = 2 x 3). The more favoured type of rectangular number is a 'long', which is equivalent to a *superparticular* numerical ratio. It has sides of unit difference. 6 is of this type. The lesser kind Ficino called 'oblong', a name which he designated to all *superpartient* types of ratio – that is, with sides of more than unit difference. 15 is of this type, with sides of 5 and 3. However,

they are all rectangular numbers. Some highly factored numbers can be rectangular in more than one way: for example, 12 can be 4 x 3 and 6 x 2.

Solid – whereas plane numbers have both length and breadth, solid numbers have the added dimension of depth. The most regular of these are cubes, which are visually 'solid'. The side of a cube is its cube root, just as the side of a square is its square root. This visual way of comprehending numbers gives an indication of how Pythagoreans approached numbers. The Lambda itself is a profound integration of Pythagorean numbers. Cubes are not the only solid numbers, for there are also all cuboid numbers. 12, for example, is also a cuboid, with sides of 2 x 2 x 3.

Numerical Ratios
  Aliquot part – an equal part of a whole.
  Double – the ratio of two to one (2:1 or 2/1).
  Multiple – a whole number or integer: for example, doubles, triples and quadruples are multiples.
  Quadruple – four to one (4:1 or 4/1).
  Subduple – the inversion of the double or one to two (1:2 or ½).
  Superbipartient – two and multiple parts of any denominator: for example, two and two thirds of one, or two and three fifths of one.
  Superparticular – one and a single part of any denominator: for example, one and one half of one, or one and one third of one.
  Superpartient – one and multiple parts of any denominator: for example, one and two thirds of one, or one and three fifths of one.
  Triple – three to one (3:1 or 3/1).

Parahypate – see **Ancient Greek Dorian Mode**.
Paramese – see **Ancient Greek Dorian Mode**.
Phthongus – a distinct musical note.
Quadruple – see **Numerical Ratios**.
Same, The – see **Five Natures of the Soul**.
Sesquialteral, sesquitertial – see **Numerical Ratios**.
Stillness – see **Five Natures of the Soul**.
Subduple – see **Numerical Ratios**.
Superparticular, superpartient, superbipartient – see **Numerical Ratios**.
Triple – see **Numerical Ratios**.
Trite – see **Ancient Greek Dorian Mode**.
Unison – see **Musical Intervals**.

BIBLIOGRAPHY

Aristotle. *The Basic Works*, edited by Richard McKeon, Random House Press.
Ficino, Marsilio. *De Numero Fatali*, from *Nuptial Arithmetic*, Michael J.B. Allen, University of California Press, 1994.
— *Philebus Commentary*, translated by Michael J.B. Allen, University of California Press, 1975.
— *Platonic Theology* (Eighteen Books in 6 Volumes), translated by Michael J.B. Allen, Harvard University Press.
— *The Letters of Marsilio Ficino* (Volumes 1-8), translated by the Language Department, The School of Economic Science, Shepheard-Walwyn (Publishers).
Greek Musical Writings: II (*Harmonic and Acoustic Theory*), Andrew Barker, Cambridge University Press.
Iamblichus. *The Theology of Arithmetic*, translated by Robin Waterfield, Phanes Press.
Nichomachus of Gerasa. *Manual of Harmonics*, translated and edited by Flora Levin, Phanes Press.
Orphic Hymns, translated and edited by Thomas Taylor, The Philosophical Research Society, Los Angeles.
Plato. *The Collected Dialogues*, edited by Hamilton and Cairns, Princetown University Press.
— *The Cosmology of Plato*, Frances Cornford, Hackett Publishing.
— *The Pythagorean Plato*, Ernest G. McClain, Nicolas Hays Ltd.
Plotinus. *The Enneads*, translated by A.H. Armstrong, Loeb Classical Library, Harvard University Press.
— *The Enneads*, translated by Stephen MacKenna, Faber and Faber.
Presocratic Philosophers. Kirk, Raven and Schofield, Cambridge University Press.
Proclus. *Platonic Theology*, translated by Thomas Taylor, The Prometheus Trust.
— *Timaeus Commentary*, Parts 1 and 2, translated and edited by Thomas Taylor, The Prometheus Trust.
— *Timaeus Commentary*, translated by Dirk Baltzly, Cambridge University Press.
Theon of Smyrna. *Mathematics Useful For Understanding Plato*, translated by R. and D. Lawlor, Wizard Bookshelf.

INDEX

abdomen 147
Ach the Egyptians revered a star called Ach 117
Acheron 40
Adeimantus 4
Alberti, Leon Battista 93
Amelius 5
Ammonius 15
Andromachus 58
Apollo 52, 53
  the source of medicine, music, and prophecy 59
  the universal absolute melody of the eighth note dedicated to Apollo 68-9
  the *disdiapason*, singing in harmony to Apollo through fifteen notes 69
Aries 7
Aristotle 3, 31, 42, 82, 83, 85, 114
  his books *On Generation* and *On Meteors* 96
arteries 145, 152
Athena an Egyptian Athena 108
Athenians at war with the men of Atlantis 5
  represent what is higher and more excellent 6
Athens two cities called Athens 108
Atlantis at war with Athens 5
Atticus 21

breath 99-100, 152-3
Bacchus 52
being and becoming 11, 12
Berlinghieri, Francesco 93
blood 151-2
body its need for exercise: the upright posture of the body is like a tribute to the heavenly posture 102
  its structure 155-6
bones 148
Brahmanas and worship 8
brain 148

Canopus 82
causes 13, 14, 144
  the threefold cause: efficient, model, final 4, 10, 108
  the unwavering view of our Plato concerning causes 91
Ceres 116
Chalcidius 31, 90
Chaldaeans 82
Cicero 98
Cocytus 40
contemplation 127
  man is born for the purpose of contemplation 90
  God made man for contemplation 149
Cornelius Celsus 98
Crantor the principal expounder of Plato at the time 5, 21
Critias 4, 5, 107

daemons 43
  conflict between the higher and the lower 5
  their genealogy and functions 117-20
  different kinds 119
  detected in Florence 119-20
Democritus 13, 59, 128, 130
destruction caused by fire and water 7
digestion 151-2, 154
disease 157-163
Difference 72, 73, 121, 126
Different 6, 47, 49. 50, 66, 67, 79
Dionysus 45
divine the divine world is the cause and model of the natural world 3
dreams 128

Earth 74, 116, 117
  never naturally departs from the centre of the world 140
Egyptian Athens 108

Egyptians 6, 7, 82, 117
Elea two Pythagoreans from Elea, Parmenides and Zeno 3
elements the four elements 35-41, 44, 110
elements and shapes 135-7
Elysian Fields 84
Empedocles 28, 39, 130
Essence 6, 47, 49, 67, 72, 73, 79
indivisible and divisible 66
eternity 112
Euclid 94
Eudoxus 7
eyes 128-9

fate and the soul 123
fever 161-2
Ficino, Marsilio references to his own writings:
'the eighth book of our letters' 65
On Life 46, 86
On Pleasure 96
Theology [i.e. *Platonic Theology*] 12, 14, 25, 47, 71, 78, 92
'our commentaries on Plotinus' 90, 111, 137
fire its properties 35-43
Fonte, Bartolomeo della 98
Francesco 'our cobbler' 120

Galen 98-101, 144
Galilea the Galilea family troubled by a daemon 110
Geber the supreme mathematician 75
George of Cyprus that outstanding physician 'often came to treat my mother' 98
genitals 147, 166
Glaucon 4
God
has composed the celestial Republic 5
is worthy of adoration and supplication 8
the creator of the world 15
made the world through His own will and goodness 24
created all things according to number, measure, and weight 31
uses harmonic proportion 67
whatever comes into being directly from God is everlasting 87

God—*continued*
there is no shadow of change within God 87
made man for contemplation 149
gods their genealogy and functions 117-18
gold 138
Good
seeking the Good 3
the final cause is the Good 4
the Good Itself 14
the Idea of the Good 17
all things yearn for the Good, which is their end 18
the Good is the creator, parent, and author of the universe 20
gums 138

hail 138
hair 150
harmonic proportion makes the dissimilar similar and joins the unequal through some common equality 67
harmony 85-6
why the soul is like a musical harmony 51-3
diseases cured by harmonies 59
musical consonance is as if alive, rational, and effective 53
definition 60
falls upon the ears like a single round, or rather, oval shape 61
the first elements 62
the ancients counted three harmonies 65
flows into the world from the harmony of the celestial soul 68
perfect human health is the mutual harmony of body and soul 101
head 149-50
man's principal part 127
and neck 151
health
perfect human health is the mutual harmony of body and soul 101
health of body and health of mind cannot co-exist unless they both harmonise with each other in due proportion 163
heart 145, 148, 166
Hebrews 39

Heraclitus 5, 13, 28, 39, 128
Hermes 54
Hermocrates 4, 5
Hipparchus 82
Hippocrates 28, 99, 100
holiness alone is the fullness of virtue 10
Homer 82
humours
  each of the four humours is composed of the four elements 156-7
  how bad humours are produced 157-9

Iamblichus 6, 21, 31, 33, 132
  his words on prayer 8-10
Ideas 86, 134
  the Idea of the Good 17
  conceived by divine intelligence 4
illness, mental 162-3
images Plato calls all perceptible things images and shadows 12
intellect
  the divine intellect, the noblest child of the Good 16
  indivisible, uniform, eternal 45
intestines 147

Jews subject to Saturn 135
Juno 118
Jupiter 45, 65, 70, 74, 81, 86, 110, 115, 118, 119, 127

Lactantius 98
light
  is the spirit and image of the world-soul 80
  fills all things instantaneously without ever becoming tainted 80
Limit 6, 19, 26, 27, 49, 50, 72, 73, 76, 121
Limitlessness 6, 18, 19, 26, 27, 49, 50, 72, 73, 76, 112, 121
liver 145-6, 148
  the Pythagorean view and images of the future 97-8
Locri a Pythagorean from Locri named Timaeus 3
lungs 145, 152, 166
Lycao of Samos 54
Lycia 82

Magi and worship 8

man is the whole world 127
  is a creature to be wondered at, being composed from the immortal and the mortal 127
marrow 147-8, 162-3
Mars 65, 70, 74, 81, 110, 115, 127
mathematical items the means between the divine world and the natural world 3
mathematics
  is like the soul, for each is deemed the mean between the divine and the natural 50
  the pathway of all liberal study 93
  natural phenomena are based on the principles of mathematics 93
  through numbers the study of mathematics indicates the divine world, and through measurements it indicates the natural world 3
matter
  its dependence on the Good 15
  not coeval with the maker of the world 20
  the matter of this world, which he names necessity 91
  the first matter 133
  matter and material forms 133
  formless matter is considered to be prior to formed matter 134
mean
  arithmetic 47
  arithmetic, geometric, harmonic 31, 56-7
Medici, Lorenzo de' 93, 103
metals 138
Mercury 70, 74, 81, 110, 111, 115, 117, 127
  the author of proportion and combination 114
mind angelic mind above the soul 51
Minerva the inscription in her temples 7
mirrors and images 130-1
Mithridates 58
Moon 4, 70, 74, 75, 81, 84, 85, 86, 110, 113, 114, 127, 128
Moses 7, 20, 24, 87, 96, 103
  harmony between Moses and Plato 40
Motion 6, 47, 49, 50, 66, 67, 72, 73, 112, 121
  seven motions in the heavens 116

movement the best movement is that by which everyone moves himself 164
Muses 52, 68
music Pythagorean and Platonic 54-8

nature
 nature is the instrument of divinity 3
 arranged in many levels: celestial, elemental, simple, compound, rational, and irrational 4
 divisible, multiform, temporary 45
Neptune 6
 signifies natural providence 7
Numenius 6
 calls Plato a second Moses 40
number
 numbers **2-7** 26
 circular numbers 26
 linear, plane, solid, equilateral, non-equilateral, square, oblong 29-31
 4 and its properties 32-40, 44-5
 5 and the soul 47-9
 musical numbers are most like the soul 50
 the ideal and metaphysical ratios of numbers 53
 1, 2, 3, 4, 7, 8, 9, 27 71-2
 linear, plane, solid 72
 means and ratios 75-6
 division of the series of harmonic numbers 78

Oceanus 40, 118
One 6
 the One Itself 14, 49
Opposition examples 6
Origen 5, 15
Orion 117
Orpheus 40, 54, 81, 86, 119

Pallas 6
 her wisdom and power 7
Parmenides 3
Peripatetics 142, 144
Phaethon his fall 7
Philo expounds *Genesis* 20
Philosophy the best gift of the Godhead 132
Phoebus 117
Phorcis 118
phthongus 54
Pier Leone of Spoleto 93

planets 85, 110-1
 the mysterious powers of the seven planets 70
 their arrangement 114
plants 150-1
Plato
 treats divinely of the natural world and of the divine world naturally 3
 his principal expounder was Crantor 5
 never exerts himself without good reason 5
 and Christian theology 16
 close to Moses 20
 praise for his eloquence 98

Platonic Solids and the elements 94-5
Plato's dialogues
 Critias 5, 6
 Epinomis 26
 Laws 10
 Parmenides 3, 14, 15
 Phaedo 48
 Philebus 96
 Politicus 82
 Republic 12, 14, 17, 29, 74, 75, 81, 122, 130
 Sophist 14, 15, 130, 132
Plotinus 21, 46, 79, 81, 90, 111, 128, 130, 137
Plutarch 21
Polemarchus 4
Porphyry 21, 81
 distinguishes three types of daemons 6
 his words on worship 8
prayer the five principal prerequisites 9
primum mobile 113
Priscian 132
Proclus 6, 7, 21, 31, 33, 79, 82, 123, 124, 132
proportion 54-8
Ptolemy 63, 75, 82
Pyriphlegethon 40
Pyroïdes 43
Pythagoras 16, 26, 29, 32, 37, 45, 59, 94, 103
 his words on creation and marriage 21
 and the smithies 61
 and the first elements of harmony 62
 forbade any continuation beyond the *double* 63
 his discovery 136

INDEX

Pythagorean
Plato is principally a Pythagorean in *Parmenides* and *Timaeus* 3
  Two Pythagoreans from Elea, Parmenides and Zeno 3

quintessence 60

ratio geometrical and musical 31
Republic the divine Republic and the celestial Republic 5
resonance 60
Rhea 118

St John 25
salt 139
Same 6, 47, 49, 50, 66, 67, 79
Sameness 72, 73, 121, 126
Saturn 45, 64, 65, 70, 74, 81, 86, 110, 113, 114, 115, 118, 127, 135
senses
  four senses in the universe 45
  through the harmony of the senses we may also impart harmony to the movements of the soul 91
  the five senses 141-4
Severus 21
shapes are the beginnings of bodies 134
  and the elements 135-7
sight its operation 127-31
Sirius 117
Socrates 5, 107
  at the Piraeus 4
Solon 108
soul
  the soul itself is and ever becomes 11
  partly indivisible, partly divisible; uniform and multiform; eternal in part and temporary in part 45
  God has placed the soul in the mean position 46
  the mean of all things 47
  its composition 47-53, 111
  is a harmony 48
  musical numbers are most like the soul 50
  the triangle is like the soul 50
  our soul contains all the proportions contained in the world-soul 53
  its harmonious composition 66-71
  its division 77

soul—*continued*
  the soul for ever turns about an intelligible axis 79
  a very close relationship between the soul and the heavens 85
  our soul and the soul of the world have been composed on a similar principle and have similar circuits 90
  why the soul becomes distorted 90
  the irrational soul 97
  its ills are divided into two groups 101-2
  how to maintain its three powers 102
  the soul of the world is prior to the body and is everywhere 110
  its shape 111
  has no difficulty in appraising whatever befalls 112
  the rational soul is divine 120
  is both rational and immortal 120
  the creation of souls 121-2
  souls and stars 121
  different kinds of soul 121-2
  soul and fate 123
  soul and brutes 123
  souls, stars, and elements 124
  soul and body 124-6
  its nature and powers 145
  its three powers 165
sphere the celestial spheres, like eight worlds 12
  the eighth sphere 13
spirit 151-2
  the three spirits 147
spleen 146
stars their nature 12-13
  stars and souls 121-2
Stillness 6, 47, 49, 50, 66, 67, 72, 73, 112, 121
Stoics 128
stones 139
Sun 70, 74, 75, 80, 81, 110, 111, 114, 115, 127
  the principal announcer of periods of time 114
Syrianus 6, 33

temperament 164-5
Terpander 54
  and the seven-stringed instrument 64
Tethys 118

Thales 13
Theodorus his words on worship 10
Theophrastus 24, 59, 130, 132
theriaca of Andromachus 58
Thrasymachus the Sophist 4
Timaeus 4, 6
   a Pythagorean from Locri 3
   examines the threefold cause of the world
   prepares to discourse upon the world 108
time 112
truth let the truth, Christian and Mosaic, persist 16

unity 121
   in all places divine unity prevails 8
   all things proceed from divine unity 9
universe the subject matter of this book
   may be said to be the very nature of the universe 3
   is not self-existent, but depends on a higher, divine cause 4
urinary tract 166
Ursa 82

vacuum the movements of nature which prevent a vacuum 153-4
Valori, Filippo 103
Varro 81
Venus 45, 52, 70, 74, 81, 110, 111, 115, 127
   the author of attraction and friendship 114
Vesta 116

war between Athens and Atlantis 5

world
   threefold: divine, celestial, human 4
   its antiquity 5
   the world never is , but always becomes 11
   the intelligible world always is and never becomes 12
   higher world, intellectual world, intelligible world, rational world, seed-world, physical world 17
   intelligible world, perceptible world 19
   two views of its origin 21
   Plato's view of its origin 22-3
   established by divine providence 24
   the world is one and spherical 25
   a creature which is alive and animated and intellectual 44
   necessarily endures some deformity 91
   is composed of mind and necessity 91
   is a single perceptible organism 109
   has two particular centres: the Moon and the Sun 110
   its spherical shape 110
   perfectly produced through the harmonious proportion of its parts 110
   composed of intelligence and necessity 132
   worlds may be numbered as five 40
world-soul 3
worship 8
   its purpose 10

year The Great Year 115, 123

Zeno 3